Dictionary of

World War II

Other titles in the Hutchinson Pocket series:

Helicon Publishing Ltd
42 Hythe Bridge Street
Oxford OX1 2EP

Printed and bound in Great Britain by
Unwin Brothers Ltd, Old Woking, Surrey

ISBN 1–85986–023–0

British Cataloguing in Publication Data

A catalogue record for this book is available
from the British Library

Acquisitions Director
Anne-Lucie Norton

Editor
Paul Davis

**Maps, Tables, and
Chronologies**
Simon Hall

Picture Research
Linda Proud

Page make-up
TechType

Production
Tony Ballsdon

Contents

About the author

Ian Vernon Hogg was born in 1926. He enlisted in the Regular Army (Royal Artillery) during World War II and served in Europe and the Far East during the Korean War with various field and Horse Artillery regiments. Qualifying as a gunnery instructor in 1953, Mr Hogg served on the staff of the Royal School of Artillery teaching artillery equipment, ammunition, and explosives. A further qualification in electronic warfare and counter–bombardment followed in 1959–60 and he became Warrant Officer in charge of trials 1961–66. Promoted to Master Gunner in 1965, he was posted to the instructional staff at the Royal Military College of Science. Reaching retirement age in 1972, Mr Hogg became a full-time writer specializing in defence journalism. Ian Hogg has written, contributed to, or edited over 100 books on military subjects and is a contributor to over 25 specialist magazines internationally.

Married with two sons and one daughter, Mr Hogg lives in Worcestershire.

Picture credits
6 and 7 courtesy of the author (Ian V Hogg) and 1, 2, 3,4, 5, 8 and 9 courtesy of Topham Picture Source.

Chronologies, tables and maps

A

A-4 rocket (also known as the V2) German ballistic missile, used to bombard England, Antwerp, and various other continental targets 1944–45. A fin-stabilized rocket, it weighed 13.6 tons at launch, carried a 1 ton warhead, and had a maximum range of about 320 km/200 mi., hitting its target at 5,000 kph/3,000 mph. Production began early 1944 and about 10,000 were made, of which 1,115 were fired against England, 1,341 against Antwerp, and 194 against other targets.

Aachen German city close to the junction of the Belgian/Netherlands/German borders. Taken by the US 1st Army after a week of hard fighting Oct 1944, it was the first German city to be taken by the Allies and its fall marked the first breakthrough in the ◊Siegfried Line.

Aberdeen code-name for the ◊Chindit base north of Indaw, Burma.

Abwehr intelligence and counter-espionage service of the German High Command. Established 1933, it was commanded by Admiral ◊Canaris 1935–44, when its duties were taken over by the ◊SS under ◊Himmler.

Achse, Operation (also called 'Operation Alarich') German disarmament of Italian forces after the Allied invasion of Italy Sept 1943 and the subsequent Italian surrender.

acoustic torpedoes and mines underwater weapons fitted with a sensor which would detect the sound of a ship's propellers. The sensor would steer a torpedo toward the ship or, if fitted to a mine, detonate it when it was close enough to the ship's hull.

Acoustic torpedoes were introduced by the German Navy 1943 but were never very successful: some even homed in on the submarine which launched them. The Allies sought to counter such weapons by towing a device behind ships which made more noise than the ship's machinery, and so either attracted the torpedo to itself rather than the ship or else triggered the mine at a non-lethal distance.

Adachi Lieutenant-General Hazato 1890–1947. Japanese soldier. He became commander of the Japanese 18th Army in New Guinea Nov 1942. Driven out of New Guinea by the Allied advance down the ◊Kokoda Trail, he made a stand in ◊Hollandia where his army was encircled by US and Australian forces. He held out until 13 Sept 1945, after the war was over, but was then sentenced to life imprisonment for war crimes and died shortly afterwards.

Addis Ababa capital of Abyssinia. Occupied by the Italians 1935 after the Abyssinian War, it was taken by British troops 6 April 1941. The Emperor ◊Haile Selassie, deposed by the Italians, returned the following month.

Adlergerät German infra-red sensor used to detect aircraft at night by the heat emitted from their engines. After detection, searchlights were directed on to the target to guide anti-aircraft fire. This system was used in the early part of the war before ◊radar fire direction became common.

Admin Box, Battle of the the 'Admin[istration] Box' was the administrative and base area of 7th Indian Division at Sinzewa, Burma, which was besieged by the 55th Japanese Division 5–23 Feb 1944. The Japanese were then taken in the rear by the 5th Indian Division advancing over the ◊Ngakyedauk Pass. The battle was the first major victory over the Japanese for British and Indian troops.

Admiralty Islands group of islands about 320 km/200 mi N of New Guinea; in 1939 they were an Australian protectorate. Taken by the Japanese 6 April 1942, they were recaptured by the US 1st Cavalry Division 29 Feb–23 March 1944. After the islands' recapture, the Japanese bases at ◊Rabaul and Kavieng were completely isolated and rendered ineffectual for the rest of the war.

Adolf Hitler Line (also called the 'Dora' or 'Senger' line) in Italy, second line of defence behind the main ◊Gustav Line about 80 km/50 mi S of Rome and stretching from ◊Cassino to the W Italian coast. It formed the principal obstacle preventing the Allied 5th Army linking up with the US VI Corps in the ◊Anzio beachhead until it was breached by Canadian forces 23 May 1944.

Aegean, Operations in the following the surrender of Italy 1943, British forces attempted to occupy various islands in the Aegean Sea, including Kos, Samos, and Leros. This provoked severe German retaliation, with heavy air attacks followed by seaborne and airborne landings. The British were under strength and so evacuated the islands Nov 1942 with severe losses, including 6 destroyers, 115 aircraft, and 4,800 men.

Afrika Korps German army corps operating in the western desert of N Africa 1941–43, commanded by Field Marshal ◊Rommel. They were driven out of N Africa by May 1943.

Agheila, El small Libyan town on the southern coast of the Gulf of Sidra, S of ◊Benghazi. A thin strip of firm ground between the sea and extensive salt marshes, it formed a natural bottleneck and so was of strategic importance to both sides. The British chose the town as their forward outpost after clearing the Italians out of Cyrenaica but lost it 24 March 1941 to a reconnaissance patrol sent out by ◊Rommel to test their defences. Rommel followed up this success and continued to push the British back to Benghazi, marking the start of his first offensive. He himself fell back on El Agheila temporarily Jan 1942 and finally Nov 1942 in his retreat after El ◊Alamein, when a deep outflanking movement through the desert by New Zealand troops drove him to continue his retreat.

Agordat town in Eritrea, about 95 km/60 mi NW of Asmera. Occupied by the Italians since the Abyssinian War 1935, it was captured by the 4th Indian Division 31 Jan 1941. The Italian garrison was partly surrounded and although it was able to escape it had to abandon most of its artillery and equipment.

Aichi Japanese aircraft, principally used by the Navy. The *B7A*, known to the Allies as 'Grace', was a torpedo-bomber produced in small numbers. The *D3A,* known as 'Val' was a carrier dive bomber of great strength and efficiency; it was the principal dive bomber used at ◊Pearl Harbor Dec 1941, and sank numerous Allied warships throughout the war. The *E13A*, 'Jake', was a floatplane used for reconnaissance; it was used in this role to prepare the way for the Pearl Harbor raid, and was carried by almost all Japanese warships.

Ainsworth Rear Admiral Walden 1886–1960. US sailor. He held various commands in the Pacific theatre of the war and is principally remembered for his part in the battles of the Kola Gulf and ◊Kolombangara, where forces under his command were able to break up Japanese attempts to reinforce their troops in the ◊Solomon Islands.

airborne radar term originally used to describe the use of radar in aircraft to detect other aircraft, e.g., night fighters looking for bombers; it was later extended to cover the use of radar to detect submarines from the air. First adopted by the Royal Air Force 1941 as an aid to night fighters.

air observation posts light unarmed aircraft used by artillery units to spot targets and report back on the accuracy of artillery fire. The aircraft did not fly over enemy territory but remained behind their own lines, merely using height to improve the observer's range of vision.

The aircraft were usually the light 'Auster' or 'Piper' high wing monoplanes, which had good visibility and were stable in the air. Air observation posts were first used by the British in N Africa 1942 and soon became an indispensable adjunct to normal ground observation. The system was adopted by the US army shortly after.

air raid precautions British term covering various forms of civil defence against air attack, such as shelters, raid wardens, rescue services, fire services, and the provision of shelter and welfare for victims of air raids. Such services were organized in all combatant countries, under various different names.

Akyab Island (now Sitwe) island off the NW coast of Burma; the Japanese built several airfields there, making it a valuable strategic target. The Allies planned an assault landing for 3 Jan 1945, but air reconnaissance on the previous day failed to see any signs of Japanese occupation. When the aircraft landed, the pilot was informed by the local residents that the Japanese had pulled out. The landing took place without opposition and the airfields were rapidly put to use by the Allies.

Alamein, El village and railway station on N coast of Egypt about 95 km/60 mi W of Alexandria; site of two decisive battles resulting in

British victory over Rommel's ◊Afrika Korps and Italian forces 1942. Rommel launched an attack from the ◊Cauldron June 1942, driving the British back to a well-prepared defensive position at El Alamein which stretched about 65 km/40 mi south from the sea across the ◊Ruweisat Ridge to the Quattara Depression, a sand sea which was completely impassable.

In the *First Battle of El Alamein* 1–27 July Rommel attacked the British line in a series of engagements, but the 8th Army under ◊Auchinleck was able to keep him at bay. Neither side can be said to have won, but the British had the strategic advantage of short supply lines and so could reinforce faster than the Germans.

Before Alamein we never had a victory. After Alamein we never had a defeat.

On the *Battles of El Alamein*,
Winston Churchill The Hinge of Fate 1951

In the *Second Battle of El Alamein* 23 Oct–4 Nov ◊Montgomery launched a diversionary British attack in the south. The aim was to draw Axis forces into the area so that the main attack in the north could cut two corridors through the extensive minefields, enabling British armoured divisions to pass through and exploit the gaps. Progress was slow however and Montgomery decided to change tactics to fight what he called a 'crumbling' battle, constantly switching the main emphasis of his attack to chip away at Rommel's front line and keep him guessing. On 26 Oct the 9th Australian Division attacked along the coastal road, drawing the Axis forces toward them. Montgomery promptly launched a fresh attack further south, forcing the German armour to react in what became a major tank battle. By 3 Nov Rommel had only 30 serviceable tanks in action and on the following day began organizing his withdrawal. He was able to disengage and escape as the British were hampered by heavy rain and a shortage of fuel.

Alam Halfa, Battle of attack by 446 German tanks under ◊Rommel against the southern sector of the Alamein defensive line 30 Aug 1942. However, General ◊Auchinleck had foreseen the possibility of such a

move and had prepared for it. His plans were implemented by General
◊Montgomery who now had 700 tanks to meet the attack. A co-ordi-
nated defence with artillery, tanks, and tactical air force stopped
Rommel and he called off the attack and retreated 2 Sept, having lost
3,000 men, 49 tanks, 60 guns, and 400 trucks.

Alanbrooke Alan Francis Brooke, 1st Viscount Alanbrooke
1883–1963. British army officer, Chief of Staff in World War II and
largely responsible for the strategy that led to the German defeat. He
served in the artillery in World War I, and in World War II, as commander of the 2nd Corps 1939–40, did much to aid the extrication of
the ◊British Expeditionary Force from Dunkirk. He was commander in
chief of the Home Forces 1940–41 and Chief of the Imperial General
Staff 1941–46. He became a field marshal 1944 and was created a
baron 1945 and viscount 1946.

Alban Hills range of hills inland from the ◊Anzio beaches which commanded the entire landing area. When the Allied landing took place 22
Jan 1944 no attempt was made to take this feature, even though it
would have denied the Germans a useful observation post and defensive line and enabled the Allies to break out of the beachhead. Instead,
the hills were rapidly occupied by German troops and remained in their
hands until May.

Albert Canal canal in Belgium which, together with the river Meuse,
formed the major Belgian defensive line 1940. The German airborne
assault on Fort ◊Eben Emael, situated at the junction of the canal and
river, breached this line and rendered it indefensible, considerably
assisting the German invasion.

Aleutian Islands volcanic island chain in the N Pacific, stretching
1,900 km/1,200 mi SW of Alaska, of which it forms part. The Japanese
occupied Attu and Kiska islands 1942–43; Attu was retaken in the only
ground fighting on North American soil of the war May 1943.

Alexander Harold Rupert Leofric George, 1st Earl Alexander of
Tunis 1891–1969. British field marshal. He commanded the 1st
Division in France 1939 and was the last person to leave during the
evacuation of ◊Dunkirk. He was then commander in chief, Southern
Command, until he became general officer commander in chief in

Burma (now Myanmar) Mar 1942, where he fought a delaying action for five months against superior Japanese forces. In Aug 1942 he went to N Africa, and in 1943 became deputy to Eisenhower in charge of the Allied forces in Tunisia. After the Axis forces in N Africa surrendered, Alexander became supreme Allied commander in the Mediterranean, and in 1944, field marshal.

After the war, he was governor general of Canada 1946–52 and UK minister of defence 1952–54. He was created Earl Alexander of Tunis 1952 and awarded the Order of Merit 1959.

Aliakmon Line Greek defensive line running some 96 km/60 mi from the Aegean coast near Mount Olympus to the Yugoslavian border north of Arnissa. It was in the process of being occupied by British troops April 1941 when it was outflanked by the Germans who passed through the gap between it and the Greek Army concentrated in Albania.

***Altmark* incident** naval skirmish off the coast of Norway Feb 1940. The *Altmark*, a German auxiliary cruiser, was intercepted by the British destroyer *Intrepid* 15 Feb while carrying the captured crews of Allied merchant ships sunk by the German battleship *Admiral Graf Spee* in the S Atlantic. The Altmark took refuge in Jösing fjord, where it was cornered by HMS *Cossack,* under Captain ◊Vian, and run aground. Vian's men rescued 299 British merchant sailors.

Amba Alagi mountain in Abyssinia where the occupying Italian forces under the Duke of ◊Aosta made a last stand against the British-led invasion May 1941. It was defended by 7,000 Italian troops with 40 guns against a mixed force of British, Indian, South African, and Abyssinian troops. The battle took place at altitudes of 3,000 m/10,000 ft and more, lasting from 3 May until the Duke's force surrendered 19 May.

Ambon Island small island in the Dutch East Indies, held by a mixed force of Dutch and Australian troops. The Japanese attacked it 31 Jan 1942, eventually taking it four days later. Some 809 Australian troops were captured, of whom over half were either murdered or allowed to die from starvation after torture.

Ambrosio General Vittorio 1897–1958. Italian soldier. Commanded the 2nd Italian Army in Yugoslavia 1941, became Chief of Staff of the Italian Army Jan 1942, and Chief of the Italian General Staff Feb 1943.

He was involved in the fall of ◊Mussolini and was opposed to German domination of Italy following the armistice Sept 1943, and so was demoted to inspector general of the army.

Anami General Korechika 1897–1945. Japanese soldier. He held several commands in China and Manchuria 1938–1943, before being sent to New Guinea to take charge of operations there. He became director-general of army aviation 1944, and was appointed minister of war April 1945. He committed suicide 15 Aug 1945.

Anders General Wladyslaw 1892–1970. Polish soldier. He commanded a cavalry brigade 1939, but was captured and imprisoned by the Soviets. Released after the German invasion June 1941, he began collecting Polish troops imprisoned in the USSR and was eventually permitted to take these men, with their families, to Palestine where he formed them into an army. The families were sent to E Africa, while the troops joined the British forces and fought at ◊Tobruk and in the desert campaigns of 1942. They then went to Italy, where they captured Monte ◊Cassino May 1944 and liberated Bologna April 1945.

After the death of General ◊Sikorski July 1943, Anders became leader of the exiled Poles but tended to ignore political problems, concentrating instead on military tasks. As a result he was politically outmanoeuvred by the Soviets in deciding the shape of postwar Poland which became a communist state, and remained in England after the war as leader of the expatriate Polish community.

anderson shelter simple air raid shelter which could be erected in a garden to provide protection for a family. Developed in England, it was named after Sir John Anderson, Home Secretary 1939–40. Tens of thousands were produced and they undoubtedly saved thousands of lives during the air raids on Britain.

Antonescu Marshal Ion 1886–1946. Romanian general and politician. Romanian minister of war from 1932, he became prime minister 1940 and seized power, forcing King Carol to abdicate and installing Carol's son Michael as monarch. He headed a pro-German government which allied Romania with Germany against the Soviet Union. King Michael had him arrested Aug 1944; he was tried 1945 and shot 1946.

Antwerp port in Belgium on the river ◊Scheldt, capital of the province of Antwerp. Occupied by the Germans 1940, it was liberated by the British 11th Armoured Division 4 Sept 1944 in the hope of securing the port in working order and thus providing the Allied forces with a supply port close to the front line. Unfortunately the banks of the river Scheldt were still held by German troops, denying the Allies use of the river, and special operations had to be mounted to remove them. It was not until 28 Nov that the first supply ships reached the port.

Anzio, Battle of beachhead invasion of Italy 22 Jan–23 May 1944 by Allied troops. Failure to exploit the initial surprise of the landing led to Allied troops being held on the beachhead for five months, before the breakthrough after Monte ◊Cassino allowed the US 5th Army to dislodge the Germans from the ◊Alban Hills and allow the Anzio force to begin its advance on Rome.

We sought to throw a raging lion ashore; what we got was a stranded whale

Winston Churchill on the *Battle of Anzio*

Anzio Annie German 28 cm K5(E) railway gun which shelled the ◊Anzio beachhead at long range. It was reputed to be kept in a tunnel when not firing so as to preserve it from air attacks. Captured at Civitavecchia, it is now an exhibit at the Aberdeen Proving Ground Museum in Maryland, USA.

Aosta Duke Amadeo 1898–1942. Italian soldier. A cousin of King Emmanuel, he was a general of the Italian Air Force and Viceroy of Abyssinia. He led an Italian army in an invasion of British Somaliland Aug 1940, but a British counterattack drove him back into Abyssinia where he took up a position at ◊Amba Alagi and was forced to surrender. He was taken prisoner and sent to a camp in Kenya where he died 1942.

Arado German aircraft. The principal model was the *AR 196*, a twin-float low-wing monoplane used as a reconnaissance machine by the German Navy and carried aboard most warships. It was also used for coastal patrolling and light bombing missions. The *AR 234* was the first

German jet bomber, a twin-jet, one-man, machine capable of flying at 740 kph/460 mph and carrying 1,500 kg/3,300 lb of bombs. It was brought into service late 1944 and was used extensively on the Western Front, notably in the Battle of the ◊Bulge and against the ◊Remagen bridges.

Arakan coastal region of Burma (now Myanmar) which offered a route for an invasion from India with access to central Burma. There were three British offensives in this area; the first, Dec 1942, had limited objectives and was largely in order to give British forces confidence in operating against the Japanese. It was halted by the Japanese at Donbaik and withdrew. The second, Dec 1943, advanced as far as Maungdaw before being halted. The third was really a continuation of the second advance which eventually resulted in the capture of ◊Rangoon 3 May 1945.

Arcadia conference meeting between Winston ◊Churchill and President ◊Roosevelt in Washington DC, 22 Dec 1941–7 Jan 1942. They agreed that Germany was to be the prime opponent and that the Combined Chiefs of Staff would be the supreme directing authority for the Allied military effort.

Arctic convoys series of supply convoys sailing from Britain to the USSR around the North Cape to ◊Murmansk, commencing Oct 1941. The natural hazards of sailing in these waters were greatly increased by the activity of German submarines and surface ships, together with German aircraft operating from bases in N Norway, and casualties were often heavy. In spite of such losses, the convoys delivered thousands of tanks and aircraft, 356,000 trucks, 50,000 jeeps, 1,500 locomotives, and 9,800 freight wagons.

Argenta Gap strip of dry land between Lake Comacchio and the Lombardy marshes in N Italy. Heavily defended by the Germans, it gave access to the Lombardy plain and NE Italy. It was breached by the 5th British Corps April 1945, using amphibious armoured vehicles to outflank the German positions, and allowed the British 6th Armoured Division to pass through the gap in the final Allied advance in Italy.

Arisaka rifle standard Japanese infantry rifle. Developed 1897, it was a 6.5 mm bolt-action magazine rifle loosely based on the German

Mauser. The design was improved 1905 and a rifle and carbine were introduced. Experience in the Sino-Japanese War and in ◊*Manchuria* in the 1930s indicated that a heavier calibre was required and a 7.7 mm design was adopted 1939, though relatively few of this pattern were ever manufactured.

***Ark Royal*, HMS** British aircraft carrier. Launched 1937 it displaced 22,000 tons and carried 72 aircraft. It went to the S Atlantic 1939 in the force sent against the ◊*Graf Spee,* then served with the Home and Mediterranean fleets 1940–41 and took part in the hunt for the ◊*Bismarck.* The *Ark Royal* was very well known and so often featured in German propaganda broadcasts which claimed the vessel had been sunk. Finally, it was torpedoed by *U-81* off Gibraltar 13 Nov 1941; an attempt was made to tow it into harbour but it sank during the tow.

Armstrong-Whitworth British aircraft. The A-W *Whitley*, designed 1934, was one of the standard bombers at the outbreak of war and was the first machine to bomb Germany and Italy. A twin-engine monoplane with a crew of five, its top speed was 366 kph/228 mph and it could carry up to 3,200 kg/7,000 lb of bombs. When no longer useful as a bomber it served in many other roles, including anti-submarine patrols, paratroop training, and glider towing. The A-W *Albemarle* was originally intended to replace the Whitley as a bomber but was not a success in that role and ended up as a glider tug for airborne operations in Sicily and France.

Arnhem, Battle of airborne operation by the Allies, 17–26 Sept 1944, to secure a bridgehead over the Rhine, thereby opening the way for a thrust toward the ◊*Ruhr* and a possible early end to the war. Arnhem itself was to be taken by the British while US troops were assigned bridges to the south of the city. Unfortunately, two divisions of the SS Panzer Corps were refitting in Arnhem when the British landed and penned the British in, while the US force captured the bridge at Nijmegen but were unable to secure the bridge at Elst. Despite the arrival of Polish reinforcements 21 Sept, Montgomery ordered a withdrawal four days after. British losses came to 1,130 killed and 6,000 taken prisoner, compared with 3,300 German casualties.

Arnim Colonel-General von Jurgen 1889–1971. German soldier. Commanded a division in the invasion of Russia 1941 and then a corps. Late in 1942 he was appointed to command the 5th Panzer Army in Africa, and in March 1943 became commander Army Group Afrika and commander in chief of German Forces in Tunisia. His appointment came too late to do any good, and with his supply lines cut, he was unable to stem the Allied advance and surrendered 12 May 1942. He remained a prisoner until the end of the war.

Arnold General Henry 'Hap' 1886–1950. US aviator. In 1936 he became assistant chief of the US Army Air Corps and in 1938 Chief of the Air Staff. He was largely responsible for preparing the US aviation industry for the war and for preparing the training programme which allowed the air corps to expand. He then served on the US Joint Chiefs of Staff Committee and the Allied Combined Chiefs of Staff Committee. He was a firm believer in the ability of bombing to win wars, though he favoured attacking specific targets rather than bombing whole areas. He was promoted to general of the army 1944, and when the US Army Air Corps was disbanded upon the formation of the US Air Force 1947, he became the first five star commanding general of the Air Force.

Arras French city, 60 km/38 mi NE of Amiens; site of a tank battle May 1940. A hastily-assembled force consisting of the 1st British Tank Brigade, 6th Durham Light Infantry, and the 3rd French Light Armoured Division, under the command of a British officer, Maj-Gen Franklyn, launched a counterattack against the German 7th Panzer Division under General ◊Rommel 21 May. The attack cut the Panzer Division in two, shattered two German rifle regiments, and caused part of the 3rd SS Division to panic and run. Rommel eventually got his troops under control and was able to beat off the British tanks using 88 mm anti-aircraft guns – the first time they had been used against tanks. His report of being attacked by 'hundreds of tanks' led to higher command ordering him to stop, and the subsequent 24-hour delay helped the British organize their retreat through ◊Dunkirk.

Arromanche-les-Bains French coastal town in Normandy, 24 km/15 mi NW of ◊Caen. The beach extending east from the town was designated 'Gold Beach' during the ◊D-Day invasion 6 June 1944 and was the landing place of the British 30th Corps.

artillery collective term for military firearms too heavy to be carried. Artillery can be mounted on tracks, wheels, ships, or aeroplanes and includes cannons and rocket launchers.

The principal advances in artillery during the war included widespread adoption of self-propelled artillery, the development of specialized anti-tank guns for the defeat of armour, and improvements in anti-aircraft artillery to match the rapid improvements in the speed and height of aircraft operations. Conventional artillery showed little technical advance on that of 1914–18 but its tactical handling was vastly improved by the introduction of radio communication.

Athens capital city of Greece, situated 8 km/5 mi NE of its port of Piraeus on the Gulf of Aegina. Occupied by the Germans 27 April 1941, it remained in their hands until 27 Oct 1944. British troops arrived two days later and were principally needed to keep the peace between rival monarchist and communist factions. Street fighting ensued, but eventually both sides agreed to a British-controlled truce Jan 1945. This lasted until May 1946 when civil war broke out, ending with the rout of the communists 1949.

Atlantic, Battle of continuous battle fought in the Atlantic Ocean by both sea and air forces to control the supply routes to the UK. The battle opened on the first night of the war 4 Sept 1939 when the ocean liner *Athenia,* sailing from Glasgow to New York, was torpedoed by a German submarine off the Irish coast.

At least 2,200 convoys of 75,000 merchant ships crossed the Atlantic, protected by US naval forces. Before the US entry into the war 1941, destroyers were supplied to the British under the ◊Lend-Lease Act 1941. Germany tried U-boats, surface-raiders, indiscriminate mine-laying, and aircraft to attack the convoys, but every method was successfully countered. U-boats were the greatest menace to Allied shipping, especially after the destruction of the German battleship *Bismarck* by British forces 27 May 1941. The Allies destroyed nearly 800 U-boats during the course of the war.

Atlantic Charter policy statement setting out British and US objectives, drawn up by Roosevelt and Churchill 12 Aug 1941. The charter declared that neither country sought any new territories and that territorial changes should not be made without the consent of the inhabitants of the area; that all nations should have the right to self-determination; that free trade and joint economic development should be encouraged; that all should be free from fear and want; that there should be freedom on the sea; and called for the abandonment of the use of force in settling disputes between nations.

Atlantic Wall fortifications built by the Germans on the North Sea and Atlantic coasts of France, Belgium, the Netherlands, Denmark, and Norway, stretching some 2,750 km/1,700 mi from the North Cape to the Spanish frontier. The defences were not in fact a continuous wall, but were grouped according to the likelihood of the area being used for landing. Millions of tons of concrete went into the construction of gun batteries, pillboxes, and tank obstacles, slave labour from Organization ◊Todt was liberally employed, and the permanent works were interspersed with barbed wire, mines, anti-tank ditches, steel underwater obstacles, and other defensive devices. All were carefully studied by the Allies, who then set about devising methods of countering them when invasion took place. In the event, Allied preparations and the experience of ◊Dieppe enabled them to overcome these obstacles.

No country without an atom bomb could properly consider itself independent.
On the *atom bomb*, General Charles de Gaulle *New York Times* 1968

---

atom bomb bomb deriving its explosive force from nuclear fission as a result of a neutron chain reaction, developed in the 1940s in the USA into a usable weapon. Research began in the UK 1940 and was transferred to the USA after its entry into the war the following year. Known as the ◊*Manhattan Project*, the work was carried out under the direction of the US physicist Oppenheimer at Los Alamos, New Mexico. After one test explosion, two atom bombs, each nominally equal to 20,000 tonnes of TNT, were dropped on the Japanese cities of

Hiroshima (6 Aug 1945) and Nagasaki (9 Aug 1945) to end Japanese resistance and hasten the end of the war. The USSR first detonated an atom bomb 1949 and the UK 1952.

ATS see ◊auxiliary territorial service.

Auchinleck General Sir Claude John Eyre 1884–1981 ('the Auk'). British soldier. He succeeded ◊Wavell as commander in chief Middle East July 1941, and in the summer of 1942 was forced back to the Egyptian frontier by the German field marshal Rommel, but then recovered to win the First Battle of El ◊Alamein in N Egypt 1942. He became commander in chief in India 1943 where he laid the foundations of the modern Indian and Pakistani armies and gave background support to the operations in Burma. His victory at El Alamein is regarded by some as more important to the outcome of the war than the Second Battle. He was promoted to field marshal 1946 and retired 1947.

Augsburg industrial city in Bavaria, Germany, at the confluence of the Wertach and Lech rivers, 52 km/32 mi NW of Munich; site of the ◊Messerschmitt aircraft works.

Auschwitz (Polish *Oswiecim*) town near Kraków in S Poland, site of a notorious ◊concentration camp used by the Nazis to exterminate Jews and other political and social minorities, as part of their ◊'final solution'. It was originally established as a transit camp but from March 1941 was expanded to a capacity of 130,000 to function as a labour camp. The nearby IG Farben factory was to use 10,000 Auschwitz prisoners as slave labour. In Sept 1941, mass executions began in four gas chambers, each of which could hold 6,000 people. It is estimated some 2 million people were killed at Auschwitz before its closure 1944.

Austen Australian sub-machine gun. Based on elements of other designs, it was intended to become the Australian equivalent of the British ◊Sten gun (hence the name) but it was never popular and was replaced by the ◊Owen gun.

auxiliary territorial service (ATS). British Army unit of non-combatant women auxiliaries. Formed 1939, it provided cooks, clerks, radar operators, searchlight operators, and undertook other light non-combat duties.

Avalanche code-name for the Allied landings at ◊Salerno, Italy, Sept 1943.

Avia Czechoslovakian aircraft. The Avia B-534 was a fast biplane single-seat fighter which was considered to be probably the best of its type when it was first produced 1934. Over 400 were built and they were adopted by the German ◊Luftwaffe as a training machine. Three Czech squadrons were organized to fight on the Eastern Front 1941 but they achieved little and most of the pilots deserted with their machines to the Soviets.

Avranches French town at the base of the Cotentin Peninsula, 110 km/70 mi S of Cherbourg. It was captured by the US 1st Army 30 July 1944 during the breakout from the Normandy beachhead. The US 3rd Army under General ◊Patton passed through this gap to begin their eastward drive.

AVRE (Armoured Vehicle, Royal Engineers) British tank specially designed to defeat various types of obstacle. Based on the ◊Churchill tank, it was armed with a special short-range mortar firing a heavy demolition charge, for use against pillboxes. The use of various modular attachments allowed it to fill ditches, lay bridges, set demolition charges, or lay tracks for soft vehicles.

Avro British aircraft made by the A. V. Roe Company. The company was famous for two aircraft during the war: the Avro *Anson,* a twin-engine reconnaissance machine which later became a trainer; and the Avro ◊*Lancaster* bomber.

Axthelm Lieutenant General Walther von 1893–1961. German airman. An officer of the ◊Luftwaffe, he was appointed inspector general of anti-aircraft artillery 1942, with considerable responsibility for the air defences of Germany. In 1944 he was in overall command of the ◊V-1 'flying bomb' campaign against Britain.

B

Bach-Zelewski General Erich von dem. German soldier. SS Obergruppenführer in charge of all anti-partisan and anti-guerrilla operations from Oct 1942. He commanded the troops which suppressed the Warsaw Rising Aug–Oct 1943, and was later a prosecution witness during the ◊Nuremberg Trials.

Bader Sir Douglas 1910–1982. British fighter pilot. He lost both legs in a flying accident 1931, but had a distinguished flying career during the war nonetheless. He was credited by the RAF with shooting down over 20 enemy aircraft before himself being shot down and captured Aug 1941. He was knighted 1976 for his work with disabled people.

Badoglio Marshal Pietro 1871–1950. Italian soldier and statesman. Badoglio served as a general in World War I and then as Chief of Staff 1919–21. He was promoted to field marshal 1925 and commanded the Italian force in the invasion of Abyssinia 1935, becoming Chief of Staff again June 1940. However, he resigned following the failure of the invasion of Greece Oct 1940. After the arrest of ◊Mussolini June 1943 he became prime minister and signed the Act of Surrender 3 Sept 1943. He resigned 1944 and retired.

Baedecker raids a series of German air raids directed at British provincial towns and cities April–Oct 1942. They were so named by the British because the targets were all places of cultural interest which appeared to have been selected from *Baedecker's Guide to Britain*.

Bagration, Operation major Soviet offensive against German Army Group Centre June 1944. Field Marshal Ernst Busch (1885–1945) had advance warning of the attack, and in order to absorb it better requested permission to fall back to a stronger defensive line on the river Beresina. Hitler refused and ordered the Group to remain in position.

Heavily outnumbered in tanks and artillery, the Germans were encircled and cut off in the Vitebsk, Mogilev, and Bobruysk areas, suffering
heavy losses. The Soviet force of over 40 tank brigades plus supporting
troops crossed E Poland and advanced as far as the line of the Vistula
river (a distance of 725 km/450 mi) in four weeks, having destroyed 25
German divisions. Soviet authorities regard this operation as being perhaps the most decisive of the war on the Eastern Front.

Bailey bridge prefabricated bridge developed by the British Army,
made from a set of standardized components so that bridges of varying
lengths and load-carrying ability could be assembled to order. Used in
every theatre of war, many remained in place for several years after the
war until the civil authorities could replace them with more permanent
structures.

Balaton, Lake lake in Hungary, scene of the last major German
offensive on the Eastern Front March 1945. On 5 March the German
2nd Army and 6th SS Panzer Army attacked the Soviet 3rd Ukrainian
Front to head off a threatened Soviet attack and try and safeguard the
Hungarian oilfields. They advanced some 32 km/20 mi into the Soviet
lines but a Soviet counterattack 16 March routed the Hungarian 3rd
Army which was on the German left flank. This exposed the Germans
who rapidly halted the operation and fell back, with losses of over
40,000 men and 500 tanks and assault guns.

Balbo Count Italo 1896–1940. Italian soldier and politician. A well-
known aviator, famed for his long-distance flights to demonstrate
Italian aviation, Balbo was one of the main figures in Mussolini's
'March on Rome' and served as minister of aviation in the 1930s. His
popularity irked Mussolini, and he was despatched as governor to
Libya 1936. This did not stop him voicing his objections to Mussolini's
growing friendship with Hitler and he tried to persuade Mussolini to
stay out of the war. Shortly after Italy's entry into the war, Balbo was
flying back to Libya from Italy when his aircraft was shot down over
Tobruk by Italian anti-aircraft guns and he was killed.

Balck General Hermann 1893–1972. German soldier. Commissioned
into the infantry 1914, he remained in the army after World War I, rising to lieutenant colonel by 1938. In 1939 he commanded a rifle

regiment in 1 Panzer Division and saw action in Poland and France. He was promoted to colonel and commanded a Panzer regiment Dec 1940, a Panzer brigade May 1941, and 11 Panzer Division May 1942. Promoted to major general Aug 1942, in Jan 1943 he was made a lieutenant general and given command of the *Grossdeutschland* Division. He commanded Army Group G in France 1944, after which he moved to command 6th Army in Hungary where he remained until the war ended.

Balikpapan town on the E coast of Borneo; a terminal for the local oil-producing area. Captured by the Japanese 24 Jan 1942, it was recaptured by Australian forces 3 July 1945.

Balkans, Operations in the Italy invaded Albania April 1939, and used it to launch an invasion of Greece Oct 1940 which was repulsed by the Greeks Nov–Dec. This defeat, together with Italian defeats in N Africa, led Hitler to plan a German invasion of Greece through Bulgaria. The plan was forestalled by an anti-Nazi coup in Yugoslavia 27 March 1941, which forced Hitler to change his plans to incorporate an invasion of Yugoslavia, securing his southern flank for the forthcoming invasion of the USSR, Operation ◊Barborossa. The invasion of Yugoslavia began 6 April, with the German 12th Army striking from Bulgaria and the 2nd Army and 1st Panzer Army from Austria and Hungary, aided by the 3rd Hungarian and 2nd Italian Armies. The Yugoslavian army, poorly armed and badly organized, surrendered 17 April.

  Greece was invaded simultaneously on 6 April, forcing the Greeks to withdraw from Albania in order to meet the new threat and thus releasing the Italians in Albania to resume their invasion. The Germans passed through the gap between the Greek forces coming out of Albania and the remaining Greek armies, outflanking both forces. British troops, who had been sent to Greece to assist, were forced to conduct a fighting retreat to the Peloponnese, where the survivors were able to embark and escape to ◊Crete. Greek forces surrendered and the 1941 campaign was over. Although it was a textbook demonstration of the ◊Blitzkrieg technique, it delayed Operation Barbarossa and so, in the long run, contributed to the German defeat outside ◊Moscow.

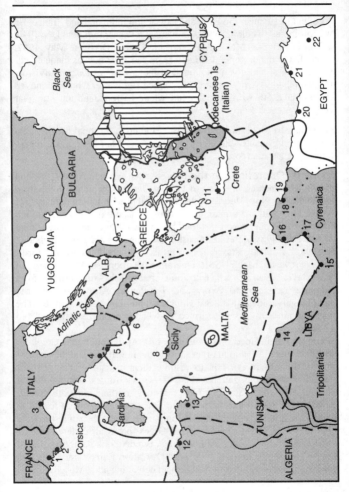

THE BALKANS, NORTH AFRICA, AND ITALY 1941–44

Key

░░░   Axis and associated powers Oct 1940

· · ·   Allied and Greek advance April 5 1941

———   Maximum Axis advance (Sept 1942)

— —   Allied advance by Jan 1 1943

—· —   Allied advance by May 1944

|||| Countries remaining neutral

Cities/towns

1	Marseille	12	Bone
2	Toulon	13	Tunis
3	Genoa	14	Tripoli
4	Rome	15	El Agheila
5	Anzio	16	Benghazi
6	Naples	17	Beda Fomm
7	Taranto	18	Gazala
8	Palermo	19	Tobruk
9	Belgrade	20	El Alamein
10	Athens	21	Alexandria
11	Maleme	22	Cairo

balloons, Japanese free-floating balloons carrying high-explosive and incendiary bombs released by Japan against mainland USA. In Nov 1944 the Japanese released several thousand balloons which were designed to rise to an altitude of about 10,000 m/35,000 ft and there be carried by the stratospheric airstream across the Pacific Ocean to the USA and Canada. The journey was expected to take three to five days, and a regulating device released gas or ballast to keep the balloons at the desired height. When the last ballast was released, this would automatically release two high explosive or incendiary bombs of about 4.5 kg/10 lb each, after which an explosive charge would destroy the balloon. It was estimated that perhaps 10% would reach their destination; in fact about 150 were reported right across the continent but strict censorship prevented any news reaching Japan and it was therefore thought that the campaign was a failure and further attempts were abandoned. The only casualties were a picnic party in Oregon who discovered a bomb which exploded and killed six people.

Baltic Campaign operations by the Soviet Army on the Baltic sector of the Eastern Front 1944–45. The 1st Baltic Front under General Bagramyan swept across Latvia to Memel (now Klaipeda), and the 2nd (under Marshal ◊Yeremenko) and 3rd (under Maslennikov) Baltic Fronts drove through Lithuania and laid siege to Riga. At the same time, troops from the Leningrad Front under Marshal ◊Govorov swept through Estonia. These moves isolated a pocket of German forces, the Army Group North, in the ◊Kurland Peninsula. In Feb 1945 Königsberg (now Kaliningrad) was surrounded, followed by Danzig (Gdansk) and Gdynia. The Germans were able to escape from ◊Kurland by sea, and a similar evacuation was carried out from Danzig and Gdynia March 1945, and Königsberg, Pillau, and Kolberg April 1945, saving about 2 million refugees and troops.

Barbarossa, Operation German code name for the plans to invade the USSR, launched 22 June 1941. The Germans deployed massive resources for the campaign, organized in three Army Groups. Army Group South (under von ◊Rundstedt), consisting of 52 divisions, with the 3rd and 4th Romanian Armies, a Hungarian and an

Italian corps, and 5 divisions of 1st Panzer Group (under von ◊Kleist), advanced southeast from S Poland in the direction of Kiev. Army Group Centre (under von ◊Bock), consisting of 42 divisions plus 9 Panzer divisions struck from the Polish border northeast toward Minsk and Smolensk. Army Group North (under von ◊Leeb) with 7 infantry and 3 Panzer divisions advanced from E Prussia through Lithuania and Latvia toward Leningrad. Some 3,330 German tanks were deployed, with four ◊Luftwaffe air fleets providing total air superiority.

Except for a check to the southern group, initial progress was rapid and immense quantities of prisoners and equipment fell into German hands, while most of the Soviet air force was destroyed on the ground. However, due to interference from Hitler, the impetus of the drive toward ◊Moscow was slowed, so that winter set in before the city could be invested. With the failure to take Moscow, Barbarossa was at an end as the German plan lay in ruins, although fighting continued in the USSR, notably the sieges of ◊Leningrad and ◊Stalingrad. The prime cause of failure was the late start to the operation due to delays caused by the ◊Balkan campaign.

Barbey Rear Admiral Daniel E 1889–1969. US sailor. Commissioned into the US Navy 1912, Barbey had a varied career, divided between sea service and administrative posts. He was a captain in the war plans section of the bureau of navigation 1937–40, where he interested himself in amphibious warfare. In 1941 he established the amphibious warfare section of the US Navy Department and was responsible for the designs of various landing ships and the ◊DUKW amphibious truck. Promoted to rear admiral 1942, in 1943 he was given command of VII Amphibious Force of the 7th Fleet and took responsibility for all amphibious operations in the SW Pacific Area. In late 1945 he became commander of 7th Fleet before retiring 1951.

Bardia (now Bardiyah) port in E Cyrenaica 95 km/60 mi E of Tobruk fortified by the Italians. It was captured 3–5 Jan 1941 by 6th Australian Division, who took 38,000 prisoners, 120 tanks, 400 guns, and 700 other vehicles. Used by the British as a supply port, it was recaptured by German troops under ◊Rommel 9 April 1941, and held until 2 Jan 1942 when it was again taken by British and South African troops.

During Rommel's advance to El ◊Alamein June 1942 the town fell into German hands once more, and was finally re-taken by British forces 11 Nov 1942.

Barents Sea, Battle of the naval action between British and German forces north of ◊Murmansk, 30 Dec 1942. A German force, including the battleship *Lutzow,* the cruiser *Admiral ◊Hipper*, and six destroyers, attacked a British convoy en route to Murmansk. The convoy was protected by six British destroyers and five smaller escort vessels which launched a vigorous counterattack, enabling it to turn away, but then themselves ran into part of the German force. The Germans were unable to tell whether they were British or German vessels due to poor visibility and hesitated long enough for the destroyers to lay a smoke screen. The British ships were severely damaged, and two were sunk, but were saved by two cruisers from Murmansk which sank one German destroyer and damaged the *Admiral Hipper.* The German commander broke off the fight and retired.

The German failure so enraged Hitler that Admiral ◊Raeder was relieved of his post as commander in chief of the German Fleet and most of the German Navy was confined to training exercises in the Baltic, some ships having their guns removed to provide coastal defences for Norway.

Bari S Italian port on the Adriatic coast, used by the Allies as a supply port. The freighter *John Harvey* was loaded with a cargo of mustard gas, intended to be held in Italy in case the Germans initiated gas warfare. However, the vessel was bombed and sunk in an air raid Dec 1943. The gas escaped and coated the sea, poisoning swimmers and survivors of the bombing. Their condition was not recognized by hospitals as the gas cargo was kept a strict secret, and many died before their injuries were correctly diagnosed and treated.

barrage balloon captive balloons, of tear-drop shape and with fins to keep them headed into the wind, which could be positioned around likely bombing targets to interfere with the probable flight paths of enemy aircraft. Their prime function was to force enemy aircraft to stay high to avoid the balloons, so placing them at the optimum height for engagement by anti-aircraft guns. Various refinements, such as stretching wire 'aprons' between balloons, or attaching aerial mines were tried from time to time but were rarely successful; the plain balloon on a cable was generally a satisfactory deterrent.

Bastogne Belgian town in the Ardennes, 80 km/50 mi S of Liège. An important road junction, it lay in the path of the German advance in the Battle of the ◊Bulge and was held by the US 101 Airborne Division and Combat Command B of the 10th US Armored Division under General ◊McAuliffe. It was besieged by German forces 18 Dec 1944 and strongly attacked; the defences were breached in two places 25 Dec. However, the attacks were repulsed and Bastogne was relieved by the US 4th Armored Division the following day, though fierce fighting continued in the area for some days.

Bataan peninsula in Luzon, in the Philippines, which was unsuccessfully defended against the Japanese by US and Filipino troops under General ◊MacArthur 1 Jan–9 April 1942. Following the surrender of Bataan MacArthur was evacuated, but Allied captives were force-marched 95 km/60 mi to the nearest railhead in the *Bataan Death March*; ill-treatment by the Japanese guards during the march killed about 16,000 US and Filipino troops.

Battleaxe, Operation British offensive in the Western Desert 15 June 1941, intended to relieve ◊Tobruk and recapture Cyrenaica. Three columns were used in the attack, one advancing toward the ◊Halfaya Pass, one to Capuzzo, and one inland to the Hafid Ridge. The tank attack on Halfaya was ambushed and destroyed by German 88 mm guns, as was the Hafid Ridge advance, though the Capuzzo attack was moderately successful. A German counterattack 16 June did more damage to British armour, and the British withdrew to their start line on the following day.

bazooka US 2.36 in calibre rocket launcher fired from the shoulder. A lightweight tube with simple sight, it was placed on the shoulder and launched a fin-stabilized rocket containing a ◊shaped charge warhead capable of penetrating up to 203 mm/8 in of armour; the maximum effective range was about 120 m/130 yds. The weapon's name came from its supposed similarity to a burlesque musical instrument played by Bob Burns, a US comedian.

Beda Fomm small town in Cyrenaica, about 190 km/120 mi S of
Benghazi on the coast road; scene of a catastrophic Italian defeat 7 Feb
1941. Elements of the British 7th Armoured Division had cut across the
desert and set up a road block in which the retreating 10th Italian Army
was ambushed. Over 25,000 prisoners, 100 tanks, 216 guns, and 1,500
other vehicles were captured.

Bedell Smith General Walter 1895–1961. US soldier. A staff officer
who had risen from the ranks, in 1941 he became secretary to the Joint
Chiefs of Staff and US secretary of the Anglo-American Combined
Chiefs of Staff. He became Chief of Staff to General ◊Eisenhower Sept
1942 and remained in this post until the end of the war. Among his
many achievements was the negotiation of the Italian surrender 1943
and the surrender of German forces in NW Europe 1945.

Belgorod Soviet city and important rail junction 80 km/50 mi N of
◊Kharkov. It was taken by the Germans in their initial advance into the
USSR Nov 1941 and was not recaptured until 9 Feb 1943 during the
Soviet offensive which followed the battle of ◊Stalingrad. It fell into
German hands once more during the German counteroffensive 18
March and was finally regained by the Soviets during their advance
after the Battle of ◊Kursk.

Bell US aircraft. The P-39 *Airacobra* first flew 1939 and was a some-
what unconventional fighter with the engine behind the pilot, driving
the propeller by a geared shaft, allowing a 20 mm cannon to fire
through the propeller boss. The French ordered several but by the time
they were built France had fallen and the planes went to England for the
RAF July 1941. They were found wanting and were withdrawn, but
later improved models, such as the P-63 *Kingcobra* which had more
power and a larger wingspan, were extensively used by the Soviet and
Free French air forces, who found them to be effective ground attack
fighters. The P-59 *Airacomet*, using two British Whittle engines, was
the first US jet to fly 1942. Production models did not appear until 1944
and it was used as a trainer.

Belsen German concentration camp on the Luneberg Heath, 48 km/30
mi NW of Celle. Established 1943 it was not officially an extermination
camp, but an outbreak of typhus 1945 caused thousands of deaths.

When captured by British troops 13 April 1945 several thousand bodies lay around the camp and the remaining inmates were barely alive. It was the first camp to be taken by the Allies and newsreel footage of the conditions appalled the general public who, until then, had assumed that these camps were ordinary labour camps, albeit with a hard regime.

Benes Eduard 1884–1948. Czechoslovak politician. He worked with Tomáš Masaryk toward Czechoslovak independence from 1918 and was Czech foreign minister and representative at the League of Nations. He was president of the republic from 1935 until forced to resign by the Germans 1939, then headed a government in exile in London during the war. He returned home as president 1945 but resigned again after the Communist coup 1948.

Benghazi historic city and industrial port in N Libya on the Gulf of Sirte. It was captured from the Italians by the British XIII Corps 6 Feb 1941, recaptured by Axis troops 4 April, re-taken by British troops Dec, and then taken again by ◊Rommel Jan 1942. It finally returned to British hands Nov 1942 during the general advance after El ◊Alamein. The frequent advances and retreats across the desert 1941–42 were sardonically known as the 'Benghazi Handicaps' by British troops.

Bennet Air Vice-Marshal Donald 1910–1968. Australian airman. In the early part of the war he controlled the 'transatlantic ferry' system of flying aircraft from the USA to Britain. He then rejoined the RAF, commanded a bomber squadron, and was shot down over Norway 1941 while attacking the ◊Tirpitz. He escaped by parachute and led his crew back to England via Sweden. He was given command of the ◊Pathfinder Force Aug 1942, which he led for the remainder of the war.

Berlin industrial city and capital of Germany; the seat of government and site of most military and administrative headquarters, it was frequently bombed by British and US forces. This and the fighting during its conquest by the Soviet Army 23 April–2 May 1945 destroyed much of the city. The city was taken in a pincer movement by ◊Zhukov's and ◊Konev's forces who had to fight street by street from the suburbs in to the centre in the face of fierce resistance. Hitler committed suicide

30 April as the Soviets closed in and General Karl Weidling surrendered the city 2 May. Soviet casualties came to about 1,000,000 dead; German casualties are unknown but some 136,000 were taken prisoner and it is believed over 100,000 civilians died in the fighting. After the war, Berlin was divided into four sectors – British, US, French, and Soviet – and until 1948 was under quadripartite government by the Allies.

Berlin, Battle of series of 16 heavy bombing attacks on Berlin by the RAF Nov 1943–March 1944. Some 9,111 bomber sorties were flown during the course of the campaign and immense damage was done to the city. However, almost 600 bombers were lost during the battle, into which the Germans threw all their air defence capability.

Bernhard Line German defensive line in Italy 1943 running from the Garigliano River to Castel di Sangri in the Apennine Mountains. Its purpose was to delay the Allied advance as it approached the main ◊Gustav Line defences; it was broken by the Allies Nov 1943. It was also known by the Germans as the 'Reinhardt Line' and by the Allies simply as the 'Winter Line'.

Bhamo town in N Burma (now Myanmar) 193 km/120 mi S of Myitkyina. Occupied by the Japanese Jan 1942 during their advance through Burma, it was attacked 10 Nov 1944 by Chinese troops of the New 1st Army as part of a drive to open communications between China and Burma. The Japanese garrison resisted until the night of 14–15 Dec when some 900 troops managed to break out and escape, and the town was occupied by the Chinese.

Bhose Subhas Chandra 1897–1945. Indian politician and nationalist; in 1939 he was President of the Indian Congress Party. He left India 1941 and went to Germany where he recruited an ◊'Indian Nationalist Army' from Indian prisoners-of-war. He repeated this in Japan 1943 but gained only a small number of recruits and the INA was ineffectual as a fighting force, most of its members defecting to the British as soon as the opportunity occurred. Bhose was killed while flying to Japan for a further recruiting drive 1945.

Biak island off the N coast of New Guinea. Used by the Japanese as an air base, it was attacked by US and Australian troops 27 May 1944.

The Japanese garrison put up strong resistance and the island was not secured until 29 June, with 2,700 Allied casualties and 9,000 Japanese.

Bialystok Polish city, 257 km/160 mi NE of Warsaw, occupied by the Soviets after their annexation of E Poland 1939. During the initial phase of Operation ◊Barbarossa it was encircled, together with Minsk, and surrendered 3 July 1941. Some 290,000 Soviet prisoners were taken together with large numbers of guns and tanks. It remained in German hands until 27 July 1944 when it was re-taken by Soviet troops during Operation ◊Bagration.

Bismarck German battleship. Launched Feb 1939, it displaced 50,153 tons and was armed with eight 38 cm guns, twelve 15 cm guns, and sixteen 105 mm and sixteen 37 mm anti-aircraft guns. It was protected by a 320 mm main armour belt and had a top speed of 29 knots.

In May 1941, together with the heavy cruiser *Prinz Eugen,* it left the Baltic to attack convoys in the Atlantic. The British anticipated their departure and two destroyers shadowed the German ships from the Denmark Strait. On 24 May they were intercepted by HMS *Hood* and HMS *Prince of Wales*. The Germans initially concentrated fire on the *Hood,* which blew up and sank, then damaged the *Prince of Wales* which managed to inflict some damage in turn on the *Bismarck* before obeying orders to break contact. The damage to the *Bismarck* resulted in its losing one-third of its oil fuel and taking on 200 tons of water. Admiral Gunther Lütjens left *Prinz Eugen* to continue patrolling and turned the *Bismarck* back toward Brest. During the evening the *Bismarck* was attacked by naval aircraft from HMS *Victorious* but sustained only minor damage. The British made contact again 26 May, when an attack by torpedo bombers from HMS *Ark Royal* damaged the *Bismarck's* steering gear. On the morning of 27 May HMS *King George V* and HMS *Rodney* caught up and opened fire, virtually wrecking Bismarck, and the final blow was a torpedo attack by HMS *Devonshire* which sank the ship. Only 107 of the 2,192 crew survived; Admiral Lütjens was among the casualties.

Bizerta seaport in N Tunisia, 64 km/40 mi N of Tunis. It served as one of the principal supply ports for the Axis forces in Tunisia. It was captured by the US II Corps 7 May 1943; together with the capture of Tunis on the same day, this effectively completed the Allied conquest of ◊Tunisia.

Blackburn British aircraft. The Blackburn *Skua* was a two-seat fighter and dive bomber used by the British Fleet Air Arm. Although successful in the early part of the war – one shot down the first German aircraft claimed by the Fleet Air Arm, and another sank the German cruiser *Königsberg* in Bergen harbour – it was withdrawn from combat duty 1941 to become a trainer. It was replaced by the Blackburn *Roc*, a similar machine but carrying a powered four-gun turret behind the pilot. It proved to be under-powered and ineffectual and was used solely as a trainer.

Blamey Thomas Albert 1884–1951. Australian field marshal. Born in New South Wales, he served at Gallipoli, Turkey, and on the Western Front in World War I and was knighted 1935. When World War II started he was appointed general officer commanding, Anzac Corps, and served in Greece and the Middle East. After his recall to Australia 1942 and appointment as commander in chief, Allied Land Forces, he commanded operations on the ◊Kokoda Trail and the recapture of Papua.

The rabbit that runs away is the rabbit that gets shot.
Field Marshal Blamey addressing his troops

Blaskowitz General Johannes von 1883–1946. German soldier. After commanding an army during the invasion of Poland 1939, Blaskowitz became military governor of the conquered territory. In 1940 he complained about the excesses of the SS in dealing with the Jews, but was politically outfoxed by ◊Himmler and relieved of his post, returning to command a field army which he later led in Operation ◊Barbarossa and subsequently on the Eastern Front. A competent if unremarkable general, he was given command of Army Group G in the south of France 1944. After Operation Dragoon, the Allied invasion of S France 1944, he conducted a fighting retreat up the Rhone valley. He was relieved of command after giving up the city of Nancy without Hitler's approval, but survived to take over Army Group H and put up a spirited defence of the Netherlands, finally surrendering to Canadian forces May 1945. He was arraigned for trial at ◊Nuremberg but committed suicide in prison.

Blitz, The (anglicization of ◊*Blitzkrieg*) British name for the German air raids against Britain which began after the failure of the Battle of ◊Britain. The first raid was against London 7-8 Sept 1940, and raids continued on all but 10 nights until 12 Nov. Then the targets became industrial cities such as Coventry (14 Nov), Southampton, Birmingham, Bristol, Cardiff, Portsmouth, and Liverpool, with occasional raids on London. In spring 1941 the air defences began to take a larger toll of the attackers, due to improvements in ◊radar for night fighters and for artillery control. The raids fell away during the early summer as Luftwaffe forces were withdrawn from the west in preparation for the invasion of the USSR. It has been estimated that about 40,000 civilians were killed, 46,000 injured, and more than a million homes destroyed and damaged in this period, together with an immense amount of damage to industrial installations.

Blitzkrieg (German 'lightning war') swift military campaign, as used by Germany 1939–41 (see map over). It was characterized by rapid movement by mechanized forces, supported by tactical air forces acting as 'flying artillery' and is best exemplified by the campaigns in ◊Poland 1939 and France 1940.

Blomberg Field Marshal Werner von 1878–1943. German soldier. After a sound but unremarkable career in World War I, Blomberg was appointed minister of war Jan 1933 as President Hindenburg hoped he would act as a counterbalance to Hitler. In the event Blomberg became a devotee of Hitler and May 1935 became commander in chief of the armed forces. In 1936 he became a field marshal but shortly afterwards married a former prostitute, which gave Hitler the chance to demand his resignation on the ground that his conduct brought the officer corps into disrepute. This, as Hitler planned, shook the confidence of the army and allowed him to replace several senior officers with his own appointees.

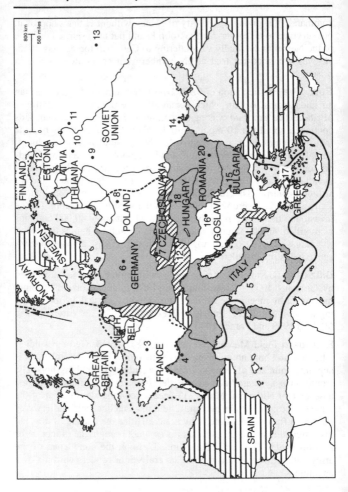

AXIS CONQUEST OF EUROPE 1939–1941

Key

▨	Occupied before Sept 1 1939
▤	Czechoslovak territory occupied by other powers 1938
– –	Axis advance by 9 May 1940
- ·-	Axis advance by 9 July 1940
▨	Axis and associated powers March 1941
——	Axis advance by end June 1941
⫿⫿⫿	Countries remaining neutral

Cities/towns

1	Madrid	11	Moscow
2	London	12	Leningrad
3	Paris	13	Stalingrad
4	Vichy	14	Odessa
5	Rome	15	Sofia
6	Berlin	16	Belgrade
7	Prague	17	Athens
8	Warsaw	18	Budapest
9	Minsk	19	Vienna
10	Smolensk	20	Bucharest

Blue Division Spanish volunteers who fought with the German army against the USSR. They were sent to join the Eastern Front April 1942 where they fought alongside regular troops.

Blumentritt General Gunther 1892–1967. German soldier. A general staff officer, he was chief of operations for von ◊Rundstedt throughout the Polish and French campaigns, and in 1942 became Chief of Staff to von ◊Kluge's 4th Army on the Eastern Front. He returned to von Rundstedt in France late 1942 and planned counter-invasion defences. After a further period as Chief of Staff to ◊Model, he was given command of 12th SS Corps 1944, of 25th Army Jan 1945, and of 1st Parachute Army March 1945. He surrendered to the British in Lübeck May 1945.

Bock Field Marshal Fedor von 1885–1945. German soldier. He commanded Army Group North during the Polish campaign 1939, then Army Group B in the invasion of Belgium and Holland 1940. He then commanded Army Group Centre in Operation ◊Barbarossa, his objective being ◊Moscow. After the failure to take Moscow and the Soviet counteroffensive, he was removed from his post, but took command of Army Group South early 1942, operating toward the Caucasus. In July 1942 he had a dispute over strategy with Hitler and was dismissed. He held no further responsible positions and was killed in an air raid.

Boeing US aircraft. Boeing made two aircraft of supreme importance in the war. The B-17 *Flying Fortress* was a four-engine bomber with a wingspan of 31 m/103 ft and a payload of 2,700 kg/6,000 lb. It was mistakenly thought that it would need no escort fighters as it was so heavily armed so the aircraft did not come into its own until it had a suitable long-range escort fighter. Numerous modifications were made to the basic design, which first flew 1935, and the final version had a speed of 505 kph/315 mph and a ceiling of 11,150 m/36,600 ft, making it a difficult target for air defence guns. The B-17 became the principal strategic bomber of the US Army Air Force; over 4,700 were in front-line service by mid-1944.

The B-29 *Superfortress* was developed as a replacement for the B-17 and first flew 1942. Designed as a pressurized high-altitude bomber, it weighed twice as much as the B-17 and used remote-controlled gun turrets. Capable of 574 kph/357 mph with a payload of 9,000 kg/ 20,000 lb, it had a range of 5,230 km/3,250 mi and was employed in the Pacific Theatre. On 6 Aug 1945 the first atomic bomb was dropped on ◊Hiroshima by the B-29 *Enola Gay*.

Bofors gun light 40 mm anti-aircraft gun designed by the Bofors company of Sweden 1929 and used by almost all combatants. It fired from four-round clips at a rate of 120 rpm (rounds per minute) and had an effective ceiling of 1,520 m/5,000 ft. Highly useful against low-flying ground attack aircraft, the original models were entirely hand operated and visually sighted, but in the latter part of the war ◊radar, predictors, and power control were added, improving the chance of hitting the target.

Bohr Niels Henrik David 1885–1962. Danish physicist who produced a new model of atomic structure, now called the Bohr model, and helped establish the validity of quantum theory. Bohr fled from the Nazis in World War II and became part of the team working on the ◊atomic bomb in the USA.

Bor-Komorowski General Tadeusz 1895–1956. Polish soldier. Komorowski joined the Polish lancers 1918 and in 1939 was colonel commanding the Cavalry Training School. After the German occupation he went underground and organized resistance groups, taking the cover-name 'Bor' and eventually becoming commander in chief of the ◊Polish Home Army. Captured by the Germans after the Warsaw Rising, he was imprisoned in ◊Colditz but survived the war and lived in Britain for the remainder of his life.

Bormann Martin 1900–1988? One of the first members of the Nazi Party, Bormann became its national organizer, and following the flight of ◊Hess 1941 was appointed head of the Party Chancery. In 1943 Hitler made him his personal secretary, a position in which he controlled access to Hitler, preventing bad news from reaching him and giving him the benefit of his opinions on various subjects; it has been suggested that some of Hitler's less intelligent actions might have been prompted by Bormann.

He made tentative overtures to the Soviets 1945 but these came to nothing and he managed to keep this from Hitler. After Hitler's suicide

Bormann vanished. He was frequently reported as being seen in various parts of the world but appears to have finally lived in South America where he reportedly died 1988.

Bougainville most northerly of the Solomon Islands, about 965 km/600 mi from Australia, now part of Papua-New Guinea. Bougainville was taken by the Japanese March 1942. It became an important refuelling and supply base for their operations against ◊Guadalcanal and the other Solomon Islands and was garrisoned by about 35,000 Japanese troops, principally in the south end of the island. The US 3rd Marine Division landed at the northern end of the island 1 Nov 1943 and established a secure beachhead, reinforced by the US 37th Infantry Division. Thereafter the Japanese, in spite of ferocious counterattacks, were neutralized and contained. In early 1944 the US troops were replaced by Australians who proceeded to hunt down the remaining Japanese and had secured the island by April 1944. An estimated 8,500 Japanese were killed in fighting on the island and a further 9,000 died of illness and malnutrition.

Boulogne French seaport on the English Channel, about 30 km/20 mi S of Calais. It was captured 25 May 1940 by the 2nd German Panzer Division who took some 5,000 Allied prisoners. It remained in German hands until liberated by Canadian 3rd Infantry Division 22 Sept 1944, but the port facilities had been so wrecked that it was unusable for several months.

bouncing bomb popular name for rotating bomb designed by Dr Barnes Wallis for attacking the ◊Ruhr dams. Cylindrical in shape, the bomb was slung beneath a ◊Lancaster bomber and rotated prior to dropping from a carefully calculated height. It then rolled or 'bounced' along the surface of the water as far as the dam and sank so as to be in contact with the dam wall. A depth-sensitive fuse detonated the bomb at the point calculated to make the most effective breach, the water in the reservoir acting as a tamping device to direct the full force of the explosion at the dam.

Bourgebus Ridge small ridge SE of ◊Caen, held 1944 by German troops amply equipped with anti-tank weapons. It was attacked by three British armoured divisions 18 July, which were beaten off with severe losses in both men and tanks. Nevertheless, the attack had the effect of making the Germans reinforce this area, weakening their hold on the southern part of the Normandy beachhead where the main Allied break-out was planned.

Bradley General Omar Nelson 1893–1981. US general. In 1943 he commanded the 2nd US Corps in their victories in Tunisia and Sicily, leading to the surrender of 250,000 Axis troops, and led US troops in the invasion of France 1944. His command, the 12th Army Group, grew to 1.3 million troops, the largest US force ever assembled. After the war, he was Chief of Staff of the US Army 1948–49 and chairman of the joint Chiefs of Staff 1949–53. He was appointed general of the army 1950.

Brandenburgers name given to German special forces and commando-style units. Originally known as the 'Lehr-Regiment Brandenburg' they were later given titles such as 'Engineer Construction Battalion' so as to conceal their true purpose. Rarely used for their intended purpose, they eventually became an ordinary mechanized infantry regiment.

Brauchitsch Walther von 1881–1948. German field marshal. A staff officer in World War I, he became commander in chief of the army and a member of Hitler's secret cabinet council 1938. He resigned after a heart attack and his failure to repel ◊Zhukov's counterattack outside Moscow 1941. Captured 1945, he died before he could be tried at the ◊Nuremburg trials.

Braun Eva 1912–45. Hitler's mistress and latterly wife. A photographer's assistant, she became Hitler's mistress 1942, but her existence was kept secret until 1944. She was married to Hitler 29 May 1945 shortly before they both committed suicide in the Berlin Führerbunker.

Braun Wernher von 1912–1977. German scientist. He became a member of the German Rocket Society in the early 1930s and then joined the army weapons department's rocket experimental section. He later became technical director of the army rocket research centre at ◊Peenemunde and was responsible for the design of a number of rockets including the ◊A-4 ballistic missile (the V2). In 1945 he was taken to the USA together with his research team to continue his researches, eventually becoming a prominent figure in the NASA space programme.

Bren gun standard light machine gun of British and Commonwealth armies. A gas-operated weapon in .303 calibre, it was of Czech design and was adopted 1936 to replace the Lewis gun. It was named after **BR**no (the Czech design factory) and **EN**field (the Royal Small Arms Factory in England which made it). Weighing 10 kg/22 lb, it used a 30-round curved box magazine mounted above the gun, and fired at 500 rpm (rounds per minute). It was probably the best light machine gun used by any army during the war, being simple, effective, and highly reliable.

Brereton General Lewis M 1890–1967. US airman. A fighter pilot in World War I, he was appointed commander of the US Far East Air Force Dec 1941, moving to India to become commander of the US Middle East Air Force 1942. He took charge of the US 9th Air Force in Tunisia Oct 1942 and after the end of that campaign took the force to England and trained it as a tactical support force, the role it fulfilled in the Normandy invasion 1944. In Aug 1944 he became commander of the 1st Allied Airborne Army and planned and executed a number of airborne operations including Operation ◊Market Garden.

Breskens pocket area S of the ◊Scheldt river, opposite the ◊Walcheren islands, where the German 6th Division was enclosed and isolated after the fall of ◊Antwerp Sept 1944. It contained a major coastal defence fort which commanded the entrance to the river which was attacked by Canadian forces 6 Oct 1944, but German resistance was strong and the attack had to be reinforced by the Canadian 4th Armoured Division and British 52nd Lowland Division. The pocket was finally taken 2 Nov along with 12,500 German prisoners.

Brest French seaport and fortified naval base in W Brittany, 275 km/170 mi NW of Nantes. Held by a strong German force, including the 2nd Parachute Division, it was attacked by US VIII Corps 25 Aug 1944. German resistance was tenacious and the fortress was not captured until 18 Sept. Some 35,000 German prisoners were taken, and US casualties amounted to some 10,000 men.

Bristol British aircraft. The Bristol *Blenheim* was a medium bomber, a twin-engine monoplane with a top speed of 400 kph/250 mph and a payload of 1,000 lb. Although originally developed 1935 as a fast executive airliner, it was found to be faster than contemporary fighters and so was modified to bomber form and adopted by the RAF 1936. It was used for day bombing in the early part of the war and many were supplied to Greece, Finland, Yugoslavia, and Turkey. It eventually became outmoded as a bomber, and many were converted into long-range radar-equipped night fighters.

The Bristol *Beaufort* resembled the Blenheim but was a heavier machine used for mine-laying and torpedo-bombing. The *Beaufighter* was a modification of the Beaufort and became the first night-fighter to be fitted with airborne radar 1940. Later versions were used in the rocket-firing ground attack role and as fast torpedo-bombers. With two extremely powerful engines it had a speed of 530 kph/330 mph, was highly manoeuvrable, and its armament of four cannon and six machine guns gave it devastating firepower.

Never in the field of human conflict was so much owed by so many to so few.

Winston Churchill speech of 20 Aug 1940

Britain, Battle of air battle between German and British air forces over Britain 10 July–31 Oct 1940.

At the outset the Germans had the advantage because they had seized airfields in the Netherlands, Belgium, and France, which were basically safe from attack and from which SE England was within easy range. On 1 Aug 1940 the Luftwaffe had about 4,500 aircraft of all kinds, compared to about 3,000 available to the RAF. The Battle of Britain had been intended as a preliminary to the German plan for the invasion of Britain *Seelöwe* (Sea Lion), which Hitler indefinitely postponed 17 Sept and abandoned 10 Oct, choosing instead to invade the USSR (see ◊Barbarossa).

The Battle of Britain has been divided into five phases: 10 July–7 Aug, the preliminary phase; 8–23 Aug, attack on coastal targets;

Battle of Britain aircraft losses: 10 July–31 Oct 1940

| period | RAF | | | Luftwaffe | |
	Fighter	Other	Bomber[1]	Fighter[2]	Other
10–30 July	75 (27)	8 (1)	116 (31)	49	9 (6)
31 July–27 Aug	284 (30)	30 (7)	306 (53)	268 (35)	21 (9)
28 Aug–1 Oct	471 (32)	12 (5)	345 (78)	400 (41)	28 (18)
2–31 Oct	174 (57)	11 (7)	194 (68)	162 (36)	19 (9)

Figures in brackets indicate aircraft lost in accidents (included in totals).
[1]Luftwaffe bombers include Ju 87 dive-bombers.
[2]Luftwaffe fighters include Me110 twin-engine fighters.

24 Aug–6 Sept, attack on Fighter Command airfields; 7–30 Sept, day-light attacks on London, chiefly by heavy bombers; and 1–31 Oct, daylight attacks on London, chiefly by fighter-bombers. The main bat-tle was between some 600 Hurricanes and Spitfires and the Luftwaffe's 800 Messerschmitt 109s and 1,000 bombers (Dornier 17s, Heinkel 111s, and Junkers 88s). Losses Aug–Sept were, for the RAF: 832 fight-ers totally destroyed; for the Luftwaffe: 668 fighters and some 700 bombers and other aircraft.

British Expeditionary Force (BEF) name for British forces sent to France 1939. By May 1940 it consisted of 10 infantry divisions, one tank brigade, and an RAF element of about 500 fighters and light bombers. After sustaining heavy losses during the French and Belgian campaigns of 1940 the remains were evacuated from ◊Dunkirk in June, leaving much of their equipment behind.

British Somaliland British colony in the Horn of Africa, S of the Gulf of Aden and now forming then part of Somalia. It was invaded by Italian forces from Abyssinia (now Ethiopia) 3 Aug 1940 and the small British force was evacuated by sea from Berbera. After the British cap-ture of Italian Somaliland (now Ethiopia and S Somalia) the Italians abandoned British Somaliland which was then re-occupied by a British force from Aden 16 March 1941.

Broadway codename given to a British base formed by the ◊Chindits E of Mohnyin, Burma (now Myanmar) March 1944. A supply dump and airstrip were set up inside a defended perimeter, and although frequently attacked from both ground and air, it remained in use until evacuated at the completion of the Chindit expedition May 1944.

Bruneval French village N of Le Havre. A German radar set was discovered there by air reconnaissance and a raid was mounted by the British Parachute Regiment to capture vital components for examination by scientists. An RAF technician jumped with the paratroops to identify the necessary parts. The raid was a success and the raiders, and their booty, were evacuated by the Royal Navy. A by-product of this raid was the removal of the British radar research establishment from close to the sea at Swanage, Dorset, to a safe inland site at Malvern, Worcestershire, in case the Germans retaliated in kind.

BT series tanks Soviet medium tanks developed in the 1930s. The design was based upon the large-wheel suspension developed by ◊Christie in the USA and culminated in the *BT-7* of 1937. This model was driven by a 350 hp aircraft engine, giving it a top speed of 56 kph/35 mph, and was armed with a 76 mm turret gun. Used in Spain, Manchuria, Finland, and in the occupation of Poland 1940, it proved no match for the German Panzers 1941, though much of this failure was due to inept tactical handling.

Buchenwald German concentration camp near Weimar, established 1937 as a labour camp for political prisoners and criminals. It was later used as a collection point for Jews and other victims en route to extermination camps.

Budapest capital of Hungary, industrial city on the Danube. When Admiral ◊Horthy, Regent of Hungary, attempted to negotiate peace terms with the Allies Oct 1944, Budapest was occupied by German troops and Horthy deposed. The city was surrounded by Soviet forces Dec 1944; the German garrison of about 40,000 was ordered to hold it until relieved, but no relief came so on 11 Feb 1945 the German commander order a break-out, abandoning his wounded. Out of some 30,000 German troops who attempted to get through the Soviet encirclement, only about 700 escaped.

Budenny Marshal Semyon 1883–1973. Soviet soldier. A sergeant-major in the Tsar's army, Budenny joined the Bolsheviks 1917 and rose rapidly, commanding a cavalry army by 1920 and being made Marshal of the Soviet Union 1935. One of Stalin's 'Old Guard', he survived the Great Purge of Red Army officers 1936–38 and after the German invasion 1941 became commander in chief in the Ukraine and Bessarabia. A man of limited military talent, Budenny was out-manoeuvred by the Germans and lost ◊Kiev together with about half the army. Surprisingly he survived this, and was made Hero of the Soviet Union and inspector of recruiting, becoming commander of cavalry forces 1943. He took no active part in the war after Kiev, his appointments being calculated to keep him in harmless positions.

Bulge, Battle of (or *Ardennes offensive*). Hitler's plan, code-named 'Watch on the Rhine', for a breakthrough by his field marshal von ◊Rundstedt aimed at the US line in the Ardennes 16 Dec 1944–28 Jan 1945. Hitler aimed to isolate the Allied forces north of the corridor which would be created by a drive through the Ardennes, creating a German salient or 'bulge'.

Three armies were employed in the operation — Sepp ◊Dietrich's 6th Panzer; the 5th Panzer; and the 7th Panzer — together with a 'Trojan Horse' force of English-speaking Germans in American uniforms, under Otto ◊Skorzeny. The offensive opened 16 Dec along a 113 km/ 70 mi sector of the front, aiming at the US 1st Army and General ◊Bradley's 12th Army Group. Initial progress was good as the Allies were unprepared for action along a section of the front hitherto so quiet it had been nicknamed 'the Ghost Front' and bad weather grounded Allied air support.

However, the Germans failed to capture vital fuel dumps and the dogged Allied defence of St Vith and ◊Bastogne seriously set the operation back. The Allies quickly recovered from the initial shock and while north of the Bulge ◊Montgomery blocked the German advance at the Meuse, to the south ◊Bradley's forces also struck back, with ◊Patton breaking through to relieve Bastogne 26 Dec. By the end of Dec the weather improved, allowing the Allied air forces to play a part in the battle and by 3 Jan 1945 the Allies took the offensive; by 16 Jan the Bulge had been eliminated.

There were 77,000 Allied casualties and 130,000 German, including Hitler's last powerful reserve, his Panzer elite. Although US troops were encircled for some weeks at Bastogne, delaying Allied operations in the West for about six weeks, the German counteroffensive failed and the loss of the reserve was a heavy price to pay.

All I had to do was cross the river, capture Brussels, and then go on to take the port of Antwerp. The snow was waist-deep and there wasn't room to deploy four tanks abreast, let alone six Panzer divisions. It didn't get light till eight and was dark again at four and my tanks can't fight at night. And all this at Christmas time!

Sepp Dietrich, commander of 6th Panzer
Army during the *Battle of the Bulge*.

Burke Rear Admiral Arleigh 1901–. US sailor. He joined the US Navy at the end of World War I and came to prominence 1943 when, as rear admiral commanding destroyers in the South Pacific, he earned the nickname '31-knot Burke' from his aggressive patrolling policy. His squadron covered the landings at ◊Bougainville and fought over 20 separate engagements with Japanese naval forces. He later became Chief of Staff to Carrier Task Force 58, and was appointed to head the research and development department in the Naval Bureau of Ordnance 1945.

ground forces casualties: SE Asia 1941–45

	killed/missing	wounded	POW
UK	5,670	12,840	53,230
India	6,860	24,200	68,890
other Allied	5,490	3,970	18,810
Japan	210,830	?	3,100

Burma, Operations in fighting between Allied and Japanese forces after the Japanese 15th Army invaded S Burma Jan 1942. The outnumbered British forces conducting a fighting retreat, finally reaching India with heavy losses May 1942. A limited British offensive was mounted in the ◊Arakan Dec 1942 but this was beaten back by the Japanese. The ◊Chindit expedition mounted an operation behind Japanese lines Feb–April 1943 which, while of negligible military worth, was a powerful morale-raiser since it showed that the Japanese did not have a monopoly on jungle operations.

In N Burma a Chinese-American force under ◊Stilwell commenced offensive operations Oct 1943. A second British offensive was launched in the Arakan Jan 1944; the Japanese response was violent but by this time the British had air superiority and were more confident of their ability and they inflicted a heavy defeat on the Japanese in the Battle of the ◊Admin Box Feb 1944.

The Japanese struck back with an offensive in central Burma toward ◊Imphal and ◊Kohima. Imphal was besieged but, thanks to supplies from the air, held out against severe attacks. At Kohima the Japanese attack was stopped and then thrown back by the British, who then went on to relieve Imphal. The Japanese, starving and disorganized, retreated behind the Chindwin river, leaving 53,000 dead behind them.

A second Chindit operation was launched which cut the Japanese supply lines, followed by renewed offensives from Stilwell in the north. The British XXX Corps crossed the Chindwin Jan–Feb 1945, attracting Japanese attacks, while IV Corps moved round to a flank, crossed the Irrawaddy river and captured Meiktila, isolating the Japanese armies in the north. The Japanese front collapsed and the British re-took Rangoon 2 May 1945 and then destroyed the Japanese 28th Army as they tried to escape across the Sittang river into Thailand.

Burma Road a transport route from Lashio in Burma to Kunming, China. With the Chinese coastline inaccessible to Allied supply ships, this was the only route by which military supplies could be sent to the Chinese Army, so cutting the route became a prime Japanese target, leading to their invasion of ◊Burma. Once the Japanese occupied the area and blocked the road, the only method of supply open to the Allies was to fly equipment from India to China, 'over the ◊Hump' of the Himalayas. The road was not reopened until a concerted effort by Chinese, US, and British forces Jan 1945.

C

Caen capital of Calvados *département*, France, on the river Orne, a major road and rail junction. Caen was one of the main objectives of the ◊D-Day landings as it held the key to breaking out of the Normandy area but it was not taken as quickly as was hoped. It was eventually captured by British forces 9 July 1944 after five weeks' fighting, during which the town was badly damaged.

Caesar Line last German line of defence in Italy before Rome. It stretched from the west coast near Ostia, over the Alban Hills south of Rome, via Valmontone to Avezzano – about half-way across the country. When it was breached by the US 5th Army 30 May 1944 the road to Rome was finally opened.

Calabria, Battle of naval action between British and Italian forces, 9 April 1940. The British Mediterranean fleet of three battleships, an aircraft carrier, and five cruisers, escorting a convoy to Alexandria, met an Italian force of two battleships and sixteen cruisers which was itself escorting a convoy to N Africa. Both sides opened fire and the British hit the Italian battleship *Guilio Cesare* at a range of 24 km/15 mi. The Italians laid a smoke screen and turned away, leaving the British force undamaged.

Calais French seaport on the Channel coast. It was taken by the German 10th Panzer Division 26 May 1940; the small British and French garrison had held out for two days before being overrun. The 3rd Canadian Division launched an attack to recover Calais 24 Sept 1944; the German garrison finally surrendered 30 Sept after thoroughly wrecking all the port facilities.

Callaghan Rear Admiral Daniel J 1809–1942. US sailor. After serving as naval aide to President ◊Roosevelt, Callaghan was given command of a cruiser, and then became Chief of Staff to the Naval Commander, South Pacific. He returned to sea commanding a squadron of five cruisers and eight destroyers. During the first battle of ◊Guadalcanal he attacked a Japanese flotilla 12 Nov 1942. He severely damaged an enemy battleship and two other warships and sunk one, so preventing Japanese reinforcements being landed on Guadalcanal. Despite the success of the action, Callaghan himself was killed during the fighting.

Canaris Admiral Wilhelm 1887–1945. German sailor and intelligence expert. A U-boat commander during World War I, he remained in the navy after the war and became an intelligence specialist. In 1935 he became head of the ◊Abwehr, the German armed forces Intelligence Service.

Never a member of the Nazi party, he appears to have flirted with various anti-Nazi factions, and there have also been suggestions that under his control the Abwehr leaked information to British intelligence, though this may well have been a British disinformation ploy to conceal their ◊Ultra source. He was arrested after the ◊July Bomb Plot against Hitler 1944, although there has never been any evidence that he was involved. In fact, it is probable that he was 'framed' by Himmler so that the SS could obtain control of all intelligence services. Canaris was executed in Flossenberg concentration camp 9 April 1945.

Cape Esperance, Battle of naval action between US and Japanese forces, 11–12 Oct 1942. A Japanese cruiser squadron of three cruisers and two destroyers was ordered to cover the landing of reinforcements on ◊Guadalcanal island, after which it was to bombard ◊Henderson Field airstrip. At the same time, a US squadron of four cruisers and five destroyers was escorting a troop and supply convoy approaching the area.

The two sides met off Savo Island; the US force opened fire first, severely damaging two Japanese cruisers and sinking one destroyer. The US destroyer *Duncan* got involved with two Japanese ships and became the target of not only their fire but that of other US ships attempting to deal with the Japanese in the dark by radar. The vessel caught fire and was abandoned; it sank the following day. The US force then pursued the Japanese out of the area and sank a further cruiser and two destroyers.

Cape Matapan, Battle of naval action between British and Italian forces 28 March 1941. An Italian force of one battleship, eight cruisers, and nine destroyers set out to disrupt British convoys between Alexandria and Greece. However the British were forewarned and Admiral Sir Andrew ♢Cunningham set out to protect the convoys with three battleships, an aircraft carrier, four cruisers, and thirteen destroyers. The two fleets met south of Crete and the British cruisers immediately opened fire and then withdrew, hoping to draw the Italians on to the main British fleet. However, having just suffered a minor air attack, the Italian commander realised the British had a carrier, and quite possibly larger vessels in the area and turned about and fled.

Cunningham ordered air and torpedo strikes against the Italian flagship *Vittorio Veneto* as the Italians were moving off. The attacks did not affect the *Vittorio Veneto* but one of the torpedoes struck and halted the cruiser *Pola*. The Italians detached two cruisers and four destroyers to assist the *Pola* then withdrew to base. The British found the *Pola* and its escort on radar, closed with them in the darkness, and opened fire at a range of 2,750 m/3,000 yds, sinking all seven Italian ships.

Cape Spartivento, Battle of naval action between British and Italian forces, 27 Nov 1940. An Italian fleet of two battleships, six cruisers, and fourteen destroyers attempted to intercept a British convoy escorted by a battleship, a battle cruiser, an aircraft carrier, five cruisers, and ten destroyers.

The British commander ordered the convoy to turn away and then took his fleet toward the Italians. The leading cruisers of both sides opened fire but the Italian commander then saw the aircraft carrier *Ark Royal* in the British force. Fearing air strikes against Italy's only two serviceable battleships, he turned about and fled for Naples.

Cape St George, Battle of naval action between five Japanese and five US destroyers, 25 Nov 1943, off the island of New Ireland. The US force was led by Capt Arleigh ♢Burke who, in his usual manner, went straight into action, sinking three Japanese destroyers and putting the other two to flight.

Carlson Lieutenant-Colonel Evans F. US Marine. After service in World War I, Carlson continued in the Marine Corps and served in

China as an observer with the Chinese Nationalist Army where he made a particular study of guerrilla operations. He applied this knowledge at ◊Guadalcanal, where he commanded the 2nd Raider Battalion who became known as 'Carlson's Raiders' after he carried out a number of lightning raids on Japanese positions. He was wounded during operations on ◊Saipan 1944 and retired shortly after the war ended.

Carolines scattered archipelago in Micronesia, Pacific Ocean, consisting of over 500 coral islets; area 1,200 sq km/463 sq mi. Mandated by the League of Nations to Japan 1919, they were fortified contrary to the terms of the mandate. They remained in Japanese hands throughout the war despite heavy Allied air attacks and then became part of the US Trust Territory of the Pacific Islands 1947–90.

Casablanca conference meeting of the US and UK leaders Roosevelt and Churchill, 14–24 Jan 1943 together with their Chiefs of Staff, at which the Allied demand for the unconditional surrender of Germany, Italy, and Japan was issued. This demand proved to be counterproductive as it only served to harden the resolve of the Axis powers and may have lengthened the war.

Matters of general strategy were also covered including agreements to give priority to the Battle of the ◊Atlantic; to continue the supply of aid to the USSR; to make joint preparations for an invasion of France from Britain (which led to the ◊D-Day invasion); to begin planning for an invasion of ◊Sicily; and to extend operations against the Japanese to retake the ◊Aleutian Islands and ◊Marshall Islands, while the British were to retake ◊Burma.

Cassino town in S Italy, 80 km/50 mi NW of Naples, at the foot of Monte Cassino. Heavily fortified by the Germans, it was the scene of heavy fighting early 1944 as it was a key position blocking the Allied advance to Rome.

It was attacked by the British X Corps, US II Corps, and the French Corps from 17 Jan–12 Feb 1944 but these assaults were all repulsed. The Allies thought the Germans had fortified the monastery above the town and so it was heavily bombed 15 Feb. Following this attack, the 4th Indian Division made some progress attacking Monastery Hill, and the 2nd New Zealand Division captured the town railway station but lost it three days later. An air raid combined with an artillery bombardment thoroughly wrecked the town 15 March, after which the railway station and Castle Hill were captured in three days of intense fighting.

The final battle began 11 May 1944 when 2,000 guns bombarded the German positions, the Polish II Corps isolated Monastery Hill, the British crossed the river Liri to cut the road west of Cassino, and US and French corps attacked south of the river. The German positions were taken despite being vigorously defended and by 18 May the town and monastery were in Allied hands. Heavy losses were suffered by both sides in the operation.

casualties

civilian it is impossible to arrive at even approximate figures for civilian casualties due to the war. It is difficult to make a connection between the war and any particular death and in the confused conditions of central Europe, ravaged by the oscillations of armies, the fate of many civilians will never be known. (For Jewish deaths see ⟩holocaust).

military casualties 1939–1945

country	dead	wounded	total
Australia	29,400	39,800	69,200
Canada	39,300	53,200	92,500
China	1,400,000	1,850,000	3,250,000
Finland	79,000	198,600	277,600
France	205,700	390,000	595,700
Germany	3,300,000	4,605,000	7,905,000
Greece	18,300	60,000	78,300
Hungary	136,000	250,000	386,000
India	36,100	64,300	100,400
Italy	226,900	500,000	726,900
Japan	1,740,000	94,000	1,834,000
New Zealand	12,200	19,300	31,500
Poland	110,800	146,700	257,500
South Africa	8,700	14,400	23,100
UK	305,800	277,100	582,900
USA	292,131	671,278	963,409
USSR (military and civilian)	6,115,000	14,012,000	20,127,000
total for all combatants:	*14,055,331*	*23,245,678*	*37,301,009*

military these figures have been derived from official sources and appear to be the most accurate available, although any such figures are inevitably best estimates as the confusion of battle does not lend itself to the accurate compilation of statistics. Note that the Soviet figures also include civilian casualties as separate figures are not available: the much-quoted figure of 'twenty million Soviet dead' is actually the grand total; the true figure for military casualties is much lower.

Caucasus, Campaigns in fighting between German and Soviet forces following German invasion of the Caucasus region June 1942. The initial invasion was by German Army Group A, intent upon seizing the oilfields around Maikop and Baku. Maikop was captured Aug 1942, but a further advance through the passes of the Caucasus mountains was beaten back by the Soviet army. The Soviet victory at ◊Stalingrad and their subsequent offensive threatened to outflank Army Group A. Hitler dismissed the commander, Field Marshal ◊List, Sept 1942, and assumed command himself until late Nov, when he appointed General von ◊Kleist as commander. The Soviets opened an offensive in Dec and von Kleist was forced to withdraw to avoid being surrounded.

Cauldron, the area in Libya S of Gazala into which ◊Rommel withdrew his forces after initial reverses in the battle of ◊Gazala, 10 May 1942. After a long delay, the British General ◊Ritchie attacked the Cauldron 5 June but by that time Rommel had reorganized and re-supplied his forces. He defeated Ritchie, broke out of the Cauldron, and defeated the British at ◊Knightsbridge.

Caumont French town in Normandy 35 km/22 mi SW of ◊Caen. Captured by US troops 1 July 1944, it was absorbed in the British 2nd Army area and used as the jumping-off point for Operation Bluecoat. This was a major attack southward aiming both to capture ground and pursue the advantage toward Vire so as to attract a counterattack by the Germans, weakening the line in front of the US forces to allow them to break out in the south. The operation failed to reach Vire but was successful in drawing off the Germans.

Cebu island in the Philippine group held by about 14,500 Japanese troops. It was attacked by the US Americal Division 26 March 1945; the Japanese retreated into prepared positions in the hills and a further three weeks of hard fighting were necessary before the island was declared secure. Even then there were numerous Japanese survivors who fled into the mountains in the north of the island and remained troublesome for the rest of the war.

Chain Home code name for the system of British ◊radar stations built around the E and S coasts of England 1938–39 to give early warning of German air attacks. The first system could only detect aircraft flying at average heights; it was later augmented by a second set of stations especially designed to detect low-flying aircraft, known as 'Chain Home Low'.

Chamberlain Arthur Neville 1869–1940. British Conservative politician, son of Joseph Chamberlain, prime minister 1937–40. He attempted to appease the demands of the European dictators, particularly Mussolini. In 1938 he went to Munich and negotiated the settlement of the Czechoslovak question with Hitler. He was ecstatically received on his return, and claimed that the ◊Munich Agreement brought 'peace in our time'. Within a year, however, Britain was at war with Germany. He resigned 1940 following the defeat of the British forces in Norway.

In war, whichever side may call itself the victor, there are no winners, but all are losers.
                    Neville Chamberlain speech at Kettering 3 July 1938

Channel Dash, the escape of three German warships through English and French waters to Germany. The battle cruisers *Gneisenau* and *Scharnhorst* and the heavy cruiser *Prinz Eugen* sailed from Brest 12 Feb 1942, through the English Channel and North Sea to the security of the Elbe river.

Aided by bad weather and radar jamming, the ships were able to evade air and sea patrols until they were near Le Toquet, when they were detected by an RAF reconnaissance flight and by coastal defence radar in Dover. The Dover coastal artillery opened fire and were able to score three hits before the warships were out of their range. Air and sea attacks by the Royal Naval Air Service, the Royal Navy, and the RAF failed to halt the ships, but the RAF hastily laid a minefield near the Frisian Islands, and both the *Scharnhorst* and *Gneisenaut* were severely damaged. Despite this, the three ships managed to make the safety of the Elbe without further attack. Although a shaming defeat for the British, it was, in fact, helpful since it was easier to keep an eye on these ships when they were in Germany than when they were in French waters.

Channel Islands group of islands in the English Channel, off the NW coast of France; dependent territories of the British crown. They comprise the islands of Jersey, Guernsey, Alderney, Great and Little Sark, with the lesser Herm, Brechou, Jethou, and Lihou. The islands were occupied by Germany June 1940–May 1945, the only British soil to be taken by the Germans.

Char B tank principal French heavy tank, developed in the 1930s. Well-armoured and carrying a 47 mm turret gun and a 75 mm howitzer in the front face, it had a speed of about 29 kph/18 mph. Like other French designs of the period it had a one-man turret, the commander being expected to command, observe, and operate the gun all by himself. It also suffered from heavy fuel consumption and a vulnerable radiator easily pierced by enemy fire. About 320 were issued, most of which were either destroyed in action or abandoned for lack of fuel during 1940.

Chase Major-General William C 1895–1986. US soldier. He was commissioned into the cavalry 1916 and served in World War I. In 1943 he took command of 1 Cavalry Brigade which recaptured the ◊Admiralty Islands March 1944. He later took part in the invasion of the ◊Philippines and led the first US troops into Manila 3 Feb 1945. He then took command of 38 Infantry Division and cleared the Japanese out of Bataan and supervised the airborne assault on ◊Corregidor.

He was given command of 1 Cavalry Division Sept 1945 and took the division to Japan where it became the first US military force to enter Tokyo. After the war he became Chief of Staff 3rd Army, then went to Taiwan as military adviser to ◊Chiang Kai-shek until his retirement 1956.

Chelmno site of the first German extermination camp, about 50 km/31 mi NE of Bydgoszcz in W Poland. Established 1941, it first used closed trucks which killed the occupants with exhaust fumes, then moved to the use of ◊Zyklon B gas. Escapees from Chelmno were the first to report that Jews were being systematically exterminated, but were not initially believed. A total of about 350,000 Jews and gypsies were killed at the camp before it was closed and destroyed 1944.

Chennault Major-General Claire L 1890–1958. US airman. A pilot in the US Army Air Corps, he was retired on medical grounds 1937 and then became an adviser and trainer on aviation for the Chinese Nationalist forces. He returned to the USA Nov 1940 and organized a 200-strong force of pilots and engineers to operate in China as the 'American Volunteer Group', who became more commonly known as the ◊'Flying Tigers'. This force was highly successful against the Japanese over S China and Burma 1941–42, destroying some 300 enemy aircraft.

Chennault returned to duty with the US Army Air Force 1942 when the Flying Tigers were absorbed in the regular forces as the 14th (Voluntary) Air Force, with him as their commander. He mounted an offensive against the Japanese 1943, but it was met with a strong counterattack which destroyed much of his force both in the air and on the ground. He resigned July 1945 after his advice on the future reorganization of the Chinese air force was rejected.

Cherbourg French seaport on northern end of the Cotentin peninsula, in the Manche *département*. It was captured by the German 7th Panzer Division, under ◊Rommel, 19 June 1940 and remained in German hands until after the ◊D-Day invasion when it became a prime target for US forces who wanted it as a supply port.

It was attacked by the US VII Corps under General ◊Collins 21 June 1944. Assisted by heavy air attacks, the defences were penetrated but pockets of German troops held out in various fortifications. The US Navy bombarded the fortifications with heavy gunfire, but it was 29 June before the last fort surrendered. About 39,000 German troops were taken prisoner, but the harbour installations had been destroyed by demolition squads as well as the Allied bombardment, and it was several months before Cherbourg was capable of operating again.

Cherwell Frederick Alexander Lindemann, Viscount Cherwell 1886–1957. British physicist. He was director of the Physical Laboratory of the RAF at Farnborough in World War I, and personal adviser to ◊Churchill on scientific and statistical matters during the war. He also served as director of the Clarendon Laboratory, Oxford, 1919–56.

Chetnik member of a Serbian nationalist group that operated underground during the German occupation of Yugoslavia. Led by Col Draza ◊Mihailovič, the Chetniks initially received aid from the Allies, but this was later transferred to the Communist partisans led by ◊Tito.

Chiang Kai-shek 1887–1975. Chinese general and politician. Leader of the nationalist Guomindang (Kuomintang), he was president of China 1928–31 and 1943–49, and of Taiwan from 1949.

Chiang was made commander in chief of the nationalist armies in S China on the death of the Guomindang leader Sun Yat-sen 1925. Cooperation with the communists under Mao was broken off 1927 but resumed 1936 as China needed to pool military strength in the struggle against the Japanese invaders. After the Japanese surrender 1945, civil war between the nationalists and communists erupted, and Chiang and his followers were expelled from the mainland Dec 1949. He took refuge on the island of Taiwan where he led an authoritarian regime with US support until his death, when he was succeeded by his son, Chiang Ching-kuo.

We shall not talk lightly about sacrifice until we are driven to the last extremity which makes sacrifice inevitable.
   Chiang Kai-shek speech to Fifth Congress of the Guomindang

---

Chindit member of a long range penetration group of the British army that carried out guerrilla operations against the Japanese in Burma (now Myanmar) under the command of Brig Gen Orde ◊Wingate. The Chindits undertook two main operations; the first was carried out by troops of 77th Brigade 1943, and the second by a specially assembled six-brigade force 1944. Wingate was killed in an air crash during the opening phase of the second operation. The unit's name derived from the mythical *Chinthe* – half lion, half eagle – placed at the entrance of Burmese pagodas to scare away evil spirits.

Christie Walter 1867–1944. US engineer. He designed naval gun mountings in the early 1900s and during World War I designed and built experimental self-propelled guns. He developed a number of prototype tanks during the 1920s, all featuring his own design of suspension, and developed the idea of a tank which could operate either on tracks or on wheels, giving the option of extremely high road speeds since his designs were all powered by aircraft engines.

The US Army purchased a handful of models from him, but found him unreliable in following up modifications and eventually abandoned his designs. He sold a number of tanks to the Soviet Army who used them as the basis for their ◊BT series and later models, and one tank was bought by the Nuffield Organisation in Britain and used as a basis for a number of British cruiser tanks 1936–42. Although his designs were often innovative they were rarely practical and he was largely ignored.

Chuikov General Vasily 1900–1982. Soviet soldier. He joined the Red Army 1918 and fought against the Poles and in the Civil War. He became an adviser to ◊Chiang Kai-shek 1926 and remained in China until 1937. He was in the War Ministry from 1941 until he was given command of the 62nd Army in ◊Stalingrad late 1942, holding the right bank of the Volga river during the siege. The 62nd was renamed the 8th Guards Army for its prowess at Stalingrad and it remained under his command for the rest of the war, fighting with distinction through to Berlin. He held several command positions following the war, finally becoming commander in chief Soviet Land Forces 1960.

Churchill Winston Leonard Spencer 1874–1965. British Conservative politician, prime minister 1940–45 and 1951–55. Churchill was an MP from 1900, as a Liberal until 1923, and held a number of ministerial offices, including First Lord of the Admiralty 1911–15 and chancellor of the Exchequer. He held no government post 1929–39, as he disagreed with mainstream Conservatives on India, rearmament, and Chamberlain's policy of appeasement.

He returned to the Admiralty Sept 1939 and became prime minister May 1940 as head of an all-party coalition, making his famous 'blood, tears, toil, and sweat' speech in the House of Commons. He had a close relationship with US president Roosevelt, and in Aug 1941 concluded the ◊Atlantic Charter with him. He travelled to Washington, ◊Casablanca, Cairo, Moscow, and ◊Tehran, meeting the other Allied leaders.

We shall go on to the end. We shall fight in France, we shall fight on the seas and oceans, we shall fight with growing confidence and growing strength in the air, we shall defend our island, whatever the cost may be. We shall fight on the beaches, we shall fight on the landing grounds, we shall fight in the fields and in the streets, we shall fight in the hills; we shall never surrender.
Winston Churchill, speech to the House of Commons 4 June 1940

His opinion that Australia was dispensable inevitably led to disputes with Australian prime minister ◊Curtin who, contrary to Churchill's demands, decided to recall Australian troops from the Middle East 1942 to help defend Australia, in cooperation with US forces, against Japanese attack. In Feb 1945 Churchill met Stalin and Roosevelt in the Crimea and agreed on the final plans for Allied victory. On 8 May he announced the unconditional surrender of Germany.

Churchill tank British heavy tank intended for trench-crossing and infantry support. First designed 1940 and then modified, the resulting model was officially the A22 but was called 'Churchill' as a morale-raising measure. Once the initial problems of early models were corrected, the Churchill went on to become a most reliable tank. Roomy, and with a remarkable cross-country performance, it was also the perfect basis for conversions into specialist vehicles such as flamethrowers (as the ◊Crocodile), bridging tanks, and engineer support vehicles.

It first saw action at ◊Dieppe, where six were landed and lost. Six took part in the battle of El ◊Alamein by way of evaluation, and two brigades were used in Tunisia. Many were also supplied to the Soviet army.

civil defence organized activities by the civilian population of a state to mitigate the effects of enemy attack. During the war civil defence efforts in Britain were centred on providing adequate warning of air raids to permit the civilian population to reach shelter; then firefighting, food, rescue, communications, and ambulance services were also needed.

The ministry of home security was established 1939 to direct air-raid precautions. The country was divided into 12 regions, each under a commissioner who would act on behalf of the central government in the event of national communications systems being destroyed. Associated with the air-raid wardens were ambulance and rescue parties, gas officers, breakdown gangs, and so on. The National Fire Service was based on existing local services, and about 5 million people enrolled as fire watchers and firefighters.

Clark General Mark Wayne 1896–1984. US soldier. He served in France in World War I and remained in the forces between the wars, becoming Chief of Staff for ground forces and deputy to General Eisenhower 1942. He led a successful secret mission by submarine to get information in N Africa to prepare for the Allied invasion, and commanded the 5th Army in the invasion of Italy. He remained in this command until the end of the war when he took charge of the US occupation force in Austria. He was commander in chief of the United Nations forces in the Korean War 1952–53.

coastwatchers Australian intelligence organization, formed 1919, a vital source of information during the war. It consisted of civilians appointed by the Royal Australian Navy who were placed in wireless-equipped stations on the mainland of Australia, islands to the N of Australia, Papua New Guinea, and the Solomon Islands.

Colditz town in E Germany, SW of Leipzig, site of a castle used as a high-security prisoner-of-war camp (Oflag IVC). It was considered escape-proof and so was used to house prisoners with important connections and those who had a record of escape from less secure camps. Although there were 130 successful escapes, only 32 managed to evade recapture. Among daring escapes was that of British Captain Patrick Reid (1910–1990) and others Oct 1942, whose story contributed much to its fame.

Collins General J Lawton 1886–1963. US soldier. He first came to prominence on ◊Guadalcanal 1942 leading the US 25th Infantry Division, which relieved the US Marines and completed the capture of the island. After service in New Guinea he went to England and took command of VII Corps, with which he assaulted ◊Utah Beach in the ◊D-Day landings 6 June 1944. Forces under his command took ◊Cherbourg, closed the ◊Falaise Gap, crossed the Seine, and advanced into Belgium. He commanded a counterattack force during the Battle of the ◊Bulge, then went on to cross the Rhine at ◊Remagen and advanced to meet the Soviet Army at Torgau 25 April 1945. His rapid manoeuvres and sound tactical sense led to his nickname 'Lightning Joe'.

Colmar pocket area in the Vosges Mountains of France where the German 17th Army was trapped by the French taking Mulhouse and US forces taking Strasbourg Nov 1944. Both French and US troops set about clearing the area Jan 1945; numbers of German troops were able to escape across the Rhine into German-held territory, but they left some 36,000 casualties behind them.

Cologne industrial and commercial port in North Rhine–Westphalia, Germany, on the left bank of the Rhine, 35 km/22 mi SE of Düsseldorf. To the N is the Ruhr coal field, on which many of Cologne's industries are based. Cologne suffered heavily from aerial bombardment, notably the British ◊'thousand bomber raid' 30 May 1942. Further damage ensued when the city was taken by General Lawton ◊Collins' US VII Corps 5 March 1945; 85% of the city and its three Rhine bridges were destroyed.

combined operations British term to denote operations in which all three services – army, navy, and air forces – were involved, notably amphibious landings. The first Chief of Combined Operations was Admiral Sir Roger Keyes Aug 1940 who was killed in an abortive attempt to kidnap Rommel. He was succeeded by Lord ◊Mountbatten Oct 1941. Combined Operations HQ were involved in planning all amphibious operations.

Comet tank British cruiser tank. One of the last wartime designs, it used the ◊Christie large wheel suspension and carried a 77 mm gun. Its greatest asset was its reliability, after a series of unreliable designs. It was first used March 1945 after the British had crossed the Rhine and remained in service for many years after the war.

commando member of a specially trained, highly mobile military unit. The term originated in South Africa in the 19th century, where it referred to Boer military reprisal raids against Africans and, in the South African Wars, against the British.

The first British commando units were the Combined Operations Command who raided enemy-occupied territory after the evacuation of ◊Dunkirk 1940. Among the commando raids were those on the Lofoten Islands (3–4 March 1941), Vaagsö, Norway (27 Dec 1941), St Nazaire (28 March 1942), and Dieppe (19 Aug 1942). In 1940 commandos were sent to the Middle East. One of their most daring exploits was the Nov 1941 raid on Rommel's headquarters in the desert. At the end of the war the army commandos were disbanded, but their role was continued by the Royal Marines.

concentration camp prison camp for civilians in wartime or under totalitarian rule. A system of hundreds of concentration camps was developed by the Nazis in Germany and occupied Europe (1933–45) to imprison Jews and political and ideological opponents after Hitler became chancellor Jan 1933. The most infamous were the extermination camps of ◊Auschwitz, ◊Belsen, ◊Dachau, ◊Maidanek, ◊Sobibor, and ◊Treblinka. The total number of people who died at the camps exceeded 6 million, and at some camps inmates were subjected to medical experimentation before being killed.

At Oswiecim (Auschwitz-Birkenau), a vast camp complex was created for imprisonment and slave labour as well as the extermination of over 4 million people in gas chambers or by other means. In addition to Jews, the victims included Gypsies, homosexuals, and other 'misfits' or 'unwanted' people. At Maidanek, about 1.5 million people were exterminated, cremated, and their ashes used as fertilizer. Many camp officials and others responsible were tried after 1945 for war crimes, and executed or imprisoned. Foremost was Adolf ◊Eichmann, the architect of the extermination system, who was tried and executed by the state of Israel 1961. See also ◊Holocaust.

Coningham Air Marshal Sir Arthur 1895–1948. British airman. After service with the New Zealand Army in World War I, he joined the Royal Flying Corps 1916 and then transferred to the Royal Air Force on its formation. By 1939 he was an Air Commodore commanding a bomber group, then went to N Africa to command the Desert Air Force. Here he developed the techniques of ground support for the army, and 1943 went to Algeria to command 1st Allied Tactical Air Force. He later commanded the air forces in the invasion of ◊Sicily and in the early part of the Italian campaign. In 1944 he returned to England to take command of 2nd Tactical Air Force which gave the army much-needed support throughout the ◊Normandy campaign.

conscription legislation for all able-bodied male citizens (and female in some countries, such as Israel) to serve with the armed forces. It originated in France 1792, and in the 19th and 20th centuries became the established practice in almost all European states. Alternatives to military service are often permitted for conscientious objectors.

In Britain conscription was first introduced in peace–time in April 1939, when all men aged 20 became liable to six months' military training. The National Service Act, passed Sept 1939, made all men between 18 and 41 liable to military service, and in 1941 women also became liable to be called up for the women's services as an alternative to industrial service. Men continued to be called up at the age of 18 until 1960.

In the USA a Selective Service Act was passed 1940 in anticipation of US entry into the war. It remained in force (except for 15 months 1947–48) until after the US withdrawal from Vietnam 1973.

Consolidated US aircraft. The *PBY Catalina* was an amphibian fly-ing-boat first developed 1935. It was relatively fast at 315 kph/195 mph, and had an enormous range of about 5,000 km/3,100 mi, making it ideal for patrolling the Atlantic. It was armed with up to six machine guns and could carry 910 kg/2,000 lb of bombs or depth charges. It was initially adopted by the US Navy, but was also used by the USSR and the Royal Air Force, who named it the Catalina; over 4,000 were built, more than any other flying boat.

The ***B-24 Liberator*** heavy bomber was designed 1939. A big four-engine machine, it was armed with 10 machine guns, could carry over 9,600 kg/8,000 lb of bombs, and flew at 480 kph/300 mph with a range of 3,500 km/2200 mi with a full bomb load. It was used as a heavy bomber, passenger and cargo carrier, fuel tanker, maritime patroller, and anti-submarine aircraft with the US, British, and Commonwealth air forces.

The ***PB4Y Privateer*** was a modification of the Liberator designed purely for maritime operations; few were built before the war ended and they were used only in the Pacific. The ***PB2Y Coronado*** was a four-engine patrol bomber developed for the US Navy 1937; some were modified into ambulance and cargo carriers but their principal use was on anti-submarine patrols.

Coral Sea part of the Pacific Ocean bounded by NE Australia, New Guinea, the Solomon Islands, Vanuatu, and New Caledonia and containing numerous coral islands and reefs. The ***Battle of the Coral Sea***, May 7–8 1942, was the first sea battle to be fought entirely by aircraft, with no engagement between the US and Japanese warships. The Japanese were attempting to move on ◊Port Moresby and ◊Tulagi but the plan was discovered by US intelligence. A US fleet led by the carrier *Yorktown* was dispatched to the area and attacked the landing force at Tulagi. A series of confusing engagements followed as aircraft from both sides attempted to attack the main carrier force of the other, picking off the many small flotillas that had broken off from the main force. The two sides finally located each other 8 May and each launched air strikes. Although the Japanese inflicted greater damage, sinking one US carrier and two major warships, the US fleet scored a strategic victory, preventing the Japanese from landing in SE New Guinea and thus threatening Australia.

Corregidor island in the entrance to ◊Manila Bay, Philippine Islands. The US Army fortified the island 1905–12 to form the major coastal defence protecting the entrance to the Bay, with 35 guns of calibres ranging from 3 inch to 12 inch distributed among 14 batteries.

After the defeat of the US forces on ◊Bataan, the island was besieged by the Japanese and suffered heavily from artillery fire and aerial bombing. Japanese infantry landed on the night of 5 May 1942 and the garrison surrendered on the following day. The island was retaken in a combined air and sea attack by US forces 16 Feb 1945.

I shall return.
General MacArthur on leaving *Corregidor* March 1942.

Coventry city in the English Midlands, about 20 miles SE of Birmingham. On the night of 14–15 Nov 1940 it was the target of a massive German air raid in which 449 bomber aircraft dropped 503 tons of high explosive bombs and 880 canisters of incendiary bombs in an attack lasting over 11 hours. Some 550 people were killed, over 1,200 were wounded, and 60,000 buildings were destroyed.

Crab tank modified ◊Sherman tank mounting a power-driven spindle in front of its nose from which chains hung. When the spindle revolved, the chains beat the ground in front of the tank, detonating any mines which were buried in the ground. The Crab could clear a lane 3 m/10 ft wide at a speed of about 2 kph/1.25 mph. When not 'flailing' for mines in this way, it could use its gun to fight as a tank.

Crerar General Henry 1888–1965. Canadian soldier. Appointed Chief of the Canadian General Staff 1940, he was sent to Britain to organize the training of Canadian troops as they arrived. He resigned 1941 and took a drop in rank to become commander of the 1st Canadian Corps, which he led in the invasion of ◊Sicily. He later took command of 1st Canadian Army, which he led in the ◊D-Day invasion of France. His force was later involved in clearing the ◊Scheldt Estuary and in Operation ◊Veritable, when they broke the ◊Siegfried Line and entered Germany.

Crete Mediterranean island, roughly halfway between Greece and Egypt. After the evacuation of ◊Greece 1941, the island held about

32,000 British and Commonwealth troops and about 10,000 Greek infantry, with little artillery or transport. The Germans had complete air superiority and were able to bomb the island at will as a prelude to an airborne attack 20 May 1941. German paratroops landed in several areas and severe fighting ensued; an attempt at landing seaborne reinforcements was thwarted by the Royal Navy. The Germans managed to capture Maleme airfield and were then able to reinforce by air, and by 28 May it was decided that the island could no longer be held and evacuation of Allied troops began.

Some 3,600 British and Commonwealth troops were killed and about 12,000 taken prisoner; German losses came to 6,000 killed and wounded and some 220 aircraft lost. The Royal Navy also suffered heavy losses in men and ships while the German 7th Air Division sustained over 50% casualties. Hitler was so appalled at this casualty rate that he forbade any further major airborne operations

Crimea peninsula in the Black Sea, USSR, the principal feature of which is the seaport and naval base of ◊Sevastopol. The Crimea was invaded by the German 11th Army Oct 1941 and the siege of Sevastopol began. In an attempt to relieve the city the 44th and 51st Soviet Armies landed near Kerch, at the eastern end of the peninsula, Dec 1941 but this force was destroyed by the Germans and Sevastopol fell 3 July 1942.

During the Soviet advances in the autumn of 1943 the German 17th Army was cut off in the peninsula and in April 1944 a Soviet army under Marshal ◊Tolbukhin struck across the isthmus while a second army made another landing near Kerch. The Germans retreated into Sevastopol and most were evacuated by the German Navy before the city was regained by the Soviet forces 9 May 1944.

Crocodile British flame-throwing tank based on the ◊Churchill tank. The flame gun was mounted in the front face of the tank, alongside the driver, and supplied from an armoured trailer holding 400 gallons of inflammable fluid. Propelled by pressurized nitrogen, also carried in the trailer, the jet of flame could reach to about 110 m/120 yds ahead of the tank. A terrifying weapon, its mere appearance on the battlefield was often sufficient to induce surrender.

Cromwell tank British cruiser tank produced 1943–44. Using the large-wheeled ◊Christie suspension it was the last of a succession of cruiser designs. One of the fastest wartime tanks, it could reach 65 kph/40 mph though later production had the engine governed so as to keep the speed down to 55 kph/35 mph. It was armed with a 75 mm gun and was widely used by British and Polish armoured regiments in NW Europe 1944–45, and many were also adapted as artillery command and observation tanks.

Crusader tank British cruiser tank, developed 1940. It was fast, armed with a 2-pounder (40 mm) gun, and initially highly unreliable. After modification to the cooling and air filtration systems its reputation improved, but it was always under-armoured and it was withdrawn from combat May 1943 and converted to use as an anti-aircraft gun carrier, artillery observation post, gun tractor, and similar tasks.

Crusader, Operation British operation in Libya Nov–Dec 1941 to relieve the besieged garrison of ◊Tobruk and destroy the ◊Afrika Korps. The plan was for three British columns to swing south through the desert and around the Axis defensive lines; one column would then swing round behind the Axis line and keep them occupied while the centre column went for Tobruk and the southern column headed west to engage the German armour.

The initial actions were confused and hard-fought: while the Tobruk garrison was fighting its way out, countered by a German force at ◊Sidi Rezegh, the Germans were themselves under attack from the south from a British force, which in turn was defending its rear against an attack by the Afrika Korps. Other British, German, and Italian units were also milling around the area, simultaneously fighting or evading each other. Amid this confusion, ◊Rommel decided to take his armour and drive eastward toward the British bases, hoping this would unnerve General Sir Alan ◊Cunningham and cause him to withdraw his troops. It may well have done, but ◊Auchinleck also considered the possibility, and replaced Cunningham with his deputy Chief of Staff Maj-Gen Neil Ritchie.

However, the absence of German armour from the main action allowed the New Zealand Division to make the junction with the Tobruk garrison, which threatened to cut off Rommel's retreat if he delayed. He had to abandon his plan and was forced to retire to ◊El Agheila, losing his garrisons at ◊Bardia, ◊Halfaya Pass, and Sollum. Axis losses in 'Crusader' amounted to 38,000 men and 300 tanks, while British losses came to 18,000 men and 278 tanks.

Cruwell General Ludwig 1892–1953. German soldier. Cruwell served in World War I and remained in the postwar Reichsheer. He was promoted to major general Dec 1939. By 1940 he commanded 11 Panzer division and became commander of the ◊Afrika Korps 1941. His aircraft was shot down while making an air reconnaissance May 1942 and he became a prisoner of the British for the rest of the war.

cryptography science of creating and reading codes; for example, those produced by the ◊Enigma coding machine used by the Germans. No method of encrypting is completely unbreakable, but decoding can be made extremely complex and time consuming.

Cunningham General Sir Alan 1887–1983. British soldier. Although he led the British offensive against the Italians in Abyssinia 1940–41 with great success, Cunningham failed to show his usual drive during Operation ◊Crusader when he was commander of the British 8th Army. He was relieved of his post by Field Marshal Auchinleck and spent the rest of the war in administrative posts before becoming the last High Commissioner in Palestine.

Cunningham Andrew Browne, 1st Viscount Cunningham of Hyndhope 1883–1963. British admiral. He served as commander in chief in the Mediterranean 1939–42, maintaining British control; as commander in chief of the Allied Naval Forces in the Mediterranean Feb–Oct 1943 he received the surrender of the Italian fleet. He then became First Sea Lord and Chief of Naval Staff until 1946.

Cunningham John 1885–1962. British admiral. In 1940 he assisted in the evacuation of Norway, taking the Norwegian king to the UK in his flagship, and, as Fourth Sea Lord in charge of supplies and transport 1941–43, prepared the way for the N African invasion 1942. He was commander in chief in the Mediterranean 1943–46, First Sea Lord 1946–48, and became admiral of the fleet 1948.

Cunningham Group Captain John 1917–. British airman. Cunningham was a test pilot for the De Havilland Aircraft company prior to the war; he was commissioned into the RAF and became an outstanding fighter pilot, and was among the first pilots to be given airborne radar for night fighting. His successes with this led to his nickname 'Cats-Eyes Cunningham', a public relations stunt to conceal the fact that radar was in use.

Curtin John Joseph 1885–1945. Australian Labor politician, prime minister 1941–45. He became Labor Party leader 1935 and then prime minister in the early years of the war when the independents in parliament transferred their allegiance from the Menzies coalition government. He proved a capable and inspirational wartime leader, mobilizing Australia's resources to meet the threat of Japanese invasion. He clashed with ◊Churchill over the latter's view that Australia was dispensable, withdrawing Australian troops from the Middle East 1942 to help defend against the Japanese threat. At the same time, he reassessed the need for US support and invited General Douglas MacArthur to establish his headquarters in Australia. He died in office before the end of the war.

Curzon line Polish-Soviet frontier proposed after World War I by the territorial commission of the Versailles conference 1919, based on the eastward limit of areas with a predominantly Polish population. It acquired its name after British foreign secretary Lord Curzon suggested in 1920 that the Poles, who had invaded the USSR, should retire to this line pending a Russo-Polish peace conference. The frontier established 1945 generally follows the Curzon Line.

D

Dachau German ◊concentration camp N of Munich, Bavaria. The first such camp to be set up, it opened early 1933 and functioned as a detention and forced labour camp until liberated 1945.

Dakar seaport and naval base in French West Africa (now Senegal). In July 1940 the French battleship *Richelieu* was stationed there with other French warships. A British naval force arrived 7 July and, wishing to deny the Germans the use of the French warships, presented them with an ultimatum: join the British against Germany; sail to a British port; sail, escorted, to the French West Indies or the USA, there to be disarmed; or be attacked in harbour. The French rejected the ultimatum and on the following day the *Richelieu* was attacked and damaged by British torpedo bombers.

It was then decided to mount a joint British-Free French operation to capture Dakar which, it was hoped, would persuade the French African colonies to join ◊de Gaulle. A force was assembled and sailed for Dakar Sept 1940, but the French governor of the colony refused all approaches from de Gaulle and it was realised that invasion would be futile. British and French warships exchanged fire, and French coastal batteries joined in, resulting in damage to both sides, and the operation was then called off. It was not known until much later that as it was abandoned, the French governor was contemplating surrender.

Daladier Edouard 1884–1970. French Radical politician. As prime minister April 1938–March 1940, he signed the ◊Munich Agreement 1938 (by which the Sudeten districts of Czechoslovakia were ceded to Germany) and declared war on Germany 1939. He resigned 1940 because of his unpopularity for failing to assist ◊Finland against the USSR. He was arrested on the fall of France 1940 and was held prisoner in Germany 1943–45. After the war he was re-elected to the Chamber of Deputies 1946–58.

Danzig (now Gdansk) Polish seaport on the Baltic at the head of the ◊Polish Corridor. Danzig had been German until 1919, and still had a large German population, many of whom were Nazi party supporters. It was the scene of several incidents fomented by the Nazis, intended to generate tension between Germany and Poland. It was taken by the Germans at the start of the Polish campaign, and was liberated by the Soviets under Marshal ◊Rokossovsky 30 March 1945.

Darlan Admiral Jean François 1881–1942. French sailor. In 1939 Darlan was commander in chief of the French Navy, and he assured Churchill 1940 that the French fleet would not fall into German hands. He then became minister of marine in Marshal Pétain's ◊Vichy government and ordered the French fleet to African ports where it was attacked by the British to ensure that it would be of no use to the Germans.

He became vice-premier of France Feb 1941 and collaborated with the Germans in the hope of obtaining better conditions for the French people, with little success. When Pétain was replaced by ◊Laval 1942 Darlan became High Commissioner in N Africa. When the Allies invaded N Africa the US Government recognized Darlan as head of the local French government, whereas the British preferred ◊de Gaulle. This problem was resolved when Darlan was murdered by a French monarchist 24 Dec 1942.

Darnand Admiral Joseph 1897–1945. French sailor and politician. Darnand had retired from the French Navy before the war to become an extreme right-wing politician. After the 1940 Armistice he supported Pétain and set up a security force 1941. In 1942 this evolved into the Milice Française, which cooperated with the German army and ◊Gestapo to counter the French ◊Resistance movement. He became an officer in the ◊Waffen SS, took the oath of allegiance to Hitler, and was among the first Frenchmen to wear a German uniform. After the liberation of France he fled to Germany, but was eventually captured by the French. He was returned to France and executed by a firing squad 3 Oct 1945.

Darwin naval base and capital of Northern Territory, Australia. It was severely damaged in an air raid 19 Feb 1942 carried out by 135 Japanese aircraft; a bomb struck a ship loaded with depth charges and the subsequent massive explosion did extensive damage to the port facilities. A US destroyer and five other ships were sunk and 240 people were killed and 150 injured. Other, less damaging, air raids followed, but the arrival of US fighters in March curtailed the attacks.

DD tanks DD (Duplex Drive) tanks were so-called because they could travel on land using their tracks and in water using a screw propeller. Developed by a British engineer, Nicholas Straussler, in the 1930s, the tank carried a canvas screen attached to its body which could be erected so as to provide the necessary buoyancy. It could then be launched into the sea some distance from shore, swim ashore, then blow away the screen with a small explosive charge, and go into action as a normal tank.

Five British, two Canadian and three US tank battalions were equipped with Sherman DD tanks in the ◊D-Day invasion. In spite of sea conditions far worse than had been encountered in training, they were generally successful, except at ◊Omaha beach where the American tanks were launched too far out to sea and most were swamped.

D-Day 6 June 1944; the day on which Allied forces landed on the coast of France to commence Operation Overlord, the invasion of German-occupied Europe. Five beaches – ◊Utah, ◊Omaha, ◊Gold, ◊Juno, and ◊Sword – were selected as the landing points for the British I and XXX Corps and US V and VII Corps. The operation was preceded by a month-long bombing campaign to disrupt communications, preventing reinforcements from moving quickly into the threatened area, and was accompanied by airborne landings to secure the flanks and destroy vital bridges and gun positions.

The landings commenced at 06.30, and by midnight 57,000 US and 75,000 British and Canadian troops and their equipment were ashore and the beachheads were being linked into a continuous front. The German response to the landings was hampered by the damage done to their communications, by a rigid command structure which required a personal directive from Hitler before any significant move could be made, and by the belief that the landing was a feint and that the major Allied attack would come in the Pas de Calais region, a belief fostered by Allied deception operations. Allied casualties during the day amounted to 2,500 killed and about 8,500 wounded. Allied air forces flew 14,000 sorties in support of the operation and lost 127 aircraft.

de Gaulle General Charles André Joseph Marie 1890–1970. French general and first president of the Fifth Republic 1958–69. He refused to accept the new prime minister ◊Pétain's truce with the Germans June 1940 and 18 June made his historic broadcast calling on the French to continue the war against Germany. He based himself in England as leader of the ◊Free French troops fighting the Germans 1940–44. In 1944 he entered Paris in triumph and was briefly head of the provisional government before resigning over the new constitution of the Fourth Republic 1946.

If I am not France, what am I doing in your office?
General de Gaulle making claim to
Winston Churchill to lead the Free French 1940

Degtyarev machine guns standard Soviet light machine gun used by infantry and mounted in tanks. A gas-operated weapon of 7.62 mm calibre, it was designed by Vasily Degtyarev and entered service 1928. Simple, reliable and robust, it used a drum magazine mounted on top of the weapon. In 1934, Degtyarev designed the PPD sub-machine gun, also of 7.62 mm calibre but using a pistol cartridge, which was produced in large numbers until 1941, after which it was replaced by simpler designs. Degtyarev himself eventually became a major general, director of technical sciences, and Deputy of the Supreme Soviet.

De Havilland British aircraft. The De Havilland company was well-known for commercial aircraft and the *Tiger Moth*, an elderly biplane which became one of the most famous training aircraft in the world, teaching thousands of pilots to fly. Their most prominent wartime product was the *Mosquito*, conceived 1938 as a fast daytime bomber, of which more than 7,700 were produced. Built almost entirely of wood to conserve scarce materials and equipped with two powerful engines, it could fly at 645 kph/400 mph, had a ceiling of 10,700 m/35,000 ft and a range of over 2,900 km/1,800 mi, and carried 2,000 kg/4,400 lb of bombs. As a bomber it was unarmed, relying upon speed for protection, but it was also used as a long-range fighter, armed with four 20 mm cannon.

de Lattre de Tassigny General Jean 1889–1952. French soldier. He served in World War I, and by 1939 was Chief of Staff of the French 5th Army, then commanded the 14th Division during the German invasion 1940. After the capitulation he was sent to Tunisia, but was recalled to France for indicating his sympathy with the Allies and sentenced to 10 years imprisonment. He escaped 1943 and made his way to Britain where he joined ◊de Gaulle, being given command of the Free French 1st Army in N Africa and later leading them in the liberation of France.

He was the French signatory to the German surrender in Berlin, 9 May 1945. Following the war he commanded NATO Land Forces Europe 1948 and was commander in chief Indo-China (now Vietnam) 1950–52.

Dempsey Lieutenant-General Sir Miles 1896–1969. British soldier. He commanded an infantry brigade in France 1939–40, then took command of an armoured division June 1941. In 1942 he was in command of XIII Corps in both ◊Sicily and ◊Italy. He returned to Britain 1944 and took command of the British 2nd Army for the ◊D-Day invasion, leading them through NW Europe to the final surrender. He then became commander in chief Allied Forces SE Asia, a post he held to the end of the war.

Demyansk Soviet town SE of Lake Ilmen, about 370 km/230 mi NW of Moscow where some 100,000 men of the German 16th Army were trapped during a Soviet offensive Jan 1942. They were resupplied and reinforced by air, about 65,000 tons of supplies and over 30,000 men being flown in and over 25,000 casualties evacuated. This was the first major airlift ever carried out, and it kept the trapped army fighting until it could be relieved by a German counterattack May 1942.

Denmark Denmark was invaded by German forces 9 April 1940, principally to acquire airfields from which the Luftwaffe could cover the invasion of ◊Norway. Danish border troops resisted the first German moves but King Christian realised that opposition was hopeless and surrendered the country. He remained in Denmark, and took an active part in resisting German demands for the surrender of Jews. A strong resistance movement grew up although in general the Germans behaved well.

The German surrender to General ◊Montgomery 4 May 1945 included Denmark in its terms and a rapid movement by the British to Lübeck ensured the country was not taken by Soviet troops.

Desert Rats nickname of the British 7th Armoured Division in N Africa. Their uniforms had a shoulder insignia bearing a jerboa (N African rodent, capable of great leaps). The term later came to include all troops of the 8th Army. The Desert Rats' most famous victories include the expulsion of the Italian army from Egypt Dec 1940 when they captured 130,000 prisoners, and the Battle of El ◊Alamein 1942.

Devers General Jacob 1887–1963. US soldier. Devers was appointed commander of US Forces in Britain 1943, but had no combat experience and so was made second-in-command to the British General ◊Wilson in the Mediterranean Theatre. After this initiation he took command of the Allied forces landing in S France 1944 and conducted a successful campaign through France to join up with the Allied armies which had landed in ◊Normandy. He then took command of the 6th Army Group and led this for the rest of the war in Europe.

Dieppe French seaport on the English Channel about 305 km/190 mi NW of Paris. It was selected as the target for a limited-objective raid Aug 1942, partly to obtain practical experience of amphibious landing techniques and German defences, but mostly to placate Stalin who was agitating for a ◊Second Front in Europe.

Some 5,000 Canadian troops and 1,000 ◊commandos took part in the landings 18–19 Aug. Eight beaches were targeted, four being used to land commandos to deal with flanking coastal defence batteries and four for the main assault parties in Dieppe itself. Apart from the commando landing on the right flank, which silenced the German coastal battery, the remainder of the operation was a failure. The Germans were in a well-defended position which was difficult to reach and were fully alert, so that the troops and tanks were scarcely able to gain a foothold. By 09.00 it was clear that the operation had failed and withdrawal was ordered, but it took three hours to remove the last of the survivors.

The Canadians lost 215 officers and 3,164 men, the commandos 24 officers and 223 men, the Royal Navy 81 officers, 469 men, and 34 ships, and the RAF lost 107 aircraft. In contrast, the Germans lost only 345 killed and 268 wounded. The whole affair was a disaster for the Allies, and strained relations between Canada and Britain for some time, but a number of valuable lessons about landing on hostile beaches were learned and applied in the ◊D-Day landings 1944.

Dietl General Eduard 1890–1944. German soldier. Dietl joined the Nazi Party 1920 and by 1939 was a major-general commanding 3rd Mountain Division which he led in ◊Poland and ◊Norway. During the invasion of the USSR 1941 (Operation ◊Barbarossa) he commanded a mountain corps which attempted unsuccessfully to seize the port of Murmansk. He was appointed commander of all German forces in Lapland 1942 and died in an air crash in the summer of 1944.

Dietrich Colonel-General Sepp 1892–1976. German SS officer. A sergeant-major during World War I, Dietrich joined the Nazi party in the 1920s and was given command of Hitler's personal bodyguard 1928. This eventually became the 'Liebstandarte SS Adolf Hitler' and he remained as commander of this unit until it became a prominent formation of the ◊Waffen SS, leading it as a regiment in Poland 1939, a combat group in France 1940, and a division in the invasion of Greece 1941. The division served two tours of duty in Russia and when resting in Belgium 1944 was called upon to fight against British and US forces in ◊Normandy. Dietrich was then promoted to colonel-general and given command of the 6th SS Panzer Army, which he led in the Battle of the ◊Bulge Dec 1944. After this he took his army to Hungary to recapture Budapest but failed to reach the city and fell back into Austria March 1945.

To ensure that his men were kept out of reach of the Soviets he surrendered his army to US forces May 1945. Arrested and charged with war crimes, notably the murder of US prisoners at Malmédy, he was convicted and received a 25-year sentence. Released 1955, he received a further 18-month sentence from a German court 1957 for his part in suppressing the ◊SA in the 'Night of the Long Knives' 1934.

Dill Field Marshal Sir John 1881–1944. British soldier. A former commandant of the Staff College and Director of Operations, he commanded British I Corps in France 1939, returning to Britain April 1940 to become Vice-Chief of the Imperial General Staff, succeeding General ◊Ironside as Chief of Staff May 1940. In Dec 1941, suffering from stress and overwork, he was replaced by General ◊Alanbrooke and went to the USA as head of the British Military Mission. He died there 1944 and was buried in Arlington National Cemetery, Washington.

displaced persons term originally used to describe those people who were left without a home country by the border changes arising from the war; e.g., the inhabitants of E Poland which was assimilated into the USSR, or citizens of the Baltic states whose countries had effectively become provinces of the USSR. Later the term was also used to describe the millions of refugees who had been uprooted by the war and transported elsewhere, so that they had no home to which they could return. Huge camps were established in Germany and other parts of Europe, into which displaced persons were shepherded so that they could be fed, housed, documented, and eventually resettled in the destination of their choice.

Dniepr river rising in the Smolensk region of the USSR and flowing south past Kiev to empty into the Black Sea at Cherson. Hitler declared it 'Germany's Eastern Rampart' Sept 1943 and defence lines were constructed along much of its length as German troops withdrew from the east to take up positions on the west bank. They were pursued by Soviet forces who managed to break through and form bridgeheads during Sept and Oct. These were rapidly expanded and by the end of 1943 the 'rampart' was completely inside Soviet territory.

Don river rising about 240 km/150 mi S of Moscow and flowing south to join the Sea of Azov at Rostov-on-Don. It was crossed by German forces in their advance to the ◊Caucasus and ◊Stalingrad, but the Soviets managed to retain a foothold on some bridgeheads on the eastern bank. From these bridgeheads they mounted a counteroffensive Nov 1942 and swung south to cut off the German 6th Army at Stalingrad. The expansion of this front forced those German units capable of escaping to cross the river and reorganize well to the west.

Dönitz, Admiral Karl 1891–1980. German sailor. He was in charge of Germany's U-boat force 1939–43 and devised the 'wolf-pack' technique of submarine warfare, which sank 15 million tonnes of Allied shipping during the course of the war. He succeeded ◊Raeder as commander in chief of the Navy Jan 1943 and devoted himself to trying to overcome Allied naval superiority. Hitler trusted him when he had lost faith in his Army and Luftwaffe commanders, and so Dönitz was appointed to succeed him May 1945. His sole deed as leader of the Reich was to negotiate its surrender. He was arrested 23 May, tried at ◊Nuremberg and was sentenced to 10 years' imprisonment.

Donovan William Joseph 1883–1959. US military leader and public official. Donovan was national security adviser to Presidents Hoover and F D Roosevelt and founded the Office of Strategic Services (◊OSS) 1942. As OSS director 1942–45, Donovan coordinated US intelligence throughout the war.

Doolittle James Harold 1896–1958. US airman. After serving as a fighter pilot in World War I, he became a famous racer and record-breaking aviator and worked with the US Army Air Force in the development of flight instruments. He returned to the service as a major 1940 and was responsible for organizing aircraft production in former car factories.

He moved to a more active post on the entry of the USA into the war, and led a flight of B-25 bombers from the aircraft carrier *Hornet* on a raid on Tokyo and other Japanese targets 18 April 1942. After the raid, the bombers flew on to airfields in China. Doolittle was awarded the Congressional Medal of Honor for his leadership and was given command of the US 12th Air Force in the invasion of N Africa. In 1944 he took command of the US 8th Air Force in England, operating a strategic bombing campaign against Germany. After the surrender in Europe he went with the 8th Air Force to the Far East to continue their work against Japan.

Dornier German aircraft. The *Do-17*, known as the 'Flying Pencil' because of its slender fuselage, was a twin-engine monoplane bomber capable of 420 kph/230 mph with 910 kg/2,000 lb of bombs. It was first used in the Spanish Civil War 1936 and was the mainstay of the ◊Luftwaffe during the air raids on Britain 1940–41. It was improved as the Do-17Z and Do-217 models with more powerful engines and better armament, and many of these were adapted as night fighters.

Dornier also produced a number of flying boats, but their most unusual machine was the *Do-335 Pfiel* ('Arrow') a single-seat fighter with an engine and propeller at each end, the front pulling and the rear pushing; it was also notable as the first production aircraft to have an ejection seat. It could reach 755 kph/470 mph and had a range of over 3,200 km/2,000 miles using a drop fuel tank. However, development took so long that no more than 20 had been issued for service before the war ended.

Douglas US aircraft. The *DC-3 Dakota*, originally intended as an air-liner, was a twin-engine monoplane capable of lifting up to 6,800 kg/15,000 lb of cargo. It was also used as a paratroop carrier and glider tug and became the universal workhorse of the Allied air forces, as well as being copied by the USSR and Japan. More aggressive machines included the *DB-7* twin-engine monoplane which saw service as the Havoc night fighter and as the Boston low-level attack bomber; the *TBD-1 Devastator* torpedo-bomber and the *A-24 Dauntless* dive bomber, both widely used by the US Navy; and the *B-26 Invader* attack bomber.

Douglas William Sholto 1893–1969. British airman. In 1939 he was assistant Chief of Air Staff and then succeeded ◊Dowding as Chief of Fighter Command Nov 1940. He took command of RAF Middle East Jan 1943 but returned to Britain 1944 to take over Coastal Command. He was then involved in much of the air planning for the ◊D-Day inva-sion of Europe, with the particular task of keeping the English Channel clear of German U-boats while the invasion fleets were assembling and crossing to Normandy.

Dowding Air Chief Marshall Hugh Caswall Tremenheere, 1st Baron 1882–1970. British airman. He was chief of Fighter Command 1939, a post he held throughout the Battle of ◊Britain 10 July–12 Oct 1940. A clear thinker, his refusal to commit more fighters to France in 1940 when he could see that the campaign was doomed proved to be a vital factor in the later Battle of Britain, but his uncompromising attitude upset Churchill and other political leaders and he was replaced in Fighter Command by William ◊Douglas Nov 1940. After undertaking a mission to the USA to procure additional aircraft, he was retired 1942 and was made a baron 1943.

Dresden German city and rail junction about 200 km/125 mi S of Berlin. It was the target of a massive air raid by the RAF 13–14 Feb 1945 in which 2,600 tons of explosive and incendiary bombs were dropped, creating the worst ◊firestorm of the war and devastating about 20 sq km/ 8 sq mi of the city. The destruction was completed on the following day in an attack by the US 8th Air Force. Since the city was crowded with refugees and troops and had few air defences the death toll was high, probably in excess of 80,000, although the precise number has never been calculated. Since that time the necessity for and morality of such an attack has been frequently debated, usually with hindsight.

Driant, Fort one of the forts defending Metz in NW France. In 1944 it was held by German NCO students from a nearby instructional school who kept the US 3rd Army at bay for about three months before it was finally surrounded and the defenders starved into surrender.

Drum, Fort US coastal defence fort at the mouth of Manila Bay, Philippines. The principal defences were on ◊Corregidor, but the mouth of the bay was so wide that an enemy force might have slipped through unseen at night, so Fort Drum was built on a tiny island across the bay. It was the last US element to surrender when Corregidor fell May 1942.

Fort Drum was retaken 1945 by a US boarding party who pumped gasoline through the fort's ventilation system and then fired explosive charges to ignite it. The subsequent fire burned for three days and none of the Japanese garrison survived.

DUKW US amphibious truck. The DUKW was basically the standard 6 x 6 GMC 2.5 ton cargo truck fitted with buoyancy tanks and with screw propulsion when in the water. Principally used to ferry supplies and men from ship to shore, these vehicles played a vital part in almost every amphibious landing performed by Allied troops.

Dunkirk seaport on the north coast of France, in Nord *département*, on the Strait of Dover. In May 1940 the surviving elements of the ◊British Expeditionary Force concentrated on Dunkirk while their evacuation by sea ('Operation Dynamo') was organized and a motley 'fleet' of over 1,000 ships, from warships down to private yachts, was assembled and sailed to Dunkirk. It was anticipated that perhaps 45,000 troops could be rescued before the Germans took the town. In the event, the Germans, thinking that the British troops penned inside Dunkirk could be safely left there, turned to complete their occupation of N France. This leeway proved vital, giving the British sufficient time to evacuate some 337,131 Allied troops, including about 100,000 French.

Dutch East Indies group of islands comprising what are now Java, Indonesia, Sumatra, Timor, Borneo, the Celebes, and the western half of New Guinea. In a two-month campaign the Japanese began landings at various places in the area 11 Jan 1942, overcoming the tiny Allied garrisons on each island with ease, until the formal Dutch surrender 8 March. The area was then neglected by the Allies for some time, as it was not on their direct route to Japan, until May 1945 when Australian and Dutch troops undertook several successful operations at Tarakan, Brunei, and Balikpapan. Following the Japanese surrender the Dutch again assumed control over the area Sept 1945, but their return was fiercely resisted by Indonesian nationalists and they eventually withdrew Sept 1949.

Dyle Belgian river running E of Brussels to join the Scheldt just before Antwerp; it formed a useful barrier against attack from Germany and the ◊British Expeditionary Force marked it as their defensive line to cover the Belgian retreat 1940. However, although the British moved up to the river, the rapidity of the German advance in the Ardennes prevented the French 1st and 7th Armies from moving into position on their flanks as planned, isolating the British and leaving them in danger of being surrounded. They were forced to abandon the position and fall back to a new line on the Scheldt and from there to ◊Dunkirk.

E

Eaker General Ira C 1898–1971. US airman. He was sent to England to command the US 8th Air Force Bomber Command 1942, succeeding General ◊Spaatz as commander at the end of the year. A strong believer in precision daylight bombing, he was initially over-optimistic about the ability of his bomber force to penetrate Germany in daylight and was forced to modify his tactics in the face of the German defences. He drew up plans for the Allied Combined Bomber Offensive, prioritizing targets for both the USAAF and RAF. He commanded the air support for Operation Dragoon, the landings in S France 1944, and then moved his force over to French airfields to give support to the Allied armies.

East Africa Campaign British conquest of Italy's colonies in Africa 1940–41. Although Italy declared war on Britain 10 June 1940 the relatively isolated garrisons in her African colonies – Eritrea, Abyssinia (now Ethiopia), and Italian Somaliland – restricted themselves to a brief foray into the Sudan and Kenya and overrunning ◊British Somaliland.

The British decided to take the initiative with two offensives: one from the south, entering Italian Somaliland from Kenya; and one from the north, entering Eritrea from the Sudan. The southern offensive began Jan 1941, capturing Mogadishu, capital of Italian Somaliland, by 25 Feb and quickly securing the rest of the country, forcing the Italians to abandon British Somaliland and fall back into Eritrea. The British swung toward Abyssinia, capturing Addis Ababa 6 April 1941 and forcing more Italians into Eritrea. The northern attack then began to take effect, putting further pressure on Eritrea, while a guerrilla force trained and commanded by Maj-Gen ◊Wingate caused unrest in the more remote areas of Abyssinia and Eritrea. Both British offensives then converged in Eritrea and trapped much of the Italian army, which surrendered 19 May. The remainder of the campaign was simply a matter of cleaning out individual pockets of Italian resistance and the final surrender came 3 July 1941.

Eastern Front battlefront between the USSR and Germany. Initially running along the line of the Polish eastern border agreed in the ◊Molotov–Ribbentrop pact 1939 (more or less where the border lies today), the front fluctuated wildly during the course of the campaign. At the time of the front's most eastern extent it ran from Petsamo in N Finland, parallel with the Finnish border, skirted Leningrad, then ran SE in front of Moscow, through Voronezh to Stalingrad, then down toward the Caucasus and looped back to the west to end on the Black Sea close to Novorossisk.

ground forces casualties: Eastern Front 1941–45

	killed/missing	wounded	POW
USSR	c. 11m	?	c. 6m
other Allied[1]	210,000		?
Germany	2,415,690	3,498,060	2
other Axis[3]	601,830	523,000	?

[1]other Allied includes Romanians and Poles fighting with Russian forces.
[2]for the period to 31 Dec 1944 only, German POWs are included as 'missing'.
[3]other Axis includes Romanians, Hungarians, and Italians.

Eastern Solomons, Battle of the naval action between US and Japanese forces 23–24 Aug 1942. The US Navy learnt of a Japanese fleet escorting troop reinforcements to ◊Guadalcanal and deployed Task Force 61 in the area. Both fleets had aircraft carriers and the Japanese had sent one of theirs ahead of the main body of the fleet to act as a decoy. A US reconnaissance plane spotted the main Japanese fleet but a strike force sent to intercept it failed to find it due to rain cloud cover. The following day another reconnaissance plane found the lone Japanese carrier and the strike force was sent out again, but was then partially diverted when another observation plane found part of the Japanese main fleet. The decoy carrier was sunk but only a few aircraft reached the main body of the fleet and did little damage. At the same time the Japanese had found the US fleet and the arrival of their strike force coincided with the return of some of the US strike force who combined with the 50 US fighters protecting the fleet, leading to considerable aerial confusion. In an inconclusive exchange, some US ships were damaged, but not seriously, and both fleets then withdrew. Meanwhile land-based US aircraft had found the transports which the Japanese were supposed to be escorting, sank one, severely damaged an escort cruiser, and drove the other two transports to shelter in the Shorland Islands where the troops had to be reloaded into destroyers for another attempt at reaching Guadalcanal. Although the naval battle was indecisive, the object of preventing the troops reaching Guadalcanal had been achieved.

Eben Emael Belgian fort placed at the junction of the Albert Canal and Maas river, N of Liège, to guard a vital crossing-point. It was considered impregnable as any assault would have to be made across either the river or the canal. It was attacked 10 May 1940 by a squad of 85 German glider troops who landed on top of the fort and used special explosive charges to put the gun turrets out of action, but were unable to get into the fort itself as they were pinned down by crossfire from neighbouring forts. The following day German troops crossed the canal by boat to relieve the glider force, who had suffered relatively low casualties (6 dead and 15 wounded), and the fort surrendered. The gliders were quickly removed so for several years it was believed that the assault had been made across the canal.

Eichelberger Lieutenant-General Robert 1886–1961. US soldier. He was commandant of West Point Military Academy when the USA entered the war and was sent to take command of US I Corps in the Pacific. He fought in New Guinea, defeating the Japanese at Buna Jan 1943, and then took command of the US 8th Army for the assault on the Philippines 1945.

Eichmann Colonel Adolf 1906–1962. German SS officer. He was in charge of the ◊Gestapo department controlling the Jewish population of all German-occupied territory. He organized the mass deportation of Jews from Germany and Bohemia to concentration camps in Poland

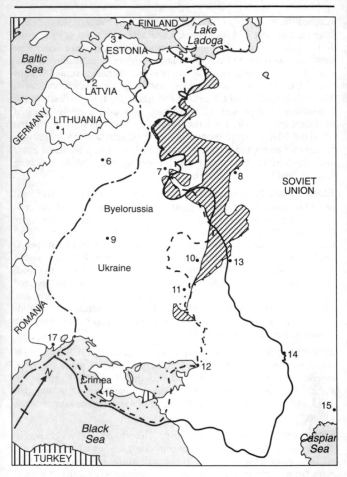

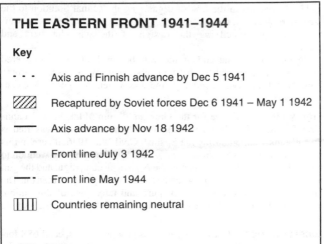

THE EASTERN FRONT 1941–1944

Key

- - -   Axis and Finnish advance by Dec 5 1941

░░░   Recaptured by Soviet forces Dec 6 1941 – May 1 1942

———   Axis advance by Nov 18 1942

— —   Front line July 3 1942

—·—   Front line May 1944

▓▓▓   Countries remaining neutral

Cities/towns

1	Kaunas	10	Kursk
2	Riga	11	Kharkov
3	Tallinn	12	Rostov
4	Helsinki	13	Voronezh
5	Leningrad	14	Stalingrad
6	Minsk	15	Astrakhan
7	Smolensk	16	Sevastopol
8	Moscow	17	Odessa
9	Kiev		

eighty-eight

1941. He was given the task of organizing the ◊Final Solution to the 'Jewish problem' at the Wannsee Conference 1942 and set up extermination camps, specifying the design of the gas chambers and crematoria.

He vanished at the end of the war but in 1960 was discovered in South America where he was abducted by an Israeli group, brought to Tel Aviv to stand trial, and was sentenced to death and executed 1962.

eighty-eight nickname for the German 88 mm ◊Flak 18 or 36 anti-aircraft guns and the later anti-tank guns. Although the gun was tried as an anti-tank weapon during the Spanish Civil War 1936, its use in this role was really proved effective at ◊Arras by ◊Rommel. He went on to use eighty-eights to good effect in the N African campaign, and the gun acquired its formidable reputation as a tank destroyer from then on. The Germans developed a number of pure anti-tank guns of this calibre which became the backbone of their anti-tank defences throughout the war.

Einsatzgruppen (German 'operations groups') four special ◊SS formations which followed up the invasion of USSR, charged with the extermination of Jews, Communists, and other 'non-Aryan elements'. Einsatzgruppe A covered the Baltic countries and N Russia; Gruppe B the central front through to Smolensk; Gruppe C the Ukraine, and Gruppe D the Crimea. Their technique was brutal but effective, simply rounding up Jews and shooting them, although a few experimental gas trucks were used. They are estimated to have executed some 2 million victims 1941–44.

Eisenhower Dwight David 1890–1969. US general and 34th president of the USA 1953–60, a Republican. He was appointed commander in chief of the US and British forces for the invasion of N Africa Nov 1942; commanded the Allied invasion of Sicily July 1943; and announced the surrender of Italy 8 Sept 1943. In Dec he became commander of the Allied Expeditionary Force for the invasion of Europe and was promoted to General of the Army Dec 1944. After the war he served as commander of the US Occupation Forces in Germany, then returned to the USA to become Chief of Staff until retiring 1948. In

1951 he returned to the army to become Supreme Commander Allied Powers, but resigned again 1952 to enter politics.

El Alamein see ◊Alamein, El.

Elefant German heavy tank destroyer, based on a design by Porsche for the ◊Tiger tank. The chassis was fitted with a fixed armoured superstructure carrying an 88 mm gun. Some 90 vehicles were built and 76 went into service July 1943, taking part in the Battle of ◊Kursk. They were not a success: the main gun could not traverse far to left or right and there was no machine gun on the hull leaving them highly vulnerable to attack from the rear with mines and explosive charges. The remaining Elefants were fitted with machine guns and sent to Italy where they fared rather better, sitting in well-defended positions and, with their 200 mm thick armour, practically impervious to any Allied anti-tank weapon.

Elephant Point peninsula commanding the sea entrance to Rangoon, Burma. The 2nd and 3rd Gurkha Parachute Battalion dropped here 1 May 1945 and eliminated the Japanese defences, clearing the way for an amphibious landing in Rangoon by 26 Indian Division. This was the only paratroop operation in the Burma campaign.

Empress Augusta Bay bay on the W coast of ◊Bougainville, Solomon Islands; site of a naval engagement between US and Japanese forces Nov 1943. A Japanese naval squadron of four cruisers and six destroyers was sent to attack the US troop and supply transports in the bay which were protected by four cruisers and eight destroyers deployed across its mouth. The Japanese approached at night but were detected by US radar and the commander had just begun turning his fleet into line when the Americans opened fire. One Japanese cruiser was sunk immediately, two destroyers collided, a third was rammed by a cruiser and sank, and the remainder of the squadron was reduced to a shambles and forced to withdraw. Only one US destroyer sustained any damage.

Enigma German enciphering machine and, by extension, the codes generated by it. The machine resembled an electric typewriter; operating a key sent a current through three rotors, the starting positions of which could be altered and 'stepped' at each keystroke. This meant that pressing the same key would not produce the same enciphered letter, making the resulting message proof against conventional code-breaking techniques.

Enzian German air defence guided missile. Launched by four solid-fuel rockets, it was sustained in flight by a liquid-fuel rocket motor and carried a 500 kg/1,100 lb explosive warhead. It was guided to the target area by radio signals and would detect and home in on the actual target by means of acoustic, infra-red, or radar systems. Although 60 experimental launches were made, the final design had not been settled when the war ended.

F

Fairey British aircraft. The Fairey company produced a number of aircraft for the Royal Navy, the most famous of which was the *Swordfish*, an elderly biplane torpedo bomber affectionately known as the 'Stringbag' because it could carry anything – bombs, depth charges, torpedoes, mines, rockets, or rescue boats. Powered by a 690 hp radial engine, it had a top speed of 215 kph/135 mph, a crew of two or three, depending upon its role, and could carry up to 500 kg/1,100 lbs of bombs or eight rockets. Although technically obsolete by 1939, it continued in service throughout the war simply because none of its promised replacements were so versatile or easily maintained. Its intended replacement, the *Albacore*, was a more modern biplane with an enclosed cockpit and more power. It entered service 1941 and was extensively used until 1943 when it was relegated to a training role. The Alabacore's successor was the *Barracuda*, a monoplane capable of 360 kph/225 mph carrying 900 kg/2,000 lbs of bombs, which proved to be moderately successful but never entirely replaced the Swordfish.

The company also produced the *Battle* for the RAF, a two-seat monoplane light day bomber which promised much but which proved to be a failure in service. Armed with one forward-firing machine gun and one free machine gun for the observer, it carried up to 450 kg/1,000 lbs of bombs and had a top speed of 385 kph/240 mph. The aircraft proved an easy target for German fighters and were shot down in such numbers during 1940 that they were hurriedly withdrawn from front line service.

Falaise Gap area between Argentan and Falaise, SE of ◊Caen, France. In Aug 1944 the Canadian 1st and British 2nd Armies were advancing south from Caen, while the US 1st and 3rd Armies were advancing east and north in their breakout from ◊Normandy. The two forces threatened to trap the German 7th Army, 5th Panzer Army, and Panzergruppe Eberbach, leaving them only the narrow gap between the two towns as an escape route. With artillery fire from three sides and constant air attacks the Germans were decimated. The gap was finally closed 19 Aug, leaving only a pocket of resistance until it too was overrun two days later. German losses were heavy – of the estimated 80,000 troops in the pocket, some 20,000 escaped, 10,000 were killed, and 50,000 surrendered, while losses of equipment included 567 tanks and assault guns, 950 artillery weapons, and 7,500 vehicles.

Falkenhausen General Alexander 1878–1966. German soldier; military governor of Belgium and N France 1940–44. He maintained strict control of his area though he deliberately ignored many ◊Gestapo directives and did his best to make life tolerable for the population. He was implicated by others in the ◊July Bomb Plot, and was recalled to Berlin and interrogated, but no evidence was found against him. At the end of the war he was arrested by the Allies and was sentenced to 12 years imprisonment by a Belgian court 1951.

Fiat Italian aircraft. After a series of open-cockpit biplane fighters, which although obsolete were still used in the early part of the war, Fiat produced the *G50 Freccia*, a low-wing monoplane fighter which first saw action in the Spanish Civil War 1936. With a top speed of 465 kph/290 mph and only two machine guns it was no match for Allied fighters, and was eventually replaced by the *G55*, an improved version capable of 620 kph/385 mph, armed with a 20 mm cannon and two heavy 12.7 mm machine guns. Most of the 100 produced were used by the Fascist Air Arm supporting the German forces in Italy after the armistice of 1943.

field artillery artillery mobile enough to accompany a field army, generally employed as the direct support of a division. The standard field artillery weapon of the war was 75–105 mm calibre with a range of about 12,000 m/13,000 yds. The British 25-pounder gun was of 87 mm calibre firing an 11 kg/25 lb shell to 12,250 m/13,400 yds; Germany and the USA used 105 mm howitzers firing 15 kg/33 lb shells to 11,000 m/12,000 yds; Italy and Japan used 75 mm guns firing 6.5 kg/14.5 lbs

shells to 9,000 m/9,800 yds and 12,000 m/13,000 yds respectively; and
the USSR had a variety of weapons of 76 mm and 85 mm calibre firing
a 6 kg/13 lb shell to 12,000 m/13,000 yds and a 9 kg/20 lb shell to
17,000 m/18,600 yds respectively.

final solution (to the 'Jewish question'; German *Endlosung der
Judenfrage*) euphemism used by the Nazis to describe the extermination of Jews (and other racial groups and opponents of the regime); see
also ◊Holocaust. The term came from a statement by ◊Himmler to
Rudolf ◊Hoess, Commandant of ◊Auschwitz, in May 1941, that Hitler
had given orders 'for the final solution of the Jewish question'.
Extermination squads (◊Einsatzgruppen) were formed to follow the
armies into Russia and murder all Jews and non-Aryan 'untermensch'
(sub-humans), communist officials and Commissars, and senior Soviet
prisoners. Extermination camps were established in Poland to which
Jews were shipped from all parts of German-occupied Europe to be
killed by gas or shooting. Accounting was slipshod, and no accurate
figure can ever be reached, but the best estimates suggest that about
5.75 million Jews, and a further million gypsies, communists, Soviet
prisoners, incurable invalids, homosexuals, and other unwanted cate-
gories were murdered.

Finland Finland was invaded by the USSR 30 Nov 1939, ostensibly
'in support of the Finnish People's Government'. The real aim of the
invasion was to gain most of the Karelian Isthmus in order to put more
distance between ◊Leningrad and the border. The Finns were hopelessly outnumbered, but nevertheless put up considerable resistance,
giving the Soviets some severe punishment before they were forced to
surrender and hand over the territory around the isthmus.

Finland allied herself with Germany 1941 and declared war on the
USSR when Germany invaded, advancing through the Karelian
Isthmus to the line of the 1939 border but no further; their refusal to
enter Soviet territory was among the factors which saved Leningrad
during the later siege. Finnish troops cooperated with German forces in
attempting to cut the railway line to ◊Murmansk and captured Petsamo
in the far north. A Soviet counteroffensive 1942 was beaten off, and the
front remained quiet until June 1944 when, with the Germans in retreat,
a Soviet offensive broke through the Finnish defences and again took

Karelia. On 4 Sept 1944 Finland signed an armistice with the USSR, after which there were a series of skirmishes against German troops and Finland finally declared war on Germany 4 March 1945.

Firefly ◊Sherman tank fitted with the British 17-pounder high velocity anti-tank gun in place of the original 75 mm medium-velocity gun. First conceived 1943, production began Feb 1944, and one was issued for every four-tank troop. Until the ◊Comet appeared it was the only tank in British service capable of taking on the German ◊Tiger and ◊Panther tanks with a reasonable chance of success. The idea was initially not taken up by US forces, who considered the normal 75 mm gun sufficient, but battle experience in Normandy soon led them to demand that US equivalents be developed. They never were, so instead British Firefly tanks were passed across to US units on the orders of General ◊Montgomery.

firestorm phenomenon arising in intense incendiary bombing raids, first seen in the RAF raid on Hamburg July 1943. When a large number of incendiary bombs are dropped in a small urban area, the intense heat of the fires causes the warm air to rise, thus drawing in fresh, cold air from the surrounding area. This cold air causes the fires to burn more fiercely, causing the hot air to rise faster, drawing in more cold air and thus forming an accelerating cycle. The incoming air soon reaches very high speeds, sufficient to knock people over or even sweep them into the fire, and the fires themselves become uncontrollable. Firestorms occurred in later raids on German and Japanese cities where large numbers of fires were started, causing immense devastation; possibly the most notorious example was at ◊Dresden Feb 1945.

flak German abbreviation for *Flugzeugabwehrkanone* – aircraft attack gun – hence an anti-aircraft gun. The term was widely adopted by Allied troops and airmen to describe German anti-aircraft fire. A 'flak jacket' was an armoured jacket worn by air crews as a defence against bullets and shell fragments.

Fletcher Vice-Admiral Frank J 1885–1973. US sailor. He commanded the US naval forces in the battle of the ◊Coral Sea 1942. During the battle of ◊Midway 1942 his flagship, USS *Yorktown,* was damaged and Admiral ◊Spruance took command of the latter part of the battle. Fletcher withdrew the three aircraft carriers which were proving cover for the US landings on ◊Guadalcanal Aug 1942, leaving the ground troops open to air attack. He later objected to providing Naval aircraft for ground support on Guadalcanal but was overruled by Admiral ◊Nimitz. He was then transferred to command of the Northern Pacific Fleet and remained there until the end of the war; he retired 1946.

Flying Tigers nickname given to the American Volunteer Group, a group of US pilots recruited to fight in China by Maj-Gen ◊Chennault 1940–41. The group proved an effective force against the Japanese in China and became the nucleus of the US 14th Air Force 1942.

Focke-Wulf German aircraft. The *FW 190* was probably the best German fighter of the war and arguably one of the best fighters in history, although it also proved itself as an attack bomber. First used 1941, it was a low-wing monoplane with a 1,700 hp radial engine giving it a top speed of 645 kph/400 mph and was armed with four 20 mm cannon and two machine guns. Performance was considerably improved with the development 1944 of the FW 190D-9, equipped with a 1,770 hp in-line engine, boosting its speed to 690 kph/430 mph, and armed with two 20 mm cannon and two 13 mm heavy machine guns. Both versions could also carry up to 500 kg/1,100 lb of bombs.

The *FW 200 Condor* was a large four-engine monoplane originally developed as a long-distance airliner. In 1938 it was converted to a maritime reconnaissance role at the request of the Japanese, and the Luftwaffe adopted it for the same task. The Condor operated mainly over the Atlantic, spotting convoys for the U-boat packs, until the Allies gained air supremacy late 1942.

Forrestal James Vincent 1892–1949. US Democratic politician. As under secretary of the navy from 1940 and secretary from 1944, he organized its war effort, accompanying the US landings on the Japanese island ◊Iwo Jima. He was the first secretary of the Department of Defense 1947–49, a post created to unify the three armed forces at the end of the war. He committed suicide after exhaustion and illness forced him to resign 1949.

Franco Francisco 1892–1975. Spanish dictator from 1939. As a general, he led the insurgent Nationalists to victory in the Spanish Civil

War 1936–39, supported by Fascist Italy and Nazi Germany, and established a dictatorship. On the outbreak of war, in spite of Spain's official attitude of 'strictest neutrality', his pro-Axis sympathies led him to send aid, later withdrawn, to the German side. In 1939 he met Hitler to discuss a Spanish-German attack on Gibraltar, but his price – Morocco and other French African territory – was one which Hitler was not prepared to pay and the proposal came to nothing. As the war progressed, Franco grew more distant from the Axis powers and managed to keep Spain out of any liaisons without upsetting either Germany or Italy to any significant degree.

Frank Hans 1900–46. German bureaucrat. A lawyer and member of the Nazi Party from its early years, he became Reichs Commissioner for Justice 1933 and in 1939 governor general of the *Generalgouvernement*, that part of Poland not incorporated into the Reich. He ran a brutal and repressive regime aimed at total subjugation of the Poles and the extraction of every possible economic advantage from the territory using slave labour and Jewish extermination. As the Soviet Army approached Aug 1944 he resigned his post and fled. Captured after the defeat of Germany he was tried at ◊Nuremberg and hanged 16 Oct 1946.

Frank Karl Hermann 1898–1946. Originally a leader of the Sudeten German Nazi Party, he became secretary of state for Bohemia and Moravia after their annexation by Germany 1939. Among other atrocities, he was responsible for the destruction of ◊Lidice and the murder of its inhabitants June 1942 as a reprisal for the assassination of ◊Heydrich. He was captured at the end of the war, tried, and publicly hanged near Prague May 1946.

Fraser Admiral Sir Bruce 1888–1982. British sailor. He was Controller of the Navy for the early part of the war before being appointed commander in chief of the Home Fleet. He directed the search for and sinking of the ◊*Scharnhorst* Dec 1943. He became commander in chief of the Eastern Fleet in the Indian Ocean Aug 1944 and Nov 1944 took command of the Pacific Fleet. He was the British representative at the signing of the Japanese surrender in Tokyo Bay 2 Sept 1945. After the war he became First Sea Lord and Chief of the Naval Staff 1948–51.

Fredendall General Lloyd. US soldier. He commanded the Center Task Force during the N African invasion, successfully taking Oran, and was put in command of 2nd US Corps in Tunisia 1943. This exposed his limited tactical grasp; he spread his troops too thinly and established his headquarters so far back as to be out of touch. Covering the sector from Fondouk to El Guettar in Tunisia, he was attacked by von ◊Arnim 15 Feb 1943 and his forces completely routed, allowing the Germans to capture the ◊Kasserine Pass. He was dismissed, returned to the USA and employed in training posts thereafter.

Free French movement formed by General Charles ◊de Gaulle in the UK June 1940, consisting of French soldiers who continued to fight against the Axis after the Franco-German armistice. They took the name *Fighting France* 1942 and served in many campaigns, among them General ◊Leclerc's advance from Chad to Tripolitania 1942, the Syrian campaigns 1941, the campaigns in the Western Desert, the Italian campaign, the liberation of France, and the invasion of Germany. Their emblem was the Cross of Lorraine, a cross with two bars.

Freyberg Bernard Cyril, Baron Freyberg, VC 1889–1963. New Zealand soldier and administrator born in England. He fought in World War I, winning the Victoria Cross and three DSOs, and was wounded nine times. During World War II he commanded the New Zealand 2nd Division in the N African desert, then went to Greece, was evacuated to ◊Crete and commanded the troops there during the German airborne attack. Returning to Libya he took the New Zealanders through to the final victory in ◊Tunisia, from where they went to Italy as part of the 8th Army. He was Corps Commander at ◊Cassino and has often, wrongly, been identified as 'the man who ordered the bombing of the monastery'. After the war he was governor general of New Zealand 1946–52.

Frick Wilhelm 1877–1946. German politician. As minister of the interior 1933–43 he was responsible for many of the laws and decrees which kept the Nazi party firmly in control of Germany. He became Reichs Protector for Bohemia and Moravia 1943, although his secretary ◊Frank actually wielded most of the power. Arrested after the war, he was tried at Nuremberg and hanged Oct 1946.

Friedeburg Admiral Hans von 1895–1945. German sailor. A relatively unknown German naval staff officer, Friedeburg succeeded ◊Dönitz as commander in chief of the German Navy April 1945 and was sent by Dönitz to negotiate surrender with General ◊Montgomery 3 May 1945. As a result it was he who signed the document which surrendered all German forces in N Europe and ended the war 7 May 1945.

Fritsch General Werner von 1880–1939. German soldier. He served with distinction in World War I and by 1934 was a general. Contemptuous of politics, he was nonetheless appointed commander in chief of the Army 1934, but his opposition to the introduction of Nazi ideology in the military soon upset Hitler and he was forced into retirement 1938 by a false charge of homosexuality. His departure removed the only obstacle to Hitler's reorganization of the Army High Command. He remained an honorary colonel of his old artillery regiment and accompanied them to Poland 1939, where he was killed by a sniper outside Warsaw.

Fritz-X German air-to-ground guided bomb. It was basically a standard 3,086 lb/1,400 kg armour-piercing bomb to which wings and a tail were added, together with a radio-control system. When dropped from an aircraft, the bomb went into a long glide during which the observer in the aircraft could steer it to its target. Developed 1939–42, it went into service 1943 and its greatest success came 9 Sept 1943 when the Italian battleship *Roma* was sunk with three of these bombs. They were also used with some success against land targets, but their use was abandoned when the Allies began jamming the radio control signals.

frogmen name give to underwater warfare specialists because of their appearance when wearing wet-suits, flippers, and masks. Usually associated with sabotage and attacks on shipping, they were also valuable in carrying out reconnaissance of beaches and underwater obstacles before any amphibious operation.

Fromm General Friedrich 1888–1945. German soldier. An officer of the German General Staff, he was responsible for all home army units, the administration of the General Staff, and maintaining a supply of trained replacements for front-line units. Although he did his job well, he became involved in the ◊July Bomb Plot through Count von ◊Stauffenberg who was on his staff. When the plot failed, Fromm attempted to cover up his involvement and display his loyalty by having his fellow conspirators rounded up, court-martialled, and shot. This did him no good; he was arrested by the Gestapo and hanged 19 March 1945.

Fuchida Commander Mitsuo 1902–1976. Japanese airman. A highly experienced naval pilot, he was selected to lead the attack on ◊Pearl Harbor 7 Dec 1941, coordinating the various elements of the operation and personally leading the first wave of the attack. He remained active in naval aviation operations throughout the war.

G

Gale General Sir Humphrey Middleton 1890–1971. British soldier. After serving in World War I, he remained in the Army and went to France with the ◊British Expeditionary Force 1939. He was promoted to major-general in charge of Administration of the Home Forces, then became administrative commander under General ◊Eisenhower for the N African landings 1942, and continued in this role through the invasions of ◊Sicily and ◊Italy. In 1944 he returned to Britain to take over the administration of Operation Overlord, the ◊D-Day landings in Normandy. He became adviser to the Supreme Commander and continued as General Eisenhower's right-hand man until the end of the war in Europe.

Gale General Sir Richard 1896–1991. British soldier. He served with the British and Indian armies prior to 1939 and was among the first to volunteer for parachute training 1940. He then raised and trained the 1st Parachute Brigade and June 1944 commanded the 6th Airborne Division. He led the small force which dropped in ◊Normandy 6 June 1944 ahead of the main invasion to capture the ◊Orne bridges flanking the British beachhead. After the war he commanded the British Army of the Rhine and later became Chief of the General Staff.

Galland Lieutenant General Adolf 1912–. German airman. Galland was a fighter pilot who saw action in the Spanish Civil War 1936–39 and then the Polish and French campaigns and the Battle of ◊Britain. By June 1941 he had claimed 70 enemy aircraft and was the first German pilot to be awarded the Swords to the Knight's Cross. In Nov 1941 he was promoted to general in charge of fighter operations on all European fronts. A fighting pilot, he found that the administrative role was not his forte, particularly as he was faced with increasing Allied air strength, bureaucratic interference, and internal political wrangling. He was relieved of his post late 1944 and at Hitler's personal request trained and led a jet fighter squadron. He raised his score to 104 enemy aircraft before injuries put an end to his flying career.

Gamelin Maurice Gustave 1872–1958. French soldier. He was commander in chief of the Allied armies in France at the outset of the war but was replaced by Maxime ◊Weygand after the German breakthrough at Sedan 1940. He was used as a scapegoat by the ◊Vichy government and tried before the 'war guilt' court 1942. He refused to defend himself and was detained in Germany until released by the Allies 1945.

Garand rifle (US rifle M1) standard rifle of the US armed forces from 1936. It was a .30 in calibre gas-operated semi-automatic weapon firing from an eight shot magazine. The first automatic rifle to be adopted as standard by any major power, its undoubted success in combat led to a reappraisal of this type of weapon by all combatants. The Garand remained in use until the late 1950s and was then replaced by the M14, a modified design in 7.62 mm NATO calibre using a 20-round magazine.

Gazala coastal town in Libya, about 95 km/60 mi W of ◊Tobruk; in 1942 the front line ran south from the town to the oasis of Bir Hacheim. ◊Rommel launched a powerful attack against Gazala 26–27 May 1942, using two Italian corps as a diversion at the northern end of the line while the Afrika Korps and another Italian corps swung around the southern end of the line and then northeast toward Tobruk. In spite of the surprise the British fought back well; Rommel sustained heavy losses and was trapped in a corner between a minefield and a British defensive 'box'. With no supplies or fuel and no apparent chance of receiving any, Rommel was contemplating surrender until the Italian Trieste Division managed to open a route through the minefield and get a supply column to him. Indecision and arguments in British headquarters also gave Rommel valuable time so that eventually, re-supplied and rested, he was able to break out of the ◊Cauldron 1 June and overwhelm the British 'box'. The British responded with uncoordinated and careless attacks 5 June which Rommel easily defeated and then resumed his offensive drive toward Tobruk. He defeated several British formations as he encountered them and the British forces were forced to abandon their positions and fall back to the El ◊Alamein line in Egypt. This was the most severe defeat inflicted on the British during the entire desert campaign.

GCI abbreviation for ◊ground controlled interception.

Gee British radio navigation and bombing device. It consisted of three transmitting stations in a line about 320 km/200 mi long and a corresponding receiving set in the bomber. Each transmitter sent out a coded signal in sequence and the aircraft's position could then be worked out from the time interval between their reception applied to a special chart. Developed 1941 it came into general use March 1942, but by the end of the year the Germans had begun jamming the special wavelength used and it was eventually replaced by other systems.

Gehlen General Reinhardt 1902–1979. German soldier and intelligence specialist. He became responsible for all intelligence relating to the Eastern Front 1942 and at the end of the war secured all the archives and files of his department and surrendered to US forces. He then set up a special intelligence agency working with the Western powers and specializing in Soviet intelligence.

Geiger Major-General Roy 1885–1947. US Marine. He saw action in ◊Guadalcanal 1942, but then was recalled to become director of Marine Aviation until Nov 1943 when he became commander of 1st Marine Amphibious Corps and took ◊Bougainville. He then commanded 3rd Marine Amphibious Corps in the assault on ◊Guam July 1944 and the assault on ◊Okinawa 1945. After General Buckner was killed on Okinawa, Geiger took command of 10th US Army for a short time, becoming the only US Marine officer ever to command a US Army in action.

Gela town on the south coast of Sicily, about 80 km/50 mi SW of Catania. It was the landing point for the US 7th Army in the invasion of ◊Sicily 10 July 1943. The landing was preceded by an advance party from the 82nd Airborne Division dropped on the hills inland, but the drop was badly executed and the troops widely scattered. Nevertheless they managed to delay a German reinforcement, allowing the US II Corps under General ◊Bradley to land with little resistance.

Germany, Surrender of the final surrender of Axis forces began in N Italy, where General Veitinghoff signed an unconditional surrender at Caserta 29 April 1945. Hitler committed suicide the next day, naming Admiral ◊Dönitz as his successor. On 4 May Dönitz sent a delegation to General ◊Montgomery which agreed the surrender of all German forces in NW Europe, Denmark, and the Low Countries 5 May 1945. German forces in S Germany surrendered to the US army 6 May. Dönitz' emissaries then reached General ◊Eisenhower at Rheims and 7 May surrendered the entire Third Reich. This final surrender was ratified in Berlin 8 May with Soviet representatives present; the war in the West officially ended midnight 8 May 1945.

Gestapo (*Geheimstaatspolizei*). German secret state police. Created 1933 by Goering to replace the political police, it was transferred to the control of Himmler's ◊SS 1934, under the command of ◊Heydrich. There was no appeal against Gestapo authority and it had sweeping powers to deal with acts or individuals it considered against the national interest. It was one of the most feared and brutal elements of the Nazi regime.

Ghormley Vice Admiral Robert L 1883–1953. US sailor. After serving in various sea and staff posts prior to 1939, in 1940 he was sent to England to study British naval procedures. He became US Commander South Pacific 1942 and was ordered to organize the capture of ◊Tulagi and ◊Guadalcanal. He complained there was not enough time for adequate preparation and although he was proved right his attitude made him enemies. He was then responsible for the decision which made Admiral ◊Fletcher withdraw his ships from Guadalcanal, leaving the ground operations exposed, which contributed to the US losses in the Battle of ◊Savo Island. He was replaced by Admiral ◊Halsey Oct 1942 and sent to a staff post in Washington, holding no further active command.

Gibson Wing Commander Guy Penrose, VC 1918–1944. British airman. He joined the RAF 1936 and in 1939 was an operational bomber pilot. In the summer of 1940 he successfully moved to flying night fighters, then did a tour as a flying instructor before returning to Bomber Command to command a squadron equipped with the new

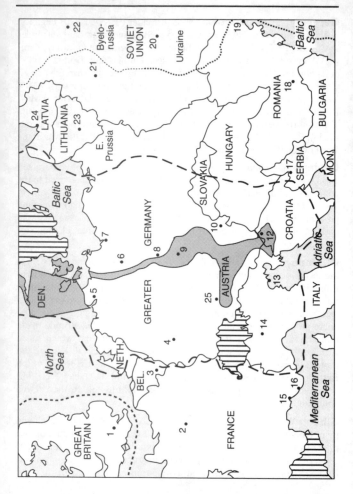

THE DEFEAT OF GERMANY 1944–45

Key

---- Front lines May 1944

— — Front lines Dec 1944

▨ German-held areas at surrender May 4 1945

|||| Countries remaining netural

Cities/towns

1	London	14	Milan
2	Paris	15	Marseille
3	Bastogne	16	Toulon
4	Frankfurt	17	Belgrade
5	Hamburg	18	Bucharest
6	Berlin	19	Odessa
7	Stettin	20	Kiev
8	Dresden	21	Minsk
9	Prague	22	Smolensk
10	Vienna	23	Kaunas
11	Budapest	24	Riga
12	Zagreb	25	Munich
13	Venice		

◊Lancaster bomber. In March 1942 he formed a special squadron (No 617) to bomb the ◊Ruhr Dams, and himself led the raid 16–17 May, dropping the first bomb on the ◊Mohne Dam. He was awarded the Victoria Cross for his leadership in this action. He was then relieved from operational duties and accompanied Churchill to Canada and the USA late 1944. On returning to Britain he obtained permission for 'one more operation', flying a ◊de Havilland Mosquito on a raid on relatively unimportant targets in Bavaria. Tragically, on the return flight his plane crashed in Holland and he was killed.

Gideon Force guerrilla force raised by Maj-Gen Orde ◊Wingate late 1940 for operations behind Italian lines in Abyssinia. It consisted of a small cadre of British officers and NCOs, 800 Sudanese troops, and 800 Abyssinian irregulars and carried out several successful operations against Italian communications and outposts.

Gilbert Islands (now Kiribati) group of islands in the Pacific Ocean about 1,600 km/1,000 mi NE of the ◊Solomon Islands. They were occupied by the Japanese 10 Dec 1941 and used as air strips. US Marine raiders assaulted Makin Atoll Aug 1943, destroyed the radio station, and killed some of the garrison, making the Japanese strengthen their defences. On 20 Nov US Army and Marine forces landed on ◊Tarawa and Makin, capturing them after heavy fighting. By 25 Nov, they had cleared the remaining islands and atolls.

Gin Drinker's Line British defensive line on the Chinese mainland in the New Territories of Hong Kong running about 18 km/11 mi from Gin Drinker's Bay to Port Shelter. It was taken by the Japanese 10 Dec 1941, forcing the garrison to give up their mainland defences and withdraw to Hong Kong island.

Giraud General Henri 1879–1949. French soldier. He commanded the French 7th Army 1940 and when this collapsed took command of the 9th Army, incorporating what was left of the 7th Army into it. Taken prisoner by the Germans 19 May 1940, he escaped two years later and made his way to Algiers, where he succeeded Admiral ◊Darlan as local commander Dec 1942. In May 1943 he became co-president, with General ◊de Gaulle, of the National Committee for Liberation and was made commander in chief of the French Army, liberating Corsica Sept

1943. However, de Gaulle was not prepared to share the stage with anyone else and refused Churchill and Roosevelt's requests to make Giraud commander in chief of the Free French Forces, so he resigned his co-presidency Oct 1943. After more pressure from de Gaulle and his faction, he resigned his command in N Africa April 1944 and refused to play any further part in the war.

Gleiwicz (now Gliwice, Poland) small German town on the border with Poland about 130 km/80 mi NW of Kraków. On 31 Aug 1939 it was reported that the town's German radio station had been raided by a group of Polish soldiers, who had conveniently all been shot dead. This 'Polish aggression' provided Hitler with the excuse he needed for the invasion of ◊Poland the next day, precipitating the start of the war. In fact, the 'Polish troops' were German concentration camp prisoners, dressed in stolen Polish uniforms and shot by the SS.

Gloster Gladiator British aircraft. The last biplane fighter to be used by the RAF, it was introduced 1936 and saw a good deal of action in the first months of the war. Sea Gladiators (the Fleet Air Arm version) took part in the defence of ◊Malta 1940. It had a top speed of 400 kph/250 mph and was armed with four machine guns.

Gloster Meteor British jet aircraft. The first British jet fighter and the only Allied jet aircraft to see combat service during the war, the Meteor began development 1941 and entered service 1944. It was a twin-engine low-wing monoplane, with a top speed of 660 kph/410 mph and four 20 mm cannon. Its speed made it capable of pursuing the V-1 flying bombs and it was sent to airstrips on the continent to deal with the Messerschmitt Me262, its German equivalent, though they never actually met in combat.

Goebbels Dr Josef 1897–1945. German politician and propagandist. An early disciple of Hitler, he joined the Nazi Party 1924 and became minister for public enlightenment and propaganda when the Nazis took power 1933. Perhaps the most intelligent of the Nazi leaders, he was totally committed to Nazism and his organizational abilities and oratory were major factors in disseminating the party line throughout Germany and abroad. He could also act if the need arose; his swift reaction to the 1944 ◊July Bomb Plot was instrumental in preventing the anti-Nazi conspirators gaining any advantage. He was appointed special plenipotentiary for total war Aug 1944 and was granted powers to draft any able-bodied person in the Reich into war work. He also fomented the myth of the last-ditch 'National Redoubt' and the ◊'Werewolf' resistance organization which gave many Allied leaders sleepless nights and led to complex military tactical dispositions to deal with threats which never actually existed. In the final days of Berlin he moved into the Führerbunker, poisoned his six children, and than ordered an SS officer to shoot him and his wife.

Goering Hermann Wilhelm 1893–1946. German politician and airman. He was a fighter pilot with Richthofen's Flying Circus during World War I, commanding it after von Richthofen's death. He joined the Nazi party 1922 as one of the original commanders of the ◊SA Storm Troops and was appointed minister of the interior for Prussia 1933. This position gave him full control of the police and security forces; he organized the ◊Gestapo and had the first ◊concentration camps built. He became minister for aviation later in 1933, organizing the clandestine formation of the ◊Luftwaffe and commanding it when it was formally revealed 1935. He then supervised the four-year economic plan to ready the country for war 1935–39.

Guns will make us powerful; butter will only make us fat.
    Goering's justification of German rearmament, radio broadcast 1936.

When war broke out he was field marshal of the Luftwaffe, but the air force's failure to break the British defences meant that Operation Sealion, the invasion of England, had to be postponed indefinitely. This was a major blow to Goering's reputation from which he never recovered and he retired to his country estate 1942, rarely appearing again in public. He remained faithful to Hitler, but after sending him an ambiguous message 1945, Hitler became convinced he was plotting a coup and had him arrested and expelled from the Nazi Party. Soon afterward he was captured by US troops and was subsequently tried at ◊Nuremberg. He was convicted and sentenced to death, but committed suicide a few hours before his execution was to take place.

Gold Beach Normandy beach on the right flank of the British sector on ◊D-Day, centred on the village of ◊Arromanche. The British 50th (Northumberland) Division made the first landing and by the end of the day some 25,000 men had been put ashore with their tanks and vehicles, contact had been made with the Canadians on the left flank, and troops had advanced 14.5 km/9 mi to the west toward US troops on ◊Omaha beach.

Gondar Abyssinian town in an exceptionally mountainous area about 320 km/200 mi SW of Asmara and N of Lake Tana. In 1941 it was held by the Italian general Nasi with about 40,000 troops, the last large body of Italian troops in the country. Access to the town was by two passes, both held by Italian garrisons which were starved into surrender in June and Sept respectively. Two brigades of the 12th African Division then converged on Gondar which held out until African troops gained the heights which commanded the Italian positions and the Kenya Armoured Car Regiment actually penetrated the outskirts of the town. General Nasi requested terms 28 Nov 1941 and the garrison surrendered.

Gort Field Marshal John Vereker, 1st Viscount 1886–1946. British soldier. He served in the Grenadier Guards during World War I, winning the VC, DSO with two bars, MC, and nine mentions in despatches. Appointed Chief of the Imperial General Staff 1936, he took command of the ◊British Expeditionary Force 1939. Although he had no experience of major command, he handled the BEF with great skill in the face of the German onslaught and French collapse, taking the vital decision 23 May 1940 to withdraw the British Army via Dunkirk before it was entirely destroyed. On returning to Britain he became inspector general of training and was then appointed governor of Gibraltar and commander in chief ◊Malta 1941.

Gothic Line German defensive line in Italy extending from south of La Spezia on the west coast, through the Apuan mountains and the Apennine passes, and then down the Foglia valley to the Adriatic Sea between Pesaro and Cattolica. The Germans retired to this line, a heavily fortified belt some 16 km/10 mi deep, after the fall of Rome June 1944. The Allies tried to break the line by using the US 5th Army to keep up pressure on the western end while the British 8th Army broke through on the east and exploited through the Po valley. The Germans defended strongly and although the British finally breached the line late Oct 1944, the winter weather was so severe that the ground became impassable and immediate exploitation was impossible.

Govorov Marshal Leonid 1897–1955. Soviet soldier. Appointed to command the 5th Soviet Army in front of Moscow Nov 1941, he played a major part in the Soviet defence and counteroffensive. He then took over the ◊Leningrad front, at the time besieged by the Germans, conducting an active defence and opening up a supply route across Lake ◊Ladoga. He eventually broke the siege Jan 1944 and pursued the retreating German forces all the way into E Prussia.

Graf Spee, **Admiral** German pocket battleship. Under Captain Langsdorff it sailed from Germany just before the outbreak of war and sank nine British merchant ships in the Atlantic. It was damaged in the Battle of the ◊River Plate Dec 1940 and sailed into Montevideo, Uruguay, for repairs. Langsdorff, fearful that the ship would be sunk as soon as it left the safety of the harbour, scuttled it 17 Dec 1940.

Grant tank US medium tank M3 (known in US service as the 'General Lee'), modified for British service. It was redesigned so that the radio could be carried in the turret where it could be operated by the vehicle commander or the gunner, removing the need for a radio operator and so reducing the crew to six. It was first used at ◊Gazala May 1942 and continued in service with the 8th Army to the end of the N African campaign, though toward the end it was being replaced by the M4 ◊Sherman. It was armed with a 37 mm turret gun and a 75 mm side-mounted gun and had a definite superiority over contemporary British tanks in both armament and reliability.

Graziani Rodolfo 1882–1955. Italian general. He was commander in chief of Italian forces in N Africa and had some initial success with an advance into Egypt until comprehensively defeated by the British Dec 1940, losing 12,000 casualties, 38,000 prisoners, and the equipment of five divisions. He resigned and returned to Italy. Following the Italian armistice 1943 he attempted to organize a republican Fascist army, was captured by the Allies 1945, and tried by an Italian military court. He was released 1950 as a result of political intrigue and remained active in neo-fascist politics until his death.

'Greater East Asian Co-Prosperity Sphere' Japanese propaganda term to convince the occupants of countries overrun 1940–41 that Japan's aims were benevolent. They remained unconvinced.

Great Marianas Turkey Shoot air battle during the naval battle of the ◊Philippine Sea, 20 June 1944. A Japanese fleet of 6 aircraft carriers with 342 aircraft set out to trap a US fleet between itself and land-based aircraft from ◊Guam. The US fleet, with 15 carriers and 956 aircraft, was aware of the plan and sent out their own aircraft, catching the Japanese some 80 km/50 mi away from their target. Over 300 Japanese were shot down and only a handful reached the US fleet, causing little or no damage.

ground controlled interception (GCI) British term for the ground command of fighter aircraft during and after the Battle of ◊Britain 1940. Using advanced radar, the British could see German air formations at considerable ranges which enabled ground controllers to direct fighter aircraft into the path of the enemy, doing away with the need to fly standing patrols across likely approaches.

Groves General Leslie 1896–1970. US soldier. An engineer who spent most of his career on civil engineering projects, Groves was appointed 1942 to supervise the engineering of the ◊'Manhattan Project', the codename for the US atomic bomb project. He was responsible for the erection of factories, towns, power stations, and the acquisition of all the raw materials necessary to complete the project. He employed over 125,000 people and had an annual budget in excess of $500 million.

Grumman US aircraft. The F4F *Wildcat* was used on aircraft carriers in all theatres of war. It had a top speed of 528 kph/328 mph, four .5 in machine guns, and could carry 100 kg/220 lbs of bombs. It was the standard US Navy fighter aircraft in 1941 and was also used by the RAF under the name Martlet.

The F6F *Hellcat* was an improved version of the Wildcat; it had a speed of 600 kph/375 mph, was armed with six .5 in machine guns, and carried 910 kg/2,000 lbs of bombs or six 5 in rockets. It was first used in action in the Pacific mid-1943.

The TBF/TBM *Avenger* was a torpedo-bomber, one of the first US aircraft to mount a power-operated gun turret and probably the first aircraft ever to carry a 22 in torpedo internally. It had a top speed of 435 kph/270 mph and was equipped with three or four machine guns.

Guadalcanal the largest of the ◊Solomon Islands; site of important US operation for control of the area 1942–43.

land campaign discovering that the Japanese were building an airfield on the island, the US 1st Marine Division landed there 7 Aug 1942, scattered the small Japanese garrison, and completed the airfield, which received its first US aircraft 20 Aug. The Japanese sent reinforcements to recapture the airfield and began naval and air attacks against the beachhead. Both sides built up strength throughout constant fighting until the Marines were relieved 8 Dec by XIV US Corps which drove the Japanese off the island, finally declaring it secure 7 Feb 1943. US casualties came to 1,600 killed, 2,400 wounded, and 12,000 hospitalized by disease; Japanese losses were 14,000 killed, 9,000 dead from disease or starvation, and 1,000 captured.

naval actions while the land battle for Guadalcanal raged, both sides were attempting to reinforce their troops by sea; prevent the other side from doing likewise, resulting in almost constant minor skirmishes and two major naval engagements. The *First Battle* began 12 Nov 1942 when the Japanese sent 2 battleships, a cruiser, 14 destroyers, and transports carrying 13,500 soldiers to the area and 5 US cruisers and 8 destroyers were sent to intercept them off Savo Island. The resulting battle was a confused affair but it ended with four US destroyers sunk, two cruisers so badly damaged that they sank later, and the rest of the US fleet damaged, whereas the Japanese lost a cruiser and two destroyers. However, they withdrew and postponed the reinforcement for 24 hours until they could assemble more cruisers to bombard the airfield. Three cruisers and two destroyers arrived and carried out a heavy bombardment, destroying 18 US aircraft but without doing much damage to the airstrip. As they withdrew they were harried by US aircraft which sank 7 of the 11 Japanese troop transports.

The *Second Battle* followed almost immediately. The Japanese ordered a further bombardment of the airfield and tried landing the remaining reinforcements 14–15 Nov. They were met by a US force of two battleships and four destroyers about midnight and a confused battle ensued in which three US destroyers were sunk and one damaged, while the US battleship *South Dakota* was severely damaged. However, the Japanese were severely punished by the US 16 in guns and the destroyers and transports withdrew at high speed out of danger, having managed to land no more than 2,000 men. Although these actions were inconclusive, they convinced the Japanese that there was no future in sending naval units to their doom for the sake of one island, and they evacuated 7 Feb 1943.

Guam island at the southern end of the Marianas group, about 1,600 km/1,000 mi N of New Guinea. It was occupied by the Japanese 10 Dec 1941 and used as a naval and air base. US forces invaded 21 July 1943 and by 10 Aug the entire island was in their hands. US losses amounted to 1,744 killed and 5,970 wounded; the Japanese lost 18,250 killed and 1,250 captured. Some of the Japanese garrison fled to the interior of the island – the last of them did not surrender until 1960.

Guderian General Heinz 1888–1954. German soldier. He created the Panzer (German 'armour') divisions that formed the ground spearhead of Hitler's Blitzkrieg attack strategy, achieving a significant breakthrough at Sedan 1940, and leading the advance to Moscow in Operation Barbarossa 1941, His initial advance was rapid but winter and determined Soviet resistance led him to make a partial withdrawal and Hitler dismissed him from his post. He was reinstated as inspector general of armoured troops 1943 and became Chief of Staff after the ◊July Bomb Plot 1944, but was dismissed by Hitler March 1945.

We have severely underestimated the Russians, the extent of the country and the treachery of the climate. This is the revenge of reality.

General Heinz Guderian letter 1941

Gustav Gerät German railway gun, the largest gun ever built. Of 80 cm (31.5 in) calibre, it weighed 1,328 tonnes and fired a 4.73 ton shell to 47 km/29.2 miles or a 7 ton shell to 38 km/23.6 miles range. When dismantled it occupied a number of railway trains and took three weeks to assemble at the firing site. The ◊Krupp company began developing the gun 1937 although it was not put into service until 1942. Two weapons, 'Gustav' and 'Dora', were built; Gustav was used at the siege of ◊Sebastopol, while Dora was sent to ◊Leningrad but arrived too late to be of any use and had to be hastily withdrawn. So far as is known, neither was ever used again. Components of both guns were found at the end of the war but not the complete equipment, which had apparently been scrapped.

Gustav Line German defensive line in Italy running from the mouth of the Garigliano river through ◊Cassino and across the Apennines to a point south of Ortona. After the US 5th Army's breakout from the ◊Salerno beachhead and the advance of the British 8th Army from Taranto, the Germans fell back to this line and put up a stubborn defence. The Allies landed at ◊Anzio 22 Jan 1944 in an attempt to outflank it, but this was quickly contained by German counterattacks and the line did not fall until the capture of Cassino May 1944.

H

Haile Selassie 1891–1976. Emperor of Abyssinia (now Ethiopia). Driven from his country by the Italian invasion 1936, he fled to Britain. He went to Egypt 1940 and with British assistance raised an army which he led into Abyssinia Jan 1941 as British forces began their offensive into Italian Somaliland and Eritrea in their ◊East Africa Campaign. Addis Ababa, capital of Abyssinia, was occupied by the British 6 April 1941 and Haile Selassie returned to his throne 5 May, precisely five years from the day the Italians had evicted him.

Halder General Franz 1884–1971. German soldier. He became Chief of Staff Sept 1938 following the resignation of General Ludwig Beck in protest at Hitler's war plans. He organized the Polish campaign competently, but was unenthusiastic about Hitler's plans for invading France, as he was convinced, wrongly, that the French Army was too strong to be beaten. He was responsible for much of the planning for Operation ◊Barbarossa, though it seems he did not dare draw attention to possible problems. He took command on the Eastern Front late 1941, but argued with Hitler Sept 1942 over the two-front policy which led to the disaster at ◊Stalingrad and was dismissed, going on to hold various staff posts. He was marginally acquainted with some of the conspirators in the ◊July Bomb Plot and so was arrested and imprisoned in ◊Dachau. Liberated by US troops 1945, he gave evidence for the prosecution at the ◊Nuremberg Trials.

Halfaya Pass pass south of ◊Bardia, on the Libya–Cyrenaica border. The pass gave access from the coastal plains through the escarpment to the inland plateau and thus to the open desert. Secured by ◊Rommel during his first offensive 1941, it became notorious when attacked by British tanks during Operation ◊Battleaxe 15 June 1941. Rommel had concealed a number of 88 mm anti-aircraft guns in the pass and deployed some of his armour to draw the British into the pass. When British tanks pursued this decoy force they were almost all destroyed by the concealed guns.

Halsey Admiral William Frederick 1882–1959. US sailor. A highly skilled naval air tactician, his handling of carrier fleets played a significant role in the eventual defeat of Japan. He was appointed commander of US Task Force 16 in the Pacific 1942 and almost immediately launched the ◊Doolittle raid on Tokyo. Appointed commander of the South Pacific Area Oct 1942 his forces fought at ◊Santa Cruz, ◊Guadalcanal, and ◊Bougainville. He took command of the US 3rd Fleet June 1943, alternating command with Admiral ◊Spruance. He led this fleet at the battle of ◊Leyte Gulf 1944; he almost fell into a Japanese trap but was saved by the timely appearance of Admiral ◊Kincaid and the 7th Fleet. He was promoted to fleet admiral 1945 and retired 1947.

Handley-Page British aircraft. The Handley-Page *Hampden* bomber, was capable of 410 kph/255 mph, could carry up to 1,800 kg/ 4,000 lbs of bombs, had a crew of four, and was equipped with four machine guns for self-defence. A twin-engine monoplane, its deep and narrow front fuselage gave rise to the nickname 'Flying Suitcase'. It was extensively used in the early part of the war, though it had to be hurriedly armoured and given additional guns when the realities of war were appreciated.

The *Halifax* was the second four-engine bomber designed to a 1936 specification, entering service March 1941. It could carry 5,900 kg/ 13,000 lb of bombs, flew at 450 kph/280 mph, had a crew of seven, and was armed with nine machine guns. Over 6,000 were built, and modified versions were used as glider tugs, transports, anti-submarine patrollers, paratroop carriers, and electronic warfare platforms.

Harbin city in Manchuria, about 480 km/300 mi NW of Vladivostok. It was the main objective of the 1945 Soviet invasion of ◊Manchuria; the 1st Far Eastern Front moved west from Vladivostok while the Trans-Baikal Front moved east from Mongolia. Soviet airborne troops landed on Harbin airport 18 Aug and the Japanese commander ordered his 43,000 men to lay down their arms while a surrender was hastily organized. The two overland fronts arrived in Harbin 20 Aug.

Harding General Sir John 1896–1989. British soldier. He served as Chief of Staff to General ◊O'Connor in Egypt 1940, then to General Godwin Austen of 30 Corps before returning to Britain to become director of military training 1942. He became Chief of Staff to General ◊Alexander in Italy Jan 1944 and later took command of 13 Corps.

Harmon General Millard F 1888–1945. US aviator. In 1942 he was placed in command of US forces in the South Pacific and was responsible for the campaigns in the ◊Solomon Islands and ◊Guadalcanal. He was appointed to command US Air Forces Pacific Ocean July 1944 with the primary task of organizing the bombing campaign against Japan. He died 1945 when his aircraft disappeared over the sea.

Harris Air Marshall Arthur Travers 1892–1984. British marshal of the Royal Air Force. Known as 'Bomber Harris', he was commander in chief of Bomber Command 1942–45. An autocratic and single-minded leader, he never lost his conviction that area bombing could, by itself, bring the war to an end. He had a flair for publicity, such as the celebrated ◊thousand-bomber raid on Cologne 30 May 1942, and he stretched his theories to the utmost with devastating raids on Hamburg, Berlin, and ◊Dresden. Although his policies were endorsed by the War Cabinet, Harris was the only senior British commander not to receive a peerage after the war, and no medal was ever struck for the men of Bomber Command.

de Hautecloque General Jacques Phillipe 1902–1947. Real name of General Phillipe ◊Leclerc.

Hawker British aircraft. The Hawker *Hurricane* was the first monoplane fighter to be adopted by the RAF and the first British aircraft to exceed 300 mph/480 kph with a top speed of 340 mph/545 kph. It was armed variously with eight or twelve machine guns, four 20 mm cannon or two 40 mm cannon, or eight rocket launchers, and could carry up to 455 kg/ 1,000 lb of bombs. It made up 60% of the RAF's fighter strength during the Battle of ◊Britain. It was produced in a naval version as the 'Sea Hurricane', was supplied to the USSR, and was modified to perform other roles such as ground attack, tank-busting, night fighting, and light bombing.

The Hawker *Typhoon* was originally designed as a fighter but became the outstanding ground attack machine of the war. With a top speed of 650 kph/405 mph, it could carry 910 kg/2,000 lbs of bombs but made its reputation in Normandy 1944. Armed with eight rockets it was highly successful at destroying German tanks attempting to reach the ◊D-Day beachheads. The *Tempest* was an improved Typhoon; a faster machine, with a speed of 700 kph/435 mph, and equipped with four 20 mm cannon, it was ideal for destroying V-1 flying bombs and also proved itself a superb fighter over Normandy.

Heinkel German aircraft. The Heinkel *He 111* was originally designed as a civil airliner 1935 but went into production almost immediately as a medium bomber. A twin-engine monoplane, it flew at 420 kph/260 mph, could carry 2,500 kg/5,500 lbs of bombs, had a crew of five, and was armed with five machine guns and one 20 mm cannon. It was used extensively in air raids over England 1940, but was found to be vulnerable to attack and so was relegated to night bombing and mine-laying.

The *He219 Uhu* ('Owl') was a high-performance night fighter which appeared late 1943. With a top speed of 665 kph/415 mph, and armed with various combinations of 20 mm and 30 mm cannons, it was highly popular with the ◊Luftwaffe and a scourge of the RAF, but internal feuding between different authorities for manufacturing priorities meant that it was never built in the numbers it deserved.

Heinkel were also the pioneers of German jet aircraft, flying their first jet Aug 1939. They produced their first jet fighter 1941, and in 1944, in response to an emergency call from the Luftwaffe, designed and produced an operational jet fighter inside three months. The *He162 Salamander* was a wooden machine with a jet engine perched on top of the fuselage and armed with two 20 mm or 30 mm cannon. It had a top speed of 835 kph/520 mph and was highly manoeuvrable, but less than 300 were built before the war ended.

Henderson Field airfield established on ◊Guadalcanal island; originally begun by the Japanese, it was completed by US forces 1942 and named after a US Marine major killed at the battle of ◊Midway. The

Guadalcanal campaign was fought over possession of the airfield, since its position was essential for command of the area around the ◊Solomon Islands.

Heraklion seaport and airfield on the island of ◊Crete. It was the objective of German parachute landings 20 May 1941 which were rapidly contained by a British counterattack. The airfield was thus denied to the Germans throughout the campaign, and the British were able to use Heraklion to evacuate many of their troops by sea when the island was finally abandoned.

Hess Rudolf 1896–1987. German politician. An early supporter of the Nazi party he was Deputy Führer until Sept 1939, when he was succeeded by ◊Goering. On 10 May 1941 he flew to Scotland on an unauthorized mission to seek a peace settlement with Britain. His proposals were ignored and he became a prisoner-of-war. Tried at ◊Nuremberg, he was sentenced to life imprisonment in Spandau Prison, Berlin, where he remained until his suicide 1987.

Hewitt Vice Admiral H Kent 1887–1972. US sailor. An expert in amphibious operations, he commanded the landings at Casablanca 1942, after which he took charge of the US 8th Fleet in N African waters. He commanded the task force which landed US troops in ◊Sicily and ◊Italy 1943, and in 1944 commanded the US landings in S France.

Heydrich General Reinhardt 1904–1942. German SS officer. He began his career in the Navy but was dismissed 1931 following a scandal involving a young woman. He then joined the ◊SS and was given the task of reorganizing and building up the ◊SD, the secret police arm of the SS. He then carried out a similar revamp of the SS and was made Deputy Commander to Himmler. He is believed to have had Jewish ancestry, although this was not wildly known at the time and seems, if anything, only to have made him a more fanatical Nazi.

Heydrich was responsible for the fake attack at ◊Gleiwicz 1939 which provided the pretext for the German invasion of Poland and went on to organize the ◊Einsatzgruppen 1941. On 31 July 1941 he was ordered by ◊Goering to draw up plans for the ◊Final Solution, which led to the establishment of extermination camps and an acceleration of the work of the Einsatzgruppen. As a reward he was appointed Reichs Protector of Bohemia and Moravia, making him the virtual ruler of Czechoslovakia. He was ambushed by a Czech resistance group 4 June 1942 and died of his wounds. The village of ◊Lidice was obliterated as part of the reprisals for his assassination.

Himmler, Heinrich 1900–1945. German SS Reichsführer. He joined the Nazi Party 1925 and became head of the elite ◊SS corps 1929, chief of the Bavarian police 1933, and head of the national police and Gestapo 1936; this accumulation of offices made him one of the most powerful people in Germany, second only to Hitler. He was one of the main instigators of the 'Knight of the Long Knives' 1934, which smashed the rival ◊SA. In his position as head of the SS he supervised the extermination of Jews in E Europe. He was appointed minister of the interior 1943 in an attempt to stamp out defeatism and following the ◊July Bomb Plot 1944 became commander in chief of the home forces. In April 1945 he proposed to the Allies that Germany should surrender to the USA and Britain but not to the USSR, but the offer was rejected. He was captured May 1945 and committed suicide.

Hipper, Admiral German heavy cruiser. It took part in the invasion of Norway 1940 and was rammed by a British destroyer, HMS *Glowworm,* which sank as a result. After this it remained in Norwegian waters as part of the German force harassing Allied convoys to the USSR. An attack led by the *Hipper* 31 Dec caused the Battle of the ◊Barents Sea, a disaster for the Germans which caused Hitler to decommission most of the German Navy's major warships.

Hirohito Emperor 1901–1989. Emperor of Japan from 1926, when he succeeded his father Taishō (Yoshihito). He is believed to have played a reluctant role in his militaristic cabinet's prewar expansion plans, preferring diplomacy to war, but was not strong enough to stand up to his government. As the war turned against Japan from June 1942, the prime minister ◊Tōjō involved him more in national life, calling upon the people to make sacrifices in his name. He belatedly began to exert more influence over his government as defeat became imminent in 1945, but was too late to act before the ◊atomic bombs were dropped on Hiroshima and Nagasaki. His speech on Japanese radio 15 Aug 1945 announcing the previous day's surrender was the first time a Japanese emperor had directly addressed his people. It was decided not to prosecute him in the Tokyo war crimes trials as he would be more use as a figurehead monarch under the US-backed 1946 constitution.

We have resolved to endure the unendurable and suffer what is insufferable.
   Emperor *Hirohito* announcing Japanese surrender, Aug 1945.

Hiroshima industrial city and port on the south coast of Honshu Island, Japan. On 6 Aug 1945 the city was utterly devastated by the first US atomic bomb dropped by the *Enola Gay*; the strike on ◊Nagasaki followed three days later. More than 10 sq km/4 sq mi were obliterated, with extensive damage outside that area. Casualties totalled at least 137,000 out of a population of 343,000: of these, 78,150 were found dead at the time, others died later.

Hitler Adolf 1889–1945. German dictator, born in Austria. He was *Führer* (leader) of the Nazi Party from 1921 and author of *Mein Kampf/My Struggle* 1925–27. As chancellor of Germany from 1933 and head of state from 1934, he created a dictatorship by playing party and state institutions against each other and continually creating new offices and appointments. His domestic position was not seriously challenged until the ◊July Bomb Plot 20 July 1944, a failed attempt to assassinate him.

The broad mass of a nation will more easily fall victim to a big lie than a small one.
           Adolf Hitler Mein Kampf 1927

In foreign affairs, he reoccupied the Rhineland and formed an alliance with the Italian fascist Mussolini 1936, annexed Austria 1938, and occupied the Sudetenland under the ◊Munich Agreement. The rest of Czechoslovakia was annexed March 1939. The ◊Molotov–Ribbentrop pact was followed 1 Sept by the invasion of Poland and the

declaration of war by Britain and France two days later. In Dec 1941 he
dismissed the commander in chief of the Army and assumed supreme
command himself; his early victories had convinced him of his military
ability but in fact he was a military amateur who was incapable of seeing the overall picture, and his assumption of command marked the end
of German strategic military superiority. He committed suicide 30
April 1945 as Berlin fell.

Hochdruckpumpe (German, 'high pressure pump') cover name for
a 15 cm (6 in) calibre multiple-chamber gun, also known as the
'Millipede', 'Busy Lizzie', or 'V-3'. The barrel was 150 m/490 ft long
and had a conventional breech and chamber at the rear, plus six auxiliary chambers arranged herring-bone fashion just in front of the breech.

A fin-stabilized shell was loaded through the breech with a conventional cartridge and additional cartridges were loaded into the auxiliary
chambers. The main cartridge fired and started the shell moving; the
auxiliary chambers then each fired in succession, adding their propul-
sive effort as the shell moved up the bore so that it left the muzzle at a
velocity of about 5,000 ft/1,500 m per second and had a maximum
range of 150 km/93 miles. Work began 1943 but although a few experimental rounds were fired from a test gun nothing practical ever came
of the project. A battery of 50 of these guns was to be built into a hill-
side at Mimoyècques, near Calais, aimed at London; it was discovered
by the RAF who suspected it was a rocket-launching site and bombed it
into ruins. The installation was finally overrun during the Allied invasion of France 1944.

Hodges General Courtney 1887–1966. US soldier. He was chief of
military intelligence until 1942, when he took over the Replacement
and Training organization for a short time before moving to take command of X Corps. He was promoted to lieutenant-general 1943 and
became deputy commander of the US 1st Army under General
◊Bradley. He organized the US landings on ◊Omaha and ◊Utah
beaches on ◊D-Day and succeeded Bradley in command of 1st Army
Aug 1944. By Oct he had led the army through Luxembourg and
Belgium, broken through the ◊Siegfried Line, and captured Aachen. He
held and eventually repulsed the main thrust of the German attack in
the Battle of the ◊Bulge and went on to cross the Rhine and link up with

9th Army in encircling the Ruhr pocket. Hodges was one of the most competent, if not so well-known, US commanders of the war.

Hoess Rudolf 1900–1947. German SS officer. In 1939 Hoess was adjutant of Sachsenhausen concentration camp and early 1940 was appointed commandant of the newly-built camp at ◊Auschwitz which began receiving its first inmates in June. Originally run simply as a forced labour camp, when he received orders to convert it into an extermination camp he installed four gas chambers and crematoria. He found that gassing by carbon monoxide, the recommended method, was inefficient and introduced the cyanide gas ◊Zyklon B, which improved his execution rate to 6,000 per day. In late 1943 he was appointed chief inspector of concentration camps and worked hard to improve the 'efficiency' of the other extermination centres. Arrested and arraigned at ◊Nuremberg, he appeared to be more upset about being thought inefficient than being thought callous. He was handed over to a Polish court, sentenced to death, and hanged at Auschwitz.

Hollandia (now Jayapura, Indonesia) seaport on the north coast of Dutch New Guinea. In 1944 it was the administrative and supply base for the Japanese 18th Army, deployed some 800 km/500 mi to the east between Wewak and Madang and threatening to be a formidable obstacle to any attack on New Guinea. ◊MacArthur therefore decided to attack Hollandia and remove the base, leaving the Japanese to starve. After a succession of heavy air raids, the US 24th and 41st Divisions landed at Hollandia with air support from the US Navy and captured all the Japanese base facilities. This effectively isolated the 18th Army which was left to its own devices until the war ended.

Holocaust the annihilation of more than 16 million people by the Nazi regime 1933–45 in the numerous extermination and ◊concentration camps, most notably Auschwitz, Sobibor, Treblinka, and Maidanek in Poland, and Belsen, Buchenwald, and Dachau in Germany. Of the victims who died during imprisonment or were exterminated, more than 6 million were Jews (over 6% of European Jewry); 10 million were Ukrainian, Polish, and Russian civilians and prisoners of war, Romanies, socialists, homosexuals, and others (labelled 'defectives'). Victims were variously starved, tortured, experimented on, and

The Holocaust 1933–45

1933	Jan	Adolf Hitler appointed chancellor of Germany. German Jewish population approximately 500,000.
	April	Official boycott of Jewish shops and businesses.
1935	Aug	Sporadic outbursts of anti-Semitic violence in several German cities.
	Sept	Reich Citizenship Law (Nuremberg Law) defined the term 'Jew' and separated Jews from other Germans.
1936		Olympic Games brought temporary halt to overt measures against Jews.
1938	March	Austrian annexation increased Jewish population of the Greater German Reich by about 200,000.
	June	Arbitrary arrests of Jews, who were sent to concentration camps.
	Oct	17,000 East European Jews deported to Poland after its government refused to renew their passports.
	Nov	*Reichskristallnacht* (Crystal Night), anti-Jewish attacks on synagogues and property, in which 91 died and 26,000 were removed to concentration camps.
	Dec	Decree for the compulsory 'Aryanization' of all Jewish businesses.
1939	Jan	Special identity cards introduced for Jews, who all had to adopt the name Israel or Sara.
	Oct	Deportations of Jews to ghettoes in the *Generalgouvernement* of Poland.
1940	April	Heinrich Himmler ordered the establishment of a concentration camp at Auschwitz.
	June	Commissar Order specified the execution of political commissars attached to Red Army units captured by German forces. Soviet Union invaded, and mass executions of Soviet prisoners of war, civilians, and Jews began.
	July	Hermann Goering issued first order for the liquidation of European Jews.
	Oct–Nov	First deportations of Jews from Germany. Mass killings of Jews in S Russia.
1942	Jan	Mass killings of gypsies from Lodz ghetto (Poland).
	July–Sept	First phase of mass deportations from occupied W Europe to extermination camps in E Poland.
1943	April	Uprising in Warsaw ghetto. Jewish resistance crushed.
	June	Himmler ordered liquidation of all Polish ghettoes.
	Aug–Dec	Deportation of remaining Russian Jews to extermination camps.
1944	April	Deportation of Greek and Hungarian Jews to extermination camps.
1945	Jan	Auschwitz closed.
	May	Last concentration camp at Mauthausen, Austria, liberated by Allied forces.

worked to death. Millions were executed in gas chambers, shot, or hanged. It was euphemistically termed the ◊final solution.

Home Guard British volunteer organization established 1940 for home defence in the event of invasion. Its members were civilians exempt from conscription who worked at their normal occupations and undertook military training in their spare time. In 1940 they were armed with a motley collection of shotguns and privately-owned weapons, but by 1942 they were a well-trained body liberally provided with automatic weapons and light artillery. They were disbanded Dec 1944.

Homma, General Masaharu 1888–1946. Japanese soldier. Homma spent most of his military career in intelligence duties and had little experience of field command. He was selected to command the invasion of the ◊Philippine Islands 1941 and was unwise enough to boast that he could do it in 45 days. MacArthur withdrew into the ◊Bataan Peninsula, prolonging the defence considerably, and Homma was reprimanded and replaced in all but name by General ◊Yamashita. Following the surrender of Bataan the captives were force-marched 95 km/60 mi to the nearest railhead; ill-treatment by the Japanese guards during the march killed about 16,000 US and Filipino troops. After the Philippine campaign was completed, Homma was recalled to Japan and held administrative posts for the rest of the war. He was arrested by US troops Sept 1945, tried for his part in the 'Bataan Death March', and executed in Manila 1946.

Honda General Masaki. Japanese soldier. He commanded the 33rd Japanese Army in ◊Burma. After the failure of the offensives at ◊Kohima and ◊Imphal 1944 he was able to extricate his forces and conduct an orderly fighting retreat to a line between Lashio and Mandalay. He managed to hold this line Jan 1945 against simultaneous attacks from US and Chinese columns attempting to re-open the ◊Burma Road. His position was then threatened by the British 14th Army advancing on Meiktila, and after a short attempt to defend the town he withdrew once more, fighting his way back into S Burma before the war ended.

Hong Kong British colony on the south coast of China comprising the island of Hong Kong and the mainland peninsula of the New

Territories. In 1941 the garrison consisted of about 11,000 men in five infantry battalions, two coastal defence artillery regiments, an anti-aircraft artillery regiment, and support troops. Too far isolated to be a safe fleet base and with little land defences, the loss of British sea and air superiority made its fall inevitable. The first Japanese patrols crossed the border from China 8 Dec 1941, followed by the main attacking force of three Japanese divisions supported by 80 aircraft and a naval squadron. Japanese air attacks soon destroyed what RAF presence there was and then subjected the entire colony to bombing attacks. The British defences on the ◊Gin Drinker's Line were soon breached and they fell back to the island. From there they turned the coastal defence guns to the mainland and bombarded the Japanese, though with little effect since the ammunition was designed for use against armoured warships. Japanese heavy artillery was emplaced in Kowloon and began bombarding the island and the first Japanese troops landed on Hong Kong itself 18 Dec. They drove a wedge between the British forces and gradually subdued the defenders until the garrison surrendered 25 Dec 1941.

Hood, HMS British battle cruiser. Of 41,200 tons displacement and armed with eight 15 in, twelve 5.5 in, and eight 4 in guns, with four torpedo tubes, it could reach a speed of 31 knots and had a crew of 1,420. It was sunk by gunfire from the German battleship ◊*Bismarck* south of Greenland 24 May 1941. Only three of the crew survived.

Hopkins Harry Lloyd 1890–1946. US government official. After a period as secretary of commerce 1938–40, he was appointed supervisor of the ◊lend-lease programme 1941, and undertook liaison missions to Britain and the USSR.

Höpner General Erich 1886–1944. German soldier. Skilled in armoured warfare, Höpner was involved in a plot to arrest Hitler if he ordered an attack on Czechoslovakia 1938, but it came to nothing when the ◊Munich Agreement allowed him to take the country without military force. Höpner then fought in the Polish and French campaigns and commanded a Panzer Group in the USSR during Operation ◊Barbarossa 1941; he got within sight of Moscow before being halted by a Soviet counterattack. Forced to withdraw, he was dismissed by

Hitler and discharged from the Army in disgrace. He then became involved with anti-Nazi groups and was designated by the conspirators in the ◊July Bomb Plot to become commander in chief of the Home Army. After the failure of the plot, Höpner was arrested and executed 8 Aug 1944.

Horrocks Lieutenant General Sir Brian Gwynne 1895–1985. British general. He served in World War I, and in the early part of World War II came to ◊Montgomery's attention while commanding a battalion under him. When Montgomery went to Africa he sent for Horrocks 1942, giving him command of XIII Corps. Horrocks repaid his confidence at ◊Alam Halfa, holding off German and Italian attacks without sustaining heavy casualties. He was given command of the British 1st Army with which he took Tunis 7 May 1943 but was wounded and returned to England. He returned to command XXX Corps at Normandy, again under Montgomery, and retained this position until the end of the war.

The British Army always fights uphill, in the rain, at the junction of two maps.

Lieutenant General Sir Brian Horrocks

Horthy Admiral Nicholas, de Nagybánya 1868–1957. Hungarian politician and admiral. Leader of the counterrevolutionary White government, he became regent 1920 on the overthrow of the communist Bela Kun regime by Romanian and Czechoslovak intervention. He ordered Hungarian forces to invade Yugoslavia Aug 1941 in support of Hitler's aims in the region and the following month formally declared an anti–Soviet alliance with Germany. He tried to retain some independence, refusing to send more troops to the Eastern Front May 1943. He went further in 1944, demanding the return of Hungarian troops from Germany and an end to the use of Hungary as a supply base and in June he attempted to halt the deportation of Hungarian Jews. He backed down on all these points when Hitler threatened to occupy Hungary and from then on began trying to remove Hungary from the war. He tried to negotiate a surrender to the

USSR 1944 but Hungary was taken over by the Nazis and he was taken prisoner. He was released by US troops May 1945 and allowed to go to Portugal, where he eventually died.

Horton Admiral Sir Max 1883–1951. British sailor. A submarine specialist, he commanded the Reserve Fleet 1937–39. On the outbreak of war he was given command of the Northern Patrol and became flag officer for submarines Jan 1940. In 1942 he became commander in chief on the Western Approaches, responsible for convoys crossing the Atlantic. He rapidly made his mark, adopting a variety of measures and tactics to neutralize the U-boat threat and eventually gained the upper hand. He remained in this post until the war ended.

Hotchkiss tanks French tanks developed by the Hotchkiss company. The light *H35* was an advanced design with a cast armour hull but like most French designs relied on one man in the turret to command, observe, and operate the 37 mm gun and machine gun. The *H39/40* model was an improved version with a more powerful gun and engine, thicker armour, and better fuel capacity, but it still suffered from a two-man crew.

Hoth General Hermann 1895–1971. German soldier. A cavalry officer in World War I, he remained in the army after the war, specializing in tank warfare. He commanded the 3rd Panzer Army in Operation ◊Barbarossa June 1941 and, together with ◊Guderian, closed the Byalystok pocket, capturing 300,000 prisoners. In Dec 1941 he got within 19 km/12 mi of Moscow but was thrown back. He managed to avoid being dismissed, unlike many generals repulsed in that battle, and was given command of 4th Panzer Army in the advance toward ◊Stalingrad. He led the last attempt to relieve the trapped 6th German Army there but was beaten back. He then led the 4th Panzer Army at the battle of ◊Kursk with little success, and after the fall of ◊Kiev he was relieved by Hitler and retired.

Hukawng Valley valley in Burma extending SW from Ledo on the Indian border in the general direction of Myitkyina. The Chinese 22nd and 38th Divisions under General ◊Stilwell advanced down the valley Oct 1943 with the intention of re-opening the ◊Burma Road but were stopped by the Japanese 18th Division. In Feb 1944 Stilwell was joined by ◊Merrill's Marauders who outflanked the Japanese position while he maintained pressure from the front. The Japanese were manoeuvred out of both positions and Stilwell was able to enter the Mogaung Valley and advance on Mytikyina.

Hull Cordell 1871–1955. US statesman. He was ◊Roosevelt's secretary of state 1933–44 and spent much of the period 1937–41 in negotiations with Japan. After Dec 1941 foreign policy was handled more directly by Roosevelt, but Hull was active in reaching agreements with ◊Vichy France, though these were largely cancelled by the rising influence of ◊de Gaulle. He took part in the early discussions which eventually led to the concept of the United Nations until ill health forced him to retire 1944.

human torpedo underwater weapon; it was basically a torpedo fitted with seats for two men and steering controls and with a detachable warhead which could be attached to a target ship. They were first used by the Italian Navy Dec 1941 in Alexandria harbour. The British battleships *Queen Elizabeth* and *Valiant* were so badly damaged in the attack that they were out of action for several months. The British had their revenge Jan 1943 with an attack on Palermo harbour in which a newly launched cruiser and a transport were sunk, and they sank another cruiser in the harbour of La Spezia June 1944.

Hump, The name given by Allied pilots to the eastern end of the Himalaya Mountains over which the Allied air supply route from Assam to China passed. The route was about 850 km/530 mi long and crossed 3,650 m/12,000 ft high mountains. It was an arduous journey but it was the only way to get supplies into China after the Japanese cut the ◊Burma Road.

Hungary the Hungarians' main ambition from 1920 was to recover the territory they lost in the peace settlements after World War I, and as ◊Hitler seemed to be good at getting his way, they allied themselves with Germany. This seemed to pay off when they regained Slovakia 1938, Ruthenia 1939, Transylvania 1940, and part of Yugoslavia (the Banat) 1941. In return, Admiral ◊Horthy sent Hungarian contingents to fight alongside the Germans on the Eastern Front. By 1944, though, Horthy could see that Germany was losing and he was preparing peace feelers to the Allies when he was deposed. Hungary therefore remained an ally of Germany until the end, and suffered accordingly when occupied by the Soviets.

Hunt's Gap pass in the Oued Mejerda mountains, about 65 km/40 mi W of Tunis. In Feb 1943 a German armoured column aimed at capturing the town of Beja was crossing the mountains while British troops were setting up a defensive position at Hunt's Gap. They put out an outpost at Sidi Nsir and the German column ran straight into it. The outpost resisted strongly, destroying 40 German tanks, before it was forced to fall back, but this delay had allowed the main position at Hunt's Gap to prepare itself, so that the Germans ran into an ambush and were almost totally destroyed.

Huntziger General Charles 1880–1941. French soldier. After a distinguished career in World War I, Huntziger was in command of the French 2nd Army 1940 when the Germans invaded. He deployed his troops to prevent an outflanking attack on the ◊Maginot Line, but his left flank was weak and was pierced by the German advance on Sedan. Huntziger then pulled his force back to protect the Maginot Line, an inexplicable decision, and was trapped in a fort at Verdun until the French collapse. He emerged to lead the French delegation which signed the armistice with Germany 22 June. He was killed in an air crash 1941.

Hyakutake General Haruyoshi 1888–1947. Japanese soldier. He was given command of the 17th Army April 1942 and was ordered to recapture ◊Guadalcanal and oversee operations in New Guinea Aug 1942. He failed to evict US troops from Guadalcanal, barely managing to escape with 10,000 of his troops. The US landings at ◊Rendova June 1943 took him by surprise and he failed to defeat the Americans on ◊Bougainville. In April 1945 he was removed from his command and employed in an administrative post for the remainder of the war.

Il Giogo Pass pass in the Apennine mountains NW of Florence, on a twisting road leading to Imola and the Lombardy plain. The US 5th Army chose this route during the battles to break the ◊Gothic Line Sept 1944 US II Corps had the task of forcing the pass, assisted by a flanking attack by the British XIII Corps. The battle was fierce and II Corps suffered over 500 killed and 2,000 wounded before taking the pass 17 Sept.

Ilyushin Soviet aircraft. The Ilyushin *Il-2 Stormovik* was probably the most famous of all wartime Soviet aircraft; over 35,000 were built. A formidable ground attack machine, it was well protected with both arms and armour, especially after the original single-seat design was found to be vulnerable to attack from behind so the cockpit was extended to make room for a rear gunner. Its top speed was 410 kph/255 mph, and it was armed with two 20 mm cannon, three 7.62 mm machine guns, and eight rockets or 590 kg/1,300 lbs of bombs.

The *Il-4* was the standard Soviet medium bomber throughout most of the war. A twin-engine monoplane it had a crew of three, three machine guns, flew at 425 kph/265 mph, and could carry 1,000 kg/2,200 lb of bombs internally plus 1,500 kg/3,300 lbs externally, or a 910 kg/2,000 lb torpedo.

Imphal town in the Manipur district of NE India, 375 miles NW of Calcutta; an important road junction. In 1944, Imphal and ◊Kohima were on the route of the Japanese invasion of India aimed at setting up a defensive line on the Naga Hills to keep the British out of Burma. General ◊Slim countered the Japanese plan by concentrating the 17th, 20th, and 23rd Indian Divisions with a tank brigade around Imphal where they established a defensive perimeter which could be resupplied by air. When the Japanese 15th Army attacked the perimeter,

Slim's plan worked, resupply went smoothly, the armour was able to move easily on the plain, and the Japanese attacks were resisted.

The ◊Chindit operations in the Japanese rear also began to have an effect upon their supply lines, exacerbated by the Allied air superiority which disrupted Japanese communications and freely bombed their positions. Finally the British 33rd Corps broke through the Japanese blocks at Kohima and were able to join up with the Imphal perimeter. The Japanese, starving and diseased, had by now lost 53,000 men and fell back to the Chindwin river, abandoning their artillery and transport. It was the turning point in the ◊Burma campaign.

INA abbreviation for ◊Indian National Army.

incendiary bomb small cylindrical bomb, usually weighing about 5.5 kg/12 lbs, made of magnesium alloy and filled with a small explosive charge and a large charge of thermite incendiary compound. They were dropped from the air in large numbers and ignited on impact; the thermite and magnesium were the source of intense fires, igniting anything capable of burning.

Indaw town in Burma about 100 miles SW of ◊Myitkyina on the railway to Mandalay, with roads leading west to ◊Imphal and ◊Kohima. An important Japanese supply base in their offensive against India, it was attacked by the ◊Chindits June 1944. This interrupted the supply line to the Japanese front and prevented troops from Indaw being used to reinforce the Imphal battle. The town was finally captured by the British 36th Division Dec 1944.

Indian National Army (INA) force recruited to fight for the Japanese from Indian prisoners of war by Subhas Chandra ◊Bhose, a disaffected Indian nationalist politician. It was intended to assist the Japanese in their conquest of India, but most of those who volunteered did so as a means of escaping the prison camps with the intention of deserting to the Allies as soon as the opportunity arose. Most did so – there are legends of one company shouldering arms and marching in ceremonial style into the British lines to 'report for duty' – but a small hard core of dissidents remained who were court-martialled and imprisoned for treason after the war.

Indo-China French colony, comprising modern Cambodia, Laos, and Vietnam. Following the fall of France 1940, the Japanese put pressure on the ◊Vichy government to allow them access to the area and Aug 1940 they established bases in the north to assist their operations in China. In July 1941 they were also give permission to establish bases in the south; this led to protests from Britain, the USA, and the Netherlands, who froze Japanese assets in their countries .The Japanese now abandoned the fiction of a joint defence of Indo–China with the French and virtually occupied the country, setting up important bases and headquarters in Saigon. In March 1945 they assumed complete control, massacring French garrisons which refused to acknowledge the Japanese government.

Much of the internal resistance to the Japanese came from Ho Chi Minh's guerrillas who received Allied backing and Aug 1945 the Japanese handed the country over to the Viet Minh. The 20th Indian Division entered Saigon 13 Sept and French troops and officials entered shortly afterwards to resume control of the country. They immediately clashed with the Viet Minh and other nationalist groups who felt the French had abandoned the country to the Japanese and now had no claims in the area.

Iran although technically a neutral country, German influence in Iran was strong and the British and Soviet governments decided to occupy it 1941 to prevent a possible German offensive from the Caucasus to seize the Iranian oilfields. There was little resistance; the Shah ordered his troops to cease fire 28 Aug and shortly after abdicated in favour of his son. Allied occupation continued throughout the war, securing both oil production and a vital supply route to the USSR.

Iraq a pre-war agreement allowed Britain to maintain two air bases in Iraq. At the outbreak of war the country was ruled by King Feisal III through a regent, but a military coup led by a pro-German politician, Rashid Ali, seized power 1 April 1941. Britain promptly sent reinforcements to Basra and Ali besieged the British bases, though his troops were quickly repulsed by the small garrisons. More reinforcements were sent, Ali was deposed, and power returned to King Feisal, and the British left a permanent garrison in the area to secure the northern oilfields and prevent further uprisings.

Ironside Field Marshal Sir Edmund 1880–1959. British soldier. After serving in the South African War and World War I, he was made Chief of the Imperial General Staff 1939 by the minister of war, Leslie Hore-Belisha (1893–1957), who found him more congenial than ◊Gort, who was sent off to command the ◊British Expeditionary Force. In May 1940 Churchill sent Ironside to France with orders for Gort to make an attack to the south in order to link up with the French. However, Gort demonstrated that it was impossible given the circumstances of the area at the time and Ironside agreed and returned to London. Churchill, now minister of defence as well as prime minister, promptly replaced him and put him in charge of the Home Forces, but he handed the post over to ◊Alanbrooke July 1940 and retired.

Irrawaddy River principal river of Burma, rising in the mountains N of ◊Myitkyina and flowing 1450 km/900 mi S to the Andaman Sea near Rangoon. After their failure at ◊Imphal and ◊Kohima 1944, the Japanese withdrew and adopted the river as a defensive line against attack from the west.

The British established three bridgeheads across the river north and south of Mandalay early 1945. While the Japanese were reacting to this, another British corps made a crossing well to the south, enabling them to expand behind the Japanese lines and capture Meiktia, the centre of Japanese communications, cutting their supply line and forcing their troops on the Irrawaddy to retreat.

Italy encouraged by the success of the German campaign in France, ◊Mussolini brought Italy into the war on Germany's side 10 June 1940, thinking it would be over quickly. Italy invaded Greece from Albania 28 Oct, but were repulsed Dec 1940 so the Germans had to take Greece themselves April 1941 (see operations in the ◊Balkans). The blows dealt at ◊Taranto as well as in Greece and N Africa, and the loss of the African colonies, soon made the war unpopular with the Italian people. German troops had to be sent to strengthen Italian defences and the Allies invaded ◊Sicily 10 July 1943, followed by landings on the Italian mainland 3 Sept. Mussolini was deposed 24 July and negotiations were opened for a separate peace with the Allies; Italy was granted a secret armistice 3 Sept, to take effect 8 Sept.

The Germans in Italy, led by Field Marshal ◊Kesselring, reacted rapidly, disarming Italian units within reach, and began a spirited defence of the country. The mountainous terrain, made worse by unseasonable weather, made the Allied progress up the peninsula slow and the attempt to outflank the Germans by a landing at ◊Anzio Jan 1944 was a failure. Rome was finally liberated 4 June 1944 and German forces in N Italy surrendered 29 April 1945.

Iwabuchi Rear Admiral Sanji. Japanese sailor. A fanatical devotee of the Emperor, he was commander of Japanese naval forces in Manila 1945, independent of Lt–Gen ◊Yamashita. When the latter ordered a withdrawal from Manila as the US forces neared the city, Sanji ignored him and ordered his 17,000-strong naval force to hold the city 'to the last man'. The subsequent battle lasted almost a month and the city was virtually destroyed, every Japanese strongpoint having to be reduced by artillery fire. There were few Japanese survivors and an estimated 100,000 civilian dead. Sanji himself was killed in one of the final engagements.

Iwo Jima island in the Bonin group, about 1,450 km/900 mi S of Tokyo. Fortified by the Japanese, it held two airfields, with a third under construction, and was a valuable strategic target for US forces as it would provide a base for land-based bombers to raid the mainland of Japan. It was assaulted by US Marines 19 Feb 1945 after a prolonged air and naval bombardment. The 22,000 Japanese troops put up a fanatical resistance but the island was finally secured 16 March. US casualties came to 6,891 killed and 18,700 wounded while only 212 of the Japanese garrison survived.

J

Jagdpanther German ◊tank destroyer, capable of destroying any Allied tank. It used a ◊Panther tank chassis with a fixed superstructure mounting an 88 mm gun. It was protected by 80 mm/3 in of well-sloped armour, weighed 45 tons, and had a speed of 72 kph/45 mph. Introduced 1944, about 385 were made.

Jagdpanzer IV German ◊tank destroyer. Based on the chassis of the PzKwIV tank, it had a long 75 mm gun in a fixed superstructure of 80 mm/3 in armour, weighed 24 tons, and had a top speed of 39 kph/24 mph. Low and easily concealed, it was a formidable weapon and some 1,300 were made from 1943 to the end of the war.

Jagdtiger German ◊tank destroyer. The most potent tank of the war, it was based on the ◊Tiger tank chassis and carried a 128 mm gun in a fixed superstructure with 10 in/250 mm thick frontal armour. It weighed 70 tons and had a top speed of 37 kph/23 mph, but its complicated electromechanical drive frequently broke down. Although only 38 of these massive vehicles were built they were virtually impervious to Allied tanks and could destroy anything on the battlefield.

Jägerfaust German air-to-air weapon. The actual weapon itself consisted of a 50 mm calibre steel tube carrying a propelling charge and a high explosive shell. This was placed in one of a number of larger tubes fitted in the aircraft's wings or fuselage. It was fired electrically when the aircraft was underneath an enemy bomber, with the shell being fired upwards and the steel tube ejected downwards, giving a recoilless effect and placing no stress on the aircraft. Several were fitted to aircraft March–April 1945 but their use in combat was inconclusive and there is no confirmation that they ever brought down an Allied bomber.

Jalo Oasis desert oasis about 400 km/250 miles S of ◊Benghazi with a small fort and airstrip. It changed hands frequently during the course of the desert campaign and at one time was used as a forward base by the ◊Long Range Desert Group.

Japanese aircraft

reporting name	type of aircraft	reporting name	type of aircraft
Alf	Kawanishi E7K2	Myrt	Nakajima C6N
Ann	Mitsubishi Ki-30	Nate	Nakajima Ki-27
Babs	Mitsubishi Ki-15	Nell	Mitsubishi G3M
Baka	Yokosuka MXY-7	Nick	Kawasaki Ki-45
Betty	Mitsubishi G4M	Norm	Kawanishi E15K1
Buzzard	Nippon Ku-7	Oscar	Nakajima Ki-43
Cherry	Yokosuka H5Y1	Patsy	Tachikawa Ki-74
Clara	Tachikawa Ki-70	Paul	Aichi E16A1
Claude	Mitsubishi A5M	Peggy	Mitsubishi Ki-67
Cypress	Nippon Ki-8	Pete	Mitsubishi F1M2
Dave	Nakajima E8N	Pine	Mitsubishi K3M
Dinah	Mitsubishi Ki-46	Randy	Kawasaki Ki-102
Emily	Kawanishi H8K	Rex	Kawanishi N1K1`
Frances	Yokosuka P1Y	Rita	Nakajima G8N1
Frank	Nakajima Ki-84	Rob	Kawasaki Ki-64
George	Kawanishi Shiden	Rufe	Mitsubishi A6M2-N
Glen	Yokosuka E14Y1	Sally	Mitsubishi Ki-21
Goose	Nippon Ku-8	Sam	Mitsubishi A7M2
Grace	Aichi B7A	Slim	Kyushu E9W1
Helen	Nakajima Ki-49	Sonia	Mitsubishi Ki-51
Hickory	Tachikawa Ki-54	Spruce	Tachikawa Ki-9
Ida	Tachikawa Ki-36	Stella	Nippon Ki-76
Irving	Nakajima J1N	Susie	Aichi D1A2-K
Jack	Mitsubishi J2M	Tabby	Showa L2D2
Jake	Aichi 13A	Thalia	Kawasaki Ki-56
Jill	Nakajima B6N	Theresa	Nippon Ki-49
Judy	Yokosuka D4Y	Thora	Nakajima Ki-34
Kate	Nakajima B5N	Tojo	Nakajima Ki-44
Lily	Kawasaki Ki-48	Tony	Kawasaki Ki-61
Liz	Nakajima G5N1	Topsy	Mitsubishi Ki-57
Lorna	Kyushu Q1W1	Val	Aichi D3A
Mary	Kawasaki Ki-32	Willow	Yokosuka K5Y
Mavis	Kawanishi H6K	Zeke	Mitsubishi A6M

Few people outside Japan had any knowledge of Japanese military aircraft in 1941, so US forces were confronted with a range of aircraft with no known titles. They gave each type a name (the 'reporting name') which was retained even when the correct designation became known, since by that time the names were well known and any change would have caused confusion.

Java Sea, Battle of the naval engagement between Japanese and Allied forces 1942. A Japanese fleet escorting the Eastern Invasion Force was intercepted 27 Feb 1942 by a mixture of British, US, Australian, and Dutch warships intent upon preventing them reaching Java. The Allied force of five cruisers and ten destroyers was severely mauled by the Japanese and while attempting to escape they ran into a second Japanese invasion force and were almost totally destroyed. Only four US destroyers, all damaged, managed to escape to the safety of Australia. This victory allowed the Japanese a free run in the waters around Java and they were able to complete their invasion without interference.

jeep US quarter-ton four-wheel-drive utility vehicle used by all Allied forces. Officially the 'Truck, 1/4 ton Willys Model MB or Ford GPW' it had been designed by Willys 1941, after which the Ford company were brought in to expand the production base. A total of 639,245 were built by the end of the war.

Jervis Bay armed British merchant ship. In Nov 1940 the *Jervis Bay* was escorting a convoy of 37 merchant ships when they encountered the German battleship *Admiral Scheer* in the North Atlantic. Captain Fegen ordered the convoy to scatter and then, hopelessly outgunned, began firing at the battleship so as to draw it away from the convoy. The end was inevitable, and the *Jervis Bay* went down fighting, but 32 of the convoy ships managed to escape. Fegen was posthumously awarded the Victoria Cross

Jeschonneck Colonel-General Hans 1899–1943. German airman. Selected by ◊Goering to help establish the Luftwaffe in the 1930s, he became Chief of Air Staff 1939, but turned out to have been over-promoted. A sound enough pilot and administrator, he was out of his depth trying to plan the air defences of Germany. His final mistake was to order his nightfighters to Berlin, where they were shot at by their own artillery, while the RAF were raiding ◊Peenemunde Aug 1943. He shot himself the next day.

Jodl General Alfred 1892–1946. German soldier. He was appointed Chief of Staff to Field Marshal ◊Keitel Aug 1939, although in practice he made most of the tactical decisions, becoming in effect commander of operations for most German operations except those in the USSR. He drew up the plans for the invasions of Yugoslavia and Greece in the ◊Balkan campaign, and also helped plan Operation ◊Barbarossa, the invasion of the USSR 1941. In Jan 1945 he formally became Chief of Staff and headed the delegation that signed Germany's surrender in Reims 7 May 1945. He was tried for war crimes at ◊Nuremberg 1945–46 and hanged.

Josef Stalin series of heavy Soviet tanks. The *JS1* was an improvement on the ◊KV design, using much the same chassis but with a new, larger turret. It initially carried an 85 mm gun but was then adapted to a powerful 122 mm gun. The *JS2* was an improved model with better-sloped armour, reduced weight, and wider track; it was the main wartime production model and some 2,250 were built.

The *JS3* was a complete re-design with a lower silhouette, ballistically shaped armour, and an 'inverted frying-pan' turret, carrying a more powerful 122 mm gun. It went into service early 1945 and caused a sensation among the Allies when they first saw it on the Berlin Victory Parade 1945.

Joyce William 1906–1946. British traitor. Born in New York, son of a naturalized Irish-born American, he carried on fascist activity in the UK as a 'British subject'. During the war he made propaganda broadcasts from Germany to the UK, his upper-class accent earning him the nickname *Lord Haw Haw*. He was captured by the British 1945, and tried and hanged for treason.

Where is the *Ark Royal*?
   rhetorical question frequently asked by *William Joyce* during his
   propaganda broadcasts which became a standing joke in Britain

---

Juin Marshal Alphonse 1888–1967. French soldier. A fellow-student of ◊de Gaulle at the St Cyr military academy, he was commanding a motorized brigade when he was captured by the Germans May 1940. He was released July and offered the post of war minister in the ◊Vichy government. He refused and instead became commander in chief N Africa, succeeding General ◊Weygand. When the Allies invaded 1942 he promptly joined them and later led French forces against the Germans in Tunisia and Italy. He became Chief of Staff and took part in the liberation of France 1944. He was posthumously appointed Marshal of France by de Gaulle.

July Bomb Plot conspiracy among a number of senior German officers to assassinate Hitler, overthrow the Nazi administration, and then sue for peace 1944. On July 20, Col von ◊Stauffenberg carried a bomb into Hitler's field headquarters in E Prussia, left it under a desk, and then left the bunker on a pretext. However, in his absence someone moved the briefcase, so when it went off Hitler was only slightly injured, though five senior officers were killed. A radio broadcast announced Hitler had survived at 18.00 the same day; the plotters in Berlin fumbled their attempt at a coup and the plot collapsed.

Mass arrests were made in the aftermath of the plot; the conspirators and those sympathetic, or merely suspected of being sympathetic, to them were given the choice of committing suicide or being hanged. At least 250 officers died this way, and some 10,000 people were sent to concentration camps.

Junkers German aircraft. The *Ju52 Iron Annie* was the German equivalent of the Allied Dakota, an all-purpose monoplane. It was originally developed 1932 as a three-engine airliner and was then adopted as a bomber. It was soon replaced in this role by faster, purpose-built machines, and settled down to its generalist role. With a speed of 265 kph/165 mph and capable of carrying up to 5.5 tonnes of cargo, over 4,800 were built in Germany and several hundred in other countries, and they remained in use in some parts of the world until the 1970s.

The *Ju87 Stuka* was a dive bomber which acted as the flying artillery for the Panzers in their ◊Blitzkrieg tactics and became one of the most famous German wartime aircraft. In a near-vertical dive, with siren screaming, and a 500 kg/1,100 lb bomb slung beneath, its effect on ground troops was a much psychological as real. A single-engine gull-winged monoplane with fixed undercarriage, its top speed was about 400 kph/250 mph and it proved to be an easy target for both fighters and anti-aircraft guns. After 1941 its dive-bombing role was much reduced, though it appeared on the Eastern front as a useful tank destroyer, carrying two 37 mm anti-tank cannon under the wings.

The *Ju88*, considered by some experts as the best all-round aircraft of the war, was designed as a high-speed medium bomber. It performed well in this role, entering service 1939, and was constantly improved with better engines, heavier armament, and a larger wingspan. A twin-engine monoplane, it could carry up to 3,000 kg/6,600 lb of bombs and had a top speed of 525 kph/325 mph. It was also converted for night fighting, photo reconnaissance, torpedo-bombing, mine-laying, dive-bombing, and ground attack.

Juno Beach Normandy beach used by Canadian troops during the ◊D-Day landings, 6 June 1944, although it was technically in the centre of the British sector. Initial resistance by the Germans caused a build-up on the beach, leading to an immense traffic jam when the troops eventually began to move inland. By midnight some 21,500 troops and their equipment had landed and the Canadian brigade had reached 11 km/7 mi inland to link up with the British on ◊Gold Beach.

K

Kaga Japanese aircraft carrier. Originally designed as a battleship, it was converted during building and completed as a carrier 1928, then modernized 1935. With a displacement of 38,100 tons and a speed of 28.5 knots, it carried 90 aircraft and was formidably armed with ten 8 in and sixteen 5 in guns.

The *Kaga* carried part of the strike force which attacked ◊Pearl Harbor 1941 and subsequently served in the South Pacific and Indian Oceans. At the Battle of ◊Midway May 1942 it was hit by four US bombs; uncontrollable fires broke out, leading to a violent explosion which sank her.

Kaiser Henry J 1882–1967. US industrialist. His shipbuilding firms became known for the mass production of vessels, including the *Liberty* ships – cheap, quickly produced transport ships built for the British.

Kaltenbrunner Ernst 1902–1946. Austrian Nazi leader. After the annexation of Austria 1938 he joined ◊Himmler's staff, and as head of the Security Police (◊SD) from 1943 was responsible for the murder of millions of Jews and Allied soldiers. After the war, he was tried at ◊Nuremberg for war crimes and hanged Oct 1946.

kamikaze (Japanese 'divine wind') Japanese suicide bombers. A special force of suicide pilots was established 1944 to crash-dive planes, loaded with bombs, onto US and British ships. Initially many different types of aircraft were used but later the *Okha,* a specifically designed piloted flying bomb, was developed (see also ◊Yokosuka, Kawasaki). Kamikaze squads caused major problems for Allied shipping, sinking or severely damaging at least six major vessels Nov 1944–Jan 1945, until their base in the Philippines was destroyed by Allied air strikes.

Kammhuber General Josef C. German airman. A skilled pilot, he was appointed to command German nightfighter defences Oct 1940. He deployed all available guns and searchlights in a line from Denmark to Belgium, adding radars and tactical controllers, so that incoming Allied bombers would be broken up by the guns and the controllers could then direct fighters to catch them as they emerged from the gun area. The system worked well until 1943 when the Allies began using electronic countermeasures. After a particularly bad period in which his fighters were largely ineffective, Kammhuber was relieved of his post.

Kasserine Pass pass in the Memetcha mountains about 240 km/150 mi W of Gafsa, Tunisia. Held by US II Corps under General ◊Fredendall, it was attacked by the German 5th Panzer Army 14 Feb 1943. The US forces were shattered, as were two US counterattacks on the following day. General ◊Alexander quickly moved British and US forces into blocking positions to halt the German thrust before it could get clear of the mountains, and Rommel withdrew so skilfully that the Allies never realised he was gone. General ◊Fredendall was subsequently relieved of his command and replaced by General ◊Patton.

Katyn Wood forest close to Smolensk, SW of Moscow, site of a Soviet massacre of Polish officers. In April 1943 German troops discovered a mass grave containing the bodies of about 4,500 Polish officers, all with their hands bound and shot in the back of the head. Germany made the most of this propaganda coup, accusing the Soviets of murdering the Poles in the hope of driving a wedge between two of the Allies. The USSR denied the accusation and blamed the Germans but the Poles believed it and the British had to work hard to play down the dispute for the sake of the common war effort.

A neutral commission examined the site and agreed with the German findings, but before they could complete their task the Soviets attacked and the Germans had to withdraw Sept 1943. The Soviets severed relations with the Polish government in exile in London and set up their own puppet government in Moscow. The question of who was really to blame was evaded during the ◊Nuremberg trials and it was not until shortly before the collapse of the Soviet Union in 1989 that the Russians finally admitted guilt.

Katyusha Soviet free-flight rocket; also called 'Stalin's Organ'. The rocket was 1.8 m/5.9 ft long and 130 mm/5.1 in diameter and weighed 42 kg/92 lb complete with a 22 kg/48 lb explosive warhead. It was fired from racks mounted in a heavy truck and had a range of about 5 km/3 mi. Each truck had 48 launcher racks and a battalion could lay down an immense rapid-fire barrage.

Kawabe Lieutenant General Masakuzo 1886–1959. Japanese soldier. A staff officer in the Kwangtung Army fighting the Chinese in the 1930s, he then became Chief of the General Staff of the Japanese Army in China. He was appointed to command the Japanese forces in Burma and planned the offensive against ◊Kohima and ◊Imphal 1944. When that failed he was recalled to Tokyo and placed in command of the Japanese Air Force.

Kawanishi Japanese aircraft. Kawanishi specialised in naval aircraft; the *H6K (Mavis)* was the military version of a pre-war commercial flying boat and was used for maritime surveillance and occasional torpedo-bombing. The *H8K (Emily)* went into production 1941 to replace the H6K and was probably the best flying boat of its day. A four-engine monoplane it had a crew of ten, five cannon, and four machine guns, could fly at 460 kph/285 mph with a range of about 6,500 km/4000 mi, and could carry up to 2,000 kg/4,400 lb of bombs.

The *N1K1 (Rex)* was one of the last floatplane fighters to be developed late 1942. Few were built because the design proved to be so good that it was converted into the *N1K2J (George)* carrier fighter. However, the conversion took time and it was not until 1944 that it appeared in service, rapidly acquiring a reputation as the best Japanese naval fighter of the war. A single-engine single-seat monoplane, it had a 2,000 hp engine, four 20 mm cannon, flew at 595 kph/370 mph and carried 500 kg/1,100 lb of bombs.

Kawasaki Japanese aircraft; Kawasaki provided aircraft for the Army air force. The *Ki45 (Nick)* was the first Japanese twin-engine fighter, entering service 1941. A two-seater with armament varying from three machine guns to combinations of 20 mm and 30 mm cannon, it served in all parts of the Pacific and also functioned as a night fighter and as a ◊kamikaze suicide machine.

The ***Ki-61 (Tony)*** was the only Japanese fighter to use an in-line engine and at first the Allies thought it was a license-built ◊Messerschmitt Bf-109, so close was the resemblance. There were difficulties in finding a suitable engine, but those which got into service proved formidable fighters with a speed of 565 kph/350 mph and armed with two 20 mm cannon and two machine guns.

The ***Ki-100*** was probably the best Japanese Army fighter to see service and was unusual in never being given a 'reporting name' (see ◊Japanese aircraft) by the Allies. It was a Ki-61 fitted with a radial engine, giving it a speed of 590 kph/367 mph; with good manoeuvrability and twin cannons and machine guns it could hold its own against any Allied fighter, but only 100 were built before the factory was bombed and production stopped. The ***Ki-102 (Randy)*** was an anti-shipping version of the Ki-45, carrying a 57 mm gun and two 20 mm cannon; again, few were built before the factory was bombed.

Keitel Field Marshal Wilhelm 1882–1946. German soldier. He was chief of the supreme command from 1938 and Hitler's chief military adviser, although he was really little better than a very efficient clerk and was totally subservient to Hitler. He dictated the terms of the French armistice 1940 and signed orders relating to the execution of prisoners of war throughout the war. He was a member of the court which sentenced many officers to death for their part in the ◊July Bomb Plot 1944. He signed Germany's unconditional surrender in Berlin 8 May 1945. He was tried at ◊Nuremberg for war crimes and hanged 16 Oct 1946.

Kenney Major General George C 1889–1952. US airman. He was commander in chief of the Far East Air Force, working with General ◊MacArthur and provided the air support for operations in the New Guinea and Solomon Islands campaigns. He pioneered the use of aircraft to supply ground troops in New Guinea 1942, and his forces supported MacArthur's assault on the ◊Philippines, where he is said to have been the first commander to use ◊napalm.

Keren town in Eritrea, about 50 miles NW of Asmara. Accessible only through a mountain gorge and surrounded by peaks, in 1941 it was held by the Italians. It was attacked Jan 1941 by the British 4th and 5th

Indian divisions, who had to isolate and attack each of the defended mountain outposts before an attempt could be made to break through the gorge with a tank column. The battle took eight weeks and the town was finally taken 26 March.

Kesselring Field Marshal Albrecht 1885–1960. German soldier. He commanded the ◊Luftwaffe 1939–40 during the invasions of Poland and the Low Countries and the early stages of the Battle of ◊Britain. He later served under Field Marshal Rommel in N Africa, took command in Italy 1943, and was commander in chief on the Western Front March 1945. His death sentence for war crimes at the ◊Nuremberg trials 1947 was commuted to life imprisonment, but he was released 1952.

Kharkov third most important city in the USSR, about 480 km/300 mi E of Kiev. It was taken by the German 6th Army 24 Oct 1941 with little resistance. In May 1942 a Soviet 'Front' of 640,000 men and 1,200 tanks set out to recapture the city, but two German armies attacked the flanks and cut off the spearhead, taking about 250,000 prisoners and destroying the remainder. It was re-taken by Soviet troops after their breakout from ◊Stalingrad Feb 1943 but was then recaptured by the German Army Group South 15 March. It was finally liberated by Soviet troops under ◊Malinovsky Aug 1943, following the failure of the German offensive against ◊Kursk.

Kiev Soviet city on the Dniepr river, about 800 km/500 mi SW of Moscow. In July 1941 Hitler changed his mind about the strategy of ◊Barbarossa and directed ◊Guderian to swing south and help von ◊Rundstedt to clear the Ukraine, instead of going straight for ◊Moscow. Following this order Guderian's force swung around the east of Kiev and, meeting von ◊Rundstedt's force, effectively cut off the Soviet South West Front which had been detailed to protect Kiev. The Soviet forces were quickly surrounded and the Germans proceeded to utterly destroy the contents of the pocket, taking 665,000 prisoners, 900 tanks, and 3,719 guns. Although this was a considerable victory, Guderian's diversion from Moscow meant that the winter descended before Moscow could be invested. Kiev remained in German hands until liberated by the 1st Ukrainian Front Nov 1943.

Kimmel Admiral Husband E 1882–1968. US sailor. Kimmel was commander in chief of the US Pacific Fleet at ◊Pearl Harbor Dec 1941. Severely criticized after the success of the Japanese attack, Kimmel complained that he had not been warned by Washington and that he had taken all the preventive measures laid down by regulations. His only positive action, sending his carriers out on a routine exercise, at least saved a crucial portion of the fleet. Nevertheless, he was relieved of his duties 10 days after the attack and held no active post thereafter.

King Admiral Ernest J 1878–1956. US sailor. Commander in chief of the US Fleet Dec 1941, in March 1942 he also became chief of naval operations and was later a member of the Joint Chiefs of Staff and the Anglo-US Combined Chiefs of Staff. Promoted to fleet admiral 1944, he organized and directed the naval forces in the Pacific; he was always reluctant to divert any resources to any other theatre and his efforts to obtain the most supplies for his Pacific Forces often caused problems in the European theatre.

Kincaid Vice Admiral Thomas C 1888–1972. US sailor. An ordnance expert, he commanded Task Force 16 in the battle of ◊Santa Cruz Oct 1942 during which the carrier *Hornet* was lost and the *Enterprise* seriously damaged. After the capture of ◊Guadalcanal 1943 he was given Task Force 67, a cruiser squadron, which he trained for night fighting to deal with Japanese convoys trying to resupply Guadalcanal at night. He then commanded the naval force in the recapture of the Aleutian Islands, and the 7th Fleet in operations to land MacArthur on the Philippines 1944, winning the battle of ◊Leyte Gulf.

Kippenberger General Howard 1897–1971. New Zealand soldier. He commanded an infantry battalion in Egypt 1939 and then saw action in Greece and Crete 1941, where he took command of a brigade. The survivors of Crete returned to Libya, reformed, and Kippenberger then led them in the desert campaigns until Dec 1941 when he was wounded and taken prisoner. He soon escaped and returned to duty, commanding 5th Infantry Brigade in the desert and then in ◊Syria. After El ◊Alamein, he commanded the New Zealand Division and led them across the desert to the final victory in Tunisia. He then commanded 5th New Zealand Brigade in Italy and the New Zealand division at ◊Cassino. He was seriously wounded by a mine 2 March 1944, losing both feet. This barred him from active duty and he then took charge of the repatriation of New Zealand prisoners after the war, returning to New Zealand to edit the national war histories.

Kleist Field Marshal Ewald von 1881–1954. German soldier. Commissioned into the cavalry 1902, he was a lieutenant-general commanding VII Army Corps by 1935 and retired 1938. He was recalled 1939 and given command of XXII Army Corps in Poland, then led Panzer Group Kleist in France 1940. He then led 1 Panzer Group in the Balkans and 1 Panzer Army in the invasion of the USSR. Promoted to field marshal Nov 1942, he commanded Army Group A in the Ukraine. He retired for the second time 30 March 1944, but when the Soviets occupied Germany he was captured and remained a prisoner until he died.

Kluge Field Marshal Gunther von 1882–1944. German soldier. He commanded 4th Army in Poland and France and was promoted to field marshal July 1940. He led 4th Army in the invasion of Russia, later succeeding von ◊Bock as commander of Army Group Centre. He was injured in an aircraft accident early 1944, and after recovering replaced von ◊Rundstedt as commander in chief in the West July 1944, with orders to throw the Allies back into the sea. After the disaster at the ◊Falaise Gap he was relieved and replaced by ◊Model. Although not involved in the ◊July Bomb Plot, he had occasionally discussed politics with some of the conspirators. Consequently, he was 'invited' to commit suicide in the aftermath of the plot's failure and did so.

knickebein German navigational aid used to permit blind bombing of targets in Britain 1940–41. The aircraft would fly along a radio beam until it was intercepted by another beam and then release its bombs. The system was susceptible to jamming, and once the British discovered it and took countermeasures it was soon abandoned.

Knightsbridge fortified area in the Libyan desert, 40 km/25 mi SW of Tobruk. It was held by the British 201st Guards Brigade during the battle of ◊Gazala 1942.

Koenig General Marie-Pierre 1898–1970. French soldier. He fought in Norway and France 1940 as a captain, and then escaped to England where he joined ◊de Gaulle. He commanded the French Brigade in the Libyan desert, defending Bir Hachiem before being evicted by ◊Rommel 1942. He later served on Eisenhower's staff to coordinate the French resistance with the invasion 1944 and after 6 June took command of the French Forces of the Interior. After the surrender of Paris he became military governor of the city and commanded the French forces of occupation in Germany 1945–49.

Koga Admiral Mineichi 1885–1943. Japanese sailor. He succeeded ◊Yamamoto as commander in chief of the Japanese fleet 1943 and followed the same policy of defending the Pacific islands. He frequently suffered defeats at the hands of the US fleets, particularly at ◊Rabaul 1943. He eventually moved to Singapore with the intention of assembling the Japanese fleet there for a final battle with the US fleet, but was killed in an aircraft accident March 1944.

Kohima town in Manipur province, NE India, about 95 km/60 mi N of ◊Imphal. It was garrisoned by an Indian infantry brigade and a British infantry battalion, with two Indian infantry battalions holding a small defensive box about two miles away. It was attacked by the 31st Japanese division 5 April 1944, isolating the British at Imphal. The battle at Kohima was among the most savage of the entire war as the Allied garrison repulsed every Japanese attack with severe casualties. On 14 April the 14th British division broke through and relieved the Kohima force, but were unable to break through the Japanese positions blocking the route to Imphal until the end of May, by which time the Japanese were weakened by disease and starvation and began to retreat.

Kokoda Trail track over the Owen Stanley Mountains of New Guinea, from Port Moresby to Buna. Little more than a muddy footpath in parts, the Kokoda Trail is generally agreed to have been the worst terrain and conditions under which any troops fought during the war. A Japanese force advanced south from Buna along it Aug 1942 and reached to within 32 km/20 miles of Port Moresby before being halted by Australian troops. They were held there and eventually withdrew on orders from Tokyo, pursued back along the trail by the Australians who carried the battle to the outskirts of Buna.

Kolombangara, Battle of naval engagement between US and Japanese forces July 1943. Four Japanese transports escorted by a cruiser and four destroyers were attempting to resupply the Japanese garrison on Kolombangara, one of the ◊Solomon Islands, when they were intercepted by three US cruisers and nine destroyers. The US vessels opened fire, sinking the Japanese cruiser; in reply the Japanese destroyers launched a torpedo attack which crippled one Allied cruiser. About two hours later the two forces met once more and the Japanese torpedoes crippled the two remaining US cruisers and sank one destroyer. By this time the Japanese had landed their men and supplies and so they withdrew.

Komandorski Islands, Battle of the naval engagement between US and Japanese forces 26 March 1943. A Japanese naval force was escorting a troop convoy to reinforce the Aleutian Islands when it was attacked by a US squadron of two cruisers and four destroyers. One cruiser on each side was damaged by long-range gunfire, and the US destroyers then closed in with a torpedo strike. The Japanese commander, fearful of the torpedoes and also apprehensive of an air strike from nearby US airfields, withdrew without landing the reinforcements. He was subsequently relieved of his command.

Kondo Vice Admiral Nobutaki 1856–1953. Japanese sailor. Kondo was the commander of the Southern Sea Force which sank the British battleships *Prince of Wales* and *Repulse* off the coast of Malaya 10 Dec 1941. He took part in the battle of ◊Midway 1942, though he withdrew without engaging the US fleet, and was also involved in the naval battles off ◊Guadalcanal and in the battle of the ◊Eastern Solomons.

Konev Marshal Ivan Stepanovich 1898–1973. Soviet soldier. He was given command of a corps 1942 and later of the 2nd Ukrainian Front. In Jan 1944 he helped ◊Zhukov encircle two German army corps and then liberated Lvov, reaching the Vistula 7 Aug. He led Soviet forces advancing on Berlin from the south, meeting up with US general ◊Bradley's forces 25 April 1945. He and Zhukov jointly attacked Berlin, taking it 2 May. After the war, he commanded all Warsaw Pact forces 1955–60.

Königsberg (now Kaliningrad, Russia) city and naval base in E Prussia; heavily fortified, it was ringed by three layers of defensive lines incorporating 15 forts. Having been cut off by Soviet advances along the ◊Baltic coast 1943, it was attacked by four Soviet armies supported by 5,000 guns, 538 tanks, and 2,400 aircraft 6 April. The battle was intense but the German commander surrendered 9 April. He was immediately sentenced to death by Hitler and his family were arrested. German casualties in the battle were high: 42,000 soldiers were killed, 92,000 captured, and an estimated 25,000 civilians were killed.

Kota Bharu seaport in N Malaya, 55 km/35 mi N of Singapore. Some 5,300 Japanese troops made a landing there 7 Dec 1941 and were met by the 8th Indian Brigade who held the airfield. The Indian troops put up the best defence they could but lost 320 dead and 538 wounded, while RAF aircraft severely damaged three troop transports. By the end of the following day the Japanese had secured their beachhead, had taken the airfield, and forced the remains of the Indian brigade to retire to the south.

Kramer Josef 1906–1945. German SS officer. A concentration camp guard since 1932, he gradually worked his way up, commanding at Natzweiler, where he inaugurated the first gas chambers, then at ◊Auschwitz May 1944, and finally Nov 1944 becoming commandant at ◊Belsen. This was a camp for invalids transferred from other camps, which could not handle the number of inmates as it rose to about 40,000. Spotted fever became rife and when the British found the camp 15 April 1945 the inmates were dying by several hundreds every day. Film of the camp shocked cinema audiences across Britain and the USA and Kramer was named the 'Beast of Belsen'. He was convicted of war crimes at Nuremberg and was hanged.

Kreipe General Karl Heinrich Georg. German soldier. A divisional commander on the Leningrad front, he was promoted to major general 1943 and sent to command the garrison in ◊Crete. In April 1944 his car was ambushed by British ◊commandos and Cretan guerrillas, and Kreipe was abducted to Egypt and remained a prisoner for the rest of the war. It was the only time that commandos or irregular forces ever achieved their ambition of capturing a German general.

Kretschmer Lieutenant Commander Otto 1912–. German sailor. A highly successful U-boat commander, he was awarded the Knights Cross for sinking seven ships on a single patrol. He is generally credited with sinking about 300,000 tons of Allied shipping in 18 months of patrolling until he was trapped by British destroyers 27 March 1941. He scuttled his boat and both he and his crew were taken prisoner.

Krueger General Walter 1881–1967. US soldier. After building his reputation as a trainer, Krueger took command of 6th US Army in Australia 1943, under ◊MacArthur. He soon made it into a highly efficient force, serving with it in ◊New Guinea, ◊New Britain, and the ◊Admiralty Islands. He invaded the Philippines Oct 1944, landing on ◊Leyte, and on Mindanao Dec, finally taking ◊Manila after a month of house-to-house fighting. Although frequently harried by MacArthur demanding some spectacular feat, Krueger refused to be hurried and conducted all his battles in a thorough and sensible manner, never stretching his troops beyond their limit.

Krupp German steelmaking armaments firm. The company developed the long-range artillery used in World War I, and supported Hitler's regime in preparation for World War II. During the war it thrived on the benefits of the forced labour of prisoners of war and concentration camp inmates and exploiting the industrial resources of occupied territories, transporting entire plants, machinery and workers, to Germany. With Germany's defeat 1945, the head of the firm, *Alfred Krupp* (1907–1967) was convicted of war crimes, sentenced to 12 years in prison, and ordered to sell 75% of his holdings. When no buyers could be found, Krupp was given a generous amnesty 1951 and was soon back in business.

Kufra Oasis oasis and fort in Cyrenaica about 800 km/500 mi S of ◊Tobruk. It was taken from the Italians by General ◊Leclerc March 1941 and was then used as a forward base by the ◊Long Range Desert Group, ◊Special Air Service, and other desert special combat units.

Kuribyashi General Todomichi 1885–1945. Japanese soldier. The commander on ◊Iwo Jima, he constructed a powerful series of defensive positions which were manned by some 23,000 troops. The US invasion of the island 1945 was not made any easier by Kuribyashi issuing orders to his men that each had to kill 10 enemy troops before they died. He signalled 'Goodbye' to his surviving troops 23 March 1945 and went into the front line to his death.

Kurile Islands chain of islands between the tip of the Kamchatka Peninsula (USSR) and the western end of the Japanese island of Hokkaido. The Soviet army began an offensive through these islands 11 Aug 1945 as part of their invasion of Japanese territory. The island garrisons fought fiercely but were overwhelmed by force of numbers and the chain was completely occupied by 1 Sept. It has remained in Russian hands ever since although it is the source of much dispute with Japan.

Kurland peninsula in Latvia, between the Gulf of Riga and the E Prussian border. In late 1944 the German Army Group North was forced into this area by the Soviet advances. It was renamed Army Group Kurland Jan 1945 when Hitler refused to allow it to evacuate by sea since it was tying up Soviet forces that might otherwise advance towards Germany. Eventually he allowed 6 of the 26 divisions to be rescued by the navy, together with wounded and refugees. The remainder of the Army Group surrendered 8 May 1945.

Kursk, Battle of battle between German and Soviet forces July 1943; the greatest tank battle in history and a turning point in the Eastern Front campaign. In spring 1943 the Soviet front line bulged out into the German front between ◊Kharkov and Orel. The Germans planned an offensive to pinch off this salient and flatten the front but the Soviets were forewarned by their intelligence service and planned to absorb the German thrust and then counterattack. They prepared for the assault with 20,000 guns, millions of mines, 3,300 tanks, 2,560 aircraft, and 1,337,000 troops; the Germans massed 10,000 guns, 2,380 tanks, 2,500 aircraft, and 900,000 troops.

The battle began 5 July in pouring rain. The northern half of the German force reached a point about 16 km/10 mi into the salient before being stopped; the southern thrust reached its climax 12 July when 700 German tanks battled with 850 Soviet tanks. But the Allies had landed in Sicily 10 July and Hitler demanded the withdrawal of troops from the USSR to reinforce Italy; on the same day the Soviets opened a massive offensive north of the Kursk salient. Hitler terminated the Kursk battle 17 July and the German forces in the area were left to extricate themselves as best they could.

Kuznetsov General Vasilly 1894–1964. Soviet soldier. A young general when he defended Kiev 1941, he was afterwards made a scapegoat for its loss, though ◊Budenny was really at fault. Remarkably, Kuznetsov survived and was given a command at ◊Stalingrad, where he performed well, and then became deputy commander of the Southwest Front, fighting from the Don to Berlin.

Kwajalien atoll in the ◊Marshall Islands; it was taken by the 4th US Marine and 7th US infantry divisions under General H M ◊Smith 4 Feb 1944. The Japanese garrison of 8,000 men fought so fanatically that there were no survivors.

KV tanks Soviet heavy tanks; the initials stood for Klimenti Voroshilov, the minister of war at the time of their approval 1940. The *KV1-A* had 80 mm/3 in armour and carried a 76.2mm/3.05 in calibre gun. The *KV1-B* was to the same design, but with additional 30 mm/1 in armour plates on front and sides. The *KV1-C* had a longer gun and 130 mm/5 in armour. Almost impervious to German anti-tank guns 1941–43, the KV was a serious threat, particularly after 1943 when the 76 mm gun was replaced by a more powerful 85 mm gun.

L

Ladoga, Lake Russian lake NE of ◊Leningrad. It formed a natural obstacle to German and Finnish forces attacking the city 1941, and when frozen was a vital supply line during the siege 1942–43.

Lancaster British bomber made by the ◊Avro company. A heavy four-engine bomber, it was capable of carrying up to 6,350 kg/14,000 lbs of bombs at a speed of 462 kph/287 mph for 2,575 km/1,600 mi. Highly adaptable, it could carry the 5,500 kg/12,000 lb Tallboy bomb and also took the ◊bouncing bomb used in the 'dambuster' raids against the ◊Ruhr dams. It was first flown June 1941 and developed into the RAF's best heavy bomber of the war, scoring many notable successes including the sinking of the ◊*Tirpitz* and the demolition of the Bielefeld viaduct.

landing ships and craft specialized ships for the transport and delivery of troops and equipment in a seaborne assault. *Landing ships* were large craft capable of long sea voyages; they carried tanks, vehicles, and landing craft. *Landing craft* were small flat-bottomed boats suitable only for use close inshore and were used to ferry troops and light equipment from landing ships and transports to the beach.

land mines explosive charges buried in the ground and fused so as to explode when disturbed. Anti-tank mines required the weight of a heavy vehicle to fire them, while anti-personnel mines required only a light footfall. Early mines were made of metal and could be located by a magnetic detector invented in Poland. Later mines were made of glass or plastic and were almost undetectable.

Latvia country in N Europe, bounded E by Russia, N by Estonia, N and NW by the Baltic Sea, S by Lithuania, and SE by Byelorussia (now Belarus). In 1939 a secret German-Soviet agreement (the ◊Molotov–

Ribbentrop pact) assigned Latvia to Soviet rule and Latvia was incorporated as a constituent republic of the USSR 1940. Latvia was occupied by German forces 1941–44, but the USSR regained control 1944.

Laval Pierre 1883–1945. French right-wing politician. He was prime minister and foreign secretary 1931–32, and again 1935–36. He joined Pétain's ◊Vichy government as vice-premier June 1940; dismissed Dec 1940, he was reinstated on Hitler's orders as head of the government and foreign minister 1942. His part in the deportation of French labour to Germany made him universally hated. When the Allies invaded, he fled the country but was arrested in Austria, tried for treason, and shot after trying to poison himself.

Lavochkin Soviet aircraft. The *LaGG-3* was a single-seat fighter which, to overcome shortages of critical metals, was largely of wood. Although over 6,000 were made, it was not notably successful. It was replaced by an improved version, the *La5*, with a more powerful engine; it was first used at ◊Stalingrad 1942. The *La7* was a further improvement, introducing metal spars to make it lighter. It had a top speed of 685 kph/425 mph and became a highly successful fighter in the final year of the war.

Leclerc General Phillipe (*nom de guerre*; real name Jacques Phillipe de Hautecloque) 1902–1947. French soldier. A captain in the 4th French Infantry Division, he deserted 1940 to avoid surrendering. He was captured and escaped twice, eventually arriving in England where he joined ◊de Gaulle. He was appointed general officer commanding French Equatorial Africa and governor of Chad and Cameroun, and changed his name to avoid repercussions against his family in France.

Leclerc led his troops across the Sahara desert to join the British 8th Army Dec 1942 and they played an important part in the battle of the ◊Mareth Line. Collecting more French troops from Tunisia, he formed the French 2nd Armoured Division which went to England and joined the US 3rd Army under ◊Patton for the ◊D-Day landings in Normandy 6 June 1944. Leclerc received the German surrender of Paris 25 Aug 1945, and then took his division to Alsace to liberate Strasbourg. He remained attached to Patton's army until the war ended. He was killed in an aircraft accident in North Africa.

Ledo Road road built by General ◊Stilwell running from Ledo, in Assam, into the ◊Hukawng Valley as an alternative to the ◊Burma Road which had been closed off by the Japanese. Work began Oct 1943 but was delayed until ◊Myitkyina had fallen, and it was only completed 27 Jan 1945. A projected oil pipeline, planned to run alongside the road, was never built.

Leeb Field Marshal Wilhelm Ritter von 1876–1956. German soldier. Retired 1938, he was recalled to command Army Group C in the invasion of France which was to mount holding attacks against the ◊Maginot Line. He then commanded Army Group North in ◊Barbarossa, the invasion of the USSR, 1941. Very much a soldier of the old school, in Jan 1942 he asked to be relieved of his post rather than have to carry out orders which were contrary to his better judgement.

Leese General Sir Oliver William 1894–1978. British soldier. He served with the ◊British Expeditionary Force in France 1940, then took command of XXX Corps of the 8th Army in N Africa shortly before El ◊Alamein. He remained one of ◊Montgomery's most trusted corps commanders, serving with him through the desert, Sicily, and Italy, and succeeding to the command of 8th Army when Montgomery left. He was appointed commander in chief Allied Land Forces Southeast Asia (ALFSEA) 1944 and held this post until succeeded by ◊Slim 1945.

Leigh light British airborne searchlight. They were carried in Wellington bombers and, guided by radar, were used to illuminate submarines prior to attacking them. First used 1942, by the end of the war 27 U-boats had been sunk and 31 severely damaged in attacks using Leigh lights.

Leigh-Mallory Air Chief Marshal Trafford 1892–1944. British airman. As commander of No 12 Fighter Group 1937–40 he took part in the Battle of ◊Britain and was responsible for the defence of the Midlands and much of East Anglia. He became head of Fighter Command Nov 1942 and 1943 was made commander of the Allied Expeditionary Air Force, the joint Anglo-US air force used during the invasion of France 1944. He ensured complete Allied air superiority during the invasion and his plan to destroy German road and rail links was crucial in isolating most of the German defence forces. He was killed in an air crash Nov 1944 while on his way to take up a new post as commander in chief of air forces in SE Asia.

Le May General Curtis 1906–. US airman. He commanded 305 Bomber Group, one of the first US units to arrive in England, and devised most of the tactics employed by the 8th Air Force. In July 1944 he became commander of 20th Bomber Command in the India-Burma-China theatre and carried out long-range B-29 raids against Formosa and W Japan. He took command of 21 Bomber Command in the ◊Marianas Jan 1945, and began a strong offensive against Japanese cities. The B-29 bombers which dropped the ◊atomic bombs Aug 1945 were under Le May's command.

lend-lease act of the US Congress passed March 1941 that gave the president power to order 'any defense article for the government of any country whose defense the president deemed vital to the defense of the USA'. The USA negotiated many lend-lease agreements in the course of the war, notably with Britain and the USSR. When lend-lease was officially halted Aug 1945, goods and services to the value of $42 billion had been supplied in this way; the British Empire had received 65% of this total and the Soviet Union 23%.

Leningrad, Siege of the German army reached Leningrad 1 Sept 1941 and were prepared to take it but Hitler ordered them to besiege the city in order to achieve a bloodless occupation. Within a week, all land communication was cut off and the city subjected to air and artillery bombardment. Before the year was out, starvation was causing 300 deaths a day although this was partially eased when Lake ◊Ladoga froze so that a truck route could be established to bring in food over the ice. Meanwhile the population laboured in munitions factories, dug defences, and served in the front line.

The siege ended 27 Jan 1944 when advancing Soviet forces drove the Germans out of artillery range. It has been estimated that about 1 million inhabitants of the city died during the 900 days of the siege, either from disease, starvation, or enemy action. Leningrad was awarded the title of 'Hero City' for withstanding the siege.

Lentaigne Major-General Walter 1899–1955. British soldier. He raised and trained the 111th Indian Infantry Brigade which became part of the ◊Chindits. When ◊Wingate was killed March 1944 he took over command of the Chindit operations and carried them to a successful conclusion.

Leyte island on the east of the Philippine group. When the Japanese realised the USA intended to invade the ◊Philippines 1944, they prepared a complex naval trap here. Their four aircraft carriers would be stationed near Leyte as bait for the US fleet while two powerful Japanese fleets would sail through the Philippine islands on different routes to execute a pincer movement when the Americans took the bait.

The *Battle of Leyte Gulf* 17–25 Oct 1944 was the biggest naval battle in history, involving 216 US warships, 2 Australian vessels, and 64 Japanese warships. There were a number of separate actions as elements of these forces met and diverged, but the overall result was the destruction of the Japanese Navy; they lost some 500 aircraft, 3 battleships, 4 carriers, 10 cruisers, 11 destroyers, and 1 submarine. Of the surviving Japanese warships, few if any had escaped damage. In contrast, the Americans lost 3 light carriers, 2 destroyers, 1 destroyer escort, and 200 aircraft. While the naval battle was raging, General ◊Krueger landed the 6th US Army on Leyte island, which was secured 25 Dec 1944.

Lidice village in Czechoslovakia, near Kladno, which was destroyed by the Germans 10 June 1942 as revenge for the assassination of ◊Heydrich by Czech partisans. All male inhabitants over 16 were shot, all females sent to ◊Ravensbruck concentration camp, and all children placed in a concentration camp at Gneisenau. There were very few survivors by the end of the war. The village's remains were preserved as a monument to Nazi atrocities.

List Field Marshal Wilhelm 1880–1971. German soldier. He commanded the 14th German Army in Poland and the 12th Army in France, and was then promoted to field marshal. He led the southern wing of the invasion of Greece and Yugoslavia 1941. Moving to the Eastern Front, he commanded Army Group A in the Caucasus 1942 but was dismissed Sept 1942 for failing to obey Hitler's directives.

He was convicted of war crimes at ◊Nuremberg 1945 and served 5 years of a life sentence.

Lithuania country in N Europe, bounded N by Latvia, E by Belarus, S by Poland and the Kaliningrad area of Russia, and W by the Baltic Sea. In 1940 Lithuania was incorporated as a constituent republic of the USSR, designated the Lithuanian Soviet Socialist Republic, in accordance with the secret agreement of the ◊Molotov–Ribbentrop pact. In 1941, when German troops had invaded the USSR, Lithuania's nationalists returned briefly to power and assisted the Nazis in the swift systematic slaughter of more than 130,000 Lithuanian Jews, communists, and other 'undesirables'. The Germans occupied Lithuania 1941–44, after which Soviet rule was restored.

Lockheed US aircraft. Lockheed produced a number of twin-engined transport and maritime reconnaissance aircraft during the war, but their greatest success was the *P-38 Lightning*. This was a unique fighter which had a short fuselage in the centre of the wing containing the pilot and guns and two long booms attached to the wings with the engines in the front and the tail unit connecting them at the rear. It was fast, at 665 kph/414 mph, and had great range (3,500 km/2,200 mi) and firepower (one 20 mm cannon and four machine guns), making it a valuable long-range escort fighter in Europe. In the Pacific, it shot down more Japanese aircraft than any other US fighter.

Lofoten Islands group of islands off the NW coast of Norway; an important source of fish and fish products for the German economy. It was the target of the first British ◊commando raid 4 March 1941, destroying some 800,000 gallons of fish oil and 18 factories. A second raid 26 Dec 1941 destroyed more factories and fishing boats.

Long Lance Japanese naval torpedo. It had a 610 mm/24 in diameter and a warhead twice the size of any comparable torpedo. Powered by an enriched oxygen motor, its range of 40 km/25 mi and speed of 50 knots outperformed any other torpedo in the world and it was responsible for many Japanese naval successes.

Long Range Desert Group highly mobile British penetration force capable of carrying out reconnaissance and raids deep in the desert of N

Africa. Formed July 1940, at its full strength March 1942, it had 25 officers, 324 soldiers, and 110 vehicles. It was redeployed March 1942 to carry out operations in Greece, Italy, and Yugoslavia. It was disbanded Aug 1945.

Los Alamos town in New Mexico, USA, where the first ◊atom bomb was designed based on data from other research stations; the hydrogen bomb was also developed there.

Luftwaffe German air force. Although Germany was not supposed to have an air force under the terms of the Treaty of Versailles, the Luftwaffe was covertly trained and organized using Lufthansa, the national airline, as a cover; its existence was officially announced 1 April 1935. It was an entirely tactical force under the command of ◊Goering but headed by Field Marshal ◊Milch from 1936, subordinated to the General Staff as a direct support arm for the army, and as such was one of the vital components of the ◊Blitzkrieg doctrine. Although some officers believed in the theories of strategic long-range bombing, they were ignored, and except for maritime reconnaissance, the Luftwaffe never operated any long-range aircraft. The Luftwaffe was also responsible for Germany's anti-aircraft defences, operating both guns and aircraft.

1. RAF Supermarine Spitfires in formation, 1943. The Spitfire was one of the most successful fighter aircraft of the war

2. Pearl Harbor, Hawaii, December 7 1941: the bridge superstructure of the US battleship *Arizona* collapses amid Japanese bomb and torpedo hits.

3. Lieutenant General (later Field Marshal) Bernard Law Montgomery, photographed on his arrival in Egypt to assume command of the British 8th Army, August 1942.

4. Field Marshal Georgi Konstantinovich Zhukov, the outstanding Soviet commander and arguably the greatest general of the entire war.

5. German Afrika Korps commander Field Marshal Erwin Rommel, pictured during the Axis siege of Tobruk, July 8 1942.

6. A German StuG III F 7.5cm assault gun accompanying infantry near the River Dniepr, Russia, 1942

7. US Generals Omar N Bradley (left) and George S Patton (right) with the Allied Supreme Commander, Dwight D Eisenhower at Bastogne, Belgium, in December 1945.

8. Belsen, Germany, 1945: bodies of concentration camp victims are removed from a communal grave.

9. The smoke cloud caused by the atomic bomb dropped on the city of Hiroshima, Japan, August 6 1945. The cloud had reached 20,000 feet by the time the photograph was taken; up to 140,000 people were killed by direct exposure to the blast.

M

MacArthur General Douglas 1880–1964. MacArthur graduated from West Point 1903, had a distinguished combat record in World War I, and rose to become Chief of Staff 1930–35. He defended the ◊Philippines against the Japanese 1941–42 and escaped to Australia when his small force was overwhelmed and he was forced to surrender. He then became commander of US forces in the Far East and, from March 1942, of the Allied forces in the SW Pacific. He was responsible for the reconquest of ◊New Guinea 1942–45 and of the Philippines 1944–45, being appointed General of the Army 1944. After the surrender of Japan 1945 he commanded the Allied occupation forces there.

McAuliffe Brigadier General Anthony 1898–1975. US soldier. He commanded the 101st US Airborne Division at ◊Bastogne during the Battle of the ◊Bulge, Dec 1944. He organized a stubborn defence 18–26 Dec before his unit was relieved by the US 3rd Army under General ◊Patton.

Nuts!

Brigadier General McAuliffe replying to a
German demand that he surrender

Mackensen Colonel General Eberhart von 1889–1968. German soldier. He became Chief of Staff 14th Army 1939 and later Chief of Staff to the 12th Army. In Jan 1941 he was given command of II Panzer Corps and took command of 1st Panzer Army Nov 1942. A year later he went to Italy to command 14th Army and remained there until he reached retirement age June 1944. It was his rapid reaction to the Allied landing at ◊Anzio which neutralized that operation. He was tried for war crimes at ◊Nuremberg and sentenced to death but this was commuted to life imprisonment, from which he was released 1952.

Maclean Brigadier Fitzroy 1911–. British soldier. An explorer in pre-war days, in 1943 he parachuted into Yugoslavia as head of the British Military Mission. On returning to London 1944 he advised that Allied support be switched from ◊Mihailovič's Chetniks to ◊Tito's communist partisans. He returned to Yugoslavia and remained there as British representative until March 1945.

Maczek Lieutenant General Stanislaw 1892– 1969. Polish soldier. He commanded Poland's only serviceable armoured brigade 1939 and managed to check the German advance in several places. Following the Polish collapse he led the brigade into Hungary and eventually to France where they reformed and fought with the French Army 1940. When France collapsed, the brigade was evacuated to Britain and re-equipped. Maczek became commander of the 1st Polish Armoured Division Feb 1942 and led the unit with distinction throughout the campaign in NW Europe. He took command of 1 Polish Corps May 1945.

Madagascar island in the Indian Ocean off the E coast of Africa. A French colony, it was controlled by the ◊Vichy government from 1940, but in 1941 it seemed likely to become a base for the Japanese which they could use to threaten the Indian Ocean. A joint force of British and South African troops landed 5 May 1942; resistance was nominal and the French governor formally surrendered the island Nov 1942.

Maginot Line French defensive line of fortification built 1929–39 to cover the Franco-German border from the Swiss border at Mulhouse to Montmedy, close to the Belgian border. It was never extended to the North Sea due to the difficulty of construction through the heavily built-up industrial areas and concern that fortifying the Belgian frontier might suggest France was abandoning the Belgians. In 1940 the line was outflanked by the Germans moving through the Ardennes and Sedan, and played little or no part in the subsequent battles.

magnetic mines sea mines which were detonated by the magnetic field of a ship passing over or alongside. Originally developed by the British 1918 but hardly used, the idea was taken up and perfected by the Germans. In late 1939 they began laying these mines in estuaries and off harbours around Britain and within a short time had sunk 27 ships and virtually stopped all shipping movements on the east coast of

Britain. A mine dropped on a mud bank was recovered intact 23 Nov 1940; it was dismantled and examined and countermeasures were soon developed.

Maidanek German ◊concentration camp near Lublin, Poland. Originally established as a labour camp 1939 it was converted to an extermination centre early 1942. Although less well-known than ◊Auschwitz, it was responsible for the deaths of about 1,380,000 Jews before being closed in the face of the advancing Soviets 1944.

Malaya (now Malaysia) British colony in SE Asia with the naval base and seaport of ◊Singapore at its southern tip. In spite of appeals from successive commanders in the 1930s, few defensive resources were allotted to the colony. A Japanese force landed in the north of the colony and in Thailand 8 Dec 1941 and began driving southwards, pushing the small British forces in the area ahead of them. The British were assembling a force to counter a Japanese landing in Thailand but the invasion of Malaya caught them off balance. Frequently outflanked, the British fell back into Singapore and surrendered 15 Feb, with 130,000 men taken prisoner.

Malinovsky Marshal Rodion Yakolevich 1898–1967. Soviet soldier and politician. He fought at ◊Stalingrad, commanded in the Ukraine, and led the Soviet advance through the Balkans to capture Budapest 1945. He then went east to lead the invasion of Japanese territory in ◊Manchuria. He was minister of defence 1957–67.

Malta island in the Mediterranean, British colony and naval base, about 80 km/50 mi from Sicily. Malta held the key to control of the Mediterranean so the British clung to it while Axis forces subjected it to heavy bombing attacks 1941–42. Heavily defended by coastal artillery, three squadrons of fighters, two of bombers, and one of torpedo bombers, the island was supplied by convoys from Gibraltar, most of which were heavily escorted and fought their way through to the island. The Italian navy attacked with ◊human torpedoes which were beaten off by coastal guns, and the island airfields acted as a base for operations against German and Italian forces in N Africa. Malta was awarded the George Cross 1942 for its fortitude in withstanding the heavy aerial bombardment.

Manchuria NE region of China, comprising the provinces of Heilongjiang, Jilin, and Liaoning. Effectively a Japanese colony from 1930 onwards, Manchuria became the Japanese puppet state of *Manchukuo* 1932–45, nominally led by the Chinese pretender to the throne Henry P'u-i. It acted as a base for Japanese operations in China and as an industrial enclave for Japan.

Manchuria was invaded by the Soviet Army 8 Aug 1945, four armies being moved from Germany to Siberia as soon as the European war ended. The invasion was by four columns, two from Mongolia and two from the Vladivostok area of Siberia, which entered Manchuria from west and east to converge on ◊Harbin and then swing southwards to the Chinese border and into Korea. With 1.5 million men and 5,000 tanks, Japanese resistance was easily swept aside and the occupation was complete within 14 days.

Manhattan project code name for the development of the ◊atom bomb in the USA, to which the physicists Enrico Fermi and J Robert Oppenheimer contributed.

Manila industrial port and capital of the ◊Philippines, on the island of Luzon. Abandoned by ◊MacArthur as indefensible, it was occupied by the Japanese 2 Feb 1942. The city was liberated 28 Feb 1945 but the old city to the S of the river Pasig was reduced to rubble in fighting between US and Japanese troops. It was replaced as capital by Quezon City 1948–76.

Mannerheim Field Marshal Carl Gustav 1867–1951. Finnish soldier. He was recalled from retirement 1939 to defend ◊Finland against the Soviet invasion, and gave the Soviets a hard fight before yielding. In 1941 Finland allied itself with Germany against Russia but by 1944 it was obvious that it was on the losing side and Mannerheim, now president of Finland, was able to disengage his country from the conflict on reasonable terms.

Manstein Field Marshal Erich von 1887–1973. German soldier. He served as Chief of Staff to von ◊Rundstedt in the Polish and French campaigns 1939–40. In 1941 he commanded a Panzer Corps of Army Group North in Operation ◊Barbarossa, then took command of the 11th Army in the ◊Crimea, being promoted to field marshal on the fall of

◊Sevastopol. He was given the task of capturing ◊Leningrad Aug 1942, but was then moved to Army Group Don and ordered to relieve the German 6th Army trapped in ◊Stalingrad. He was unable to help the trapped army but dealt with the subsequent Soviet offensive and captured ◊Kharkov. He fought at ◊Kursk July 1943, after which he conducted the withdrawal of Army Group South. After a series of arguments with Hitler over this withdrawal he was dismissed and took no further part in the war.

Maquis French ◊resistance movement that fought covert actions against the German occupation of France throughout the war.

Mareth Line German defensive line in N Africa running from the sea close to Mareth to the Matmata Hills, about 50 km/30 mi away. It followed the Wadi Zigzau, a dried river bed which made an excellent defence against tanks. ◊Rommel retired to this line March 1943, and frontal attacks by the British had no effect on him. He was finally manoeuvred out of the position by a force of New Zealand troops which made a wide flanking movement around the Matmata Hills accompanied by the British 1st Armoured Division. A hastily organized blocking operation by 21 Panzer Division managed to hold off the threat for long enough to allow ◊Rommel and the rest of his forces to retire from the line into Tunisia.

Marianas group of islands about halfway between New Guinea and Japan, containing the islands of Guam, Saipan, and Tinian. They were an important target for US forces since they would provide airfields close enough to Japan to permit B-29 bombers to raid it. Operations in the area commenced with the capture of Saipan 15 June 1944 and ended with the capture of Guam 10 Aug.

Market Garden operation by British and US forces to cross the Meuse, Waal, and Neder-Rijn rivers in Holland. An essential part of the operation was the capture of vital bridges at ◊Arnhem by British airborne forces, which would then be exploited by an armoured thrust from the south. In the event the airborne operation failed and the armoured force was prevented from reaching Arnhem.

Marshall General George Catlett 1880–1959. Marshall became army Chief of Staff 1939 with the rank of general. He foresaw the inevitability of US involvement in the war and so prepared the army well for it. Following ◊Pearl Harbor he was made Chairman of the new Joint Chiefs of Staff Committee and maintained a close liaison with ◊Roosevelt throughout the war. Following the end of the war, he initiated the *Marshall Plan* 1947 of massive US aid to restore Europe's economy and received the Nobel Peace Prize 1953.

Marshall Islands group of Pacific islands about 1,300 km/800 mi long, lying about 1,900 km/1,200 mi NE of New Guinea; the principal islands of the group are Eniwetok, at the north end, Kwajalien in the middle, and Majuro toward the south. Operation 'Flintlock' 30 Jan 1944 secured the group from south to north, with Eniwetok, the most difficult objective, being secured by 23 Feb. The Marshalls were the first Japanese possessions to be taken by Allied troops.

Martin US aircraft. The *PBM Mariner* was ordered by the US Navy 1937 as a patrol and transport aircraft and was also used by the RAF. A twin-engine flying boat, it stayed in production for 10 years.

The *Maryland* was a twin-engine bomber refused by the USAF but bought by the French 1939. It performed well, with a speed of 480 kph/300 mph and carrying 900 kg/2,000 lb of bombs; some escaped to Britain 1940 to be adopted by the RAF. The *A-30 Baltimore* was the result of the RAF's suggestions on how to improve the Maryland with more powerful engines and more defensive armament.

The *B-26 Marauder* was developed to meet a USAF demand 1939 and became one of the best light bombers of the war. A twin-engine machine with a speed of 525 kph/325 mph it could carry 2,500 kg/5,500 lb of bombs and was armed with 12 machine guns.

Masaryk Jan 1886–1948. Czechoslovak politician, son of the first Czech president, Tomáš Masaryk. He was foreign minister from 1940, when the Czechoslovak government was exiled in London. He returned 1945, retaining the post, but committed suicide as a result of political pressure from the communists.

Matilda tank British 'infantry' tank, slow and heavily armoured to accompany an infantry assault. The *Matilda I* appeared 1937 and was used in France 1940. It was an 11 ton tank with a crew of two, armed with a single machine gun but with 60 mm/2.5 in armour plate. *Matilda*

II was a far better tank, a 26-tonner with crew of four, armed with a two-pounder or 3 in gun plus a machine gun, and 78 mm/3 in of armour. It was used extensively in N Africa and the Middle East and later in Borneo and Hew Guinea. Several were also sent to the USSR.

Matsuoka Yosuke 1880–1946. Japanese politician, foreign minister 1940–41. A fervent nationalist, Matsuoka led Japan out of the League of Nations when it was condemned for the seizure of ◊Manchuria. As foreign minister, he allied Japan with Germany and Italy. At the end of the war, he was arrested as a war criminal but died before his trial.

Mauthausen German ◊concentration camp near Linz, Austria, established 1941. Although not actually an extermination camp, an estimated 180,000 prisoners died there.

Medenine town in Tunisia, S of the Gabes Gulf. After occupation by the British army Jan 1943 it was used as a forward supply and rest area, and ◊Rommel decided that an attack would disrupt ◊Montgomery's plans for advancing further. Deciphered messages warned the British and when Rommel attacked 6 March 1943 he was met by a fierce artillery barrage which shredded his infantry and powerful anti-tank defences which destroyed over 50 of his tanks. This was the last straw for Rommel, and he withdrew, resigned his command, and returned to Germany.

Medjerda river valley in Tunisia running NE from Souq Ahras to Tunis and a natural route through difficult country. It was strongly defended by the Germans but a night attack by 4th Indian Division 6 May 1943 broke through and opened a clear route into Tunis. The German commander, von ◊Arnim, surrendered 12 May.

Mellenthin Major-General F W von 1904–. German soldier. A staff officer in the Polish, French, and ◊Balkan campaigns 1939–41, he then moved to N Africa 1942 and then became Chief of Staff to XLVIII Panzer corps on the Eastern Front Nov 1942. He served as Chief of Staff to the 4th Panzer Army 15 Aug–14 Sept 1944 before moving to the Western Front as Chief of Staff Army Group G. He was appointed Chief of Staff 5th Panzer Army 1945 and was still in that position when the war ended. He was a foremost expert in the handling of armoured forces and his postwar book *Panzer Battles* became a standard work on armoured warfare in the 1940s.

Merrill Brigadier General Frank 1903–1955. US soldier. Enlisted as a private, he attended West Point and was commissioned 1929. He became assistant military attaché in Tokyo 1938 and studied the Japanese language and military system. He served with ◊Stilwell in the retreat from Burma. In Jan 1944 he was given command of 5307 Composite Unit (Provisional), a US group formed for long-range penetration behind the Japanese lines. This unit, later known as 'Merrill's Marauders', fought in the ◊Hukawng Valley and ◊Myitkyina but due to Stilwell's neglect of their supply line and his insistence on continuing in action too long, it was virtually destroyed by overstress and disease. Merrill, together with most of his men, was hospitalized but later became deputy US Commander in Burma and then Chief of Staff to the 10th Army in the Pacific.

Mers-el-Kebir (now El Marsa el Kebir) French naval base in Algeria near Oran (now Wahran). In July 1940 a major part of the French fleet was here and the British, fearful that these ships would be added to the German fleet in spite of French promises to the contrary, demanded that they either sail to a British port, to a neutral port, or be destroyed. The French commander rejected all alternatives and the British therefore opened fire, sinking several warships. There was a similar situation about the same time in ◊Dakar.

Messerschmitt German aircraft. The designs of Willy Messerschmitt were the most famous German machines of the war, notably the *Bf 109*, more or less the German equivalent of the British ◊Supermarine Spitfire. In 1937 this aircraft held the world speed record of 610 kph/379 mph; it carried a variety of cannon and machine guns and was a formidable fighter which was constantly improved through the war years. The *Bf 110* was a twin-engine fighter with insufficient power and manoeuvrability to survive, though it performed moderately well as a night bomber.

The *Me163 Komet* was a defensive fighter propelled by a liquid-fuel rocket. It was shot into the air at 965 kph/600 mph into the path of attacking bombers and before the rocket burned out would shoot something down and land. No flight lasted longer than 15 minutes and so it was not particularly successful. A more practical fighter was the *Me262* jet fighter, produced 1944, too late to be really effective, though it wreaked havoc among US day bombers during 1945.

Middleton Major-General Troy H 1889–1976. US soldier. He commanded the US 45th Infantry division in ◊Sicily and ◊Italy 1943, then took command of US VIII Corps, leading them for the rest of the war. After fighting in Normandy and capturing Brest, his Corps was involved in the Battle of the ◊Bulge 1944 and Middleton's skill in deploying his troops and reserves so as to break up various German movements was a major factor in the Allied victory.

midget submarines small one- or two-man submersibles capable of carrying one or two torpedoes. They were used by Britain, Germany, Japan, and Italy, for entering restricted waters inaccessible to conventional submarines. The Germans used them in the Scheldt estuary, the British in Norwegian fjords, and the Italians against the harbours of Gibraltar and Malta, all with success. The Japanese used them principally in a defensive role around ◊Okinawa and the ◊Philippines, and sometimes as suicide craft.

Midway, Battle of decisive US naval victory over Japan June 1942. Midway island lies NW of the Hawaiian islands, and in May 1942 the Japanese planned to expand their conquests by landing troops in the Aleutian islands and on Midway.

The Japanese attack involved two task forces; the Aleutian force was to draw the US fleet north, allowing the Midway force a free hand. The Americans deciphered the Japanese naval codes and so were able to deploy their fleet to surprise the Midway force. Both launched aircraft and the Americans sank one Japanese carrier and so damaged another two that they were abandoned. The sole remaining Japanese carrier managed to launch a strike which sank the USS *Yorktown*, but later in the day another US strike damaged it so badly that it had to be scuttled. With no aircraft carriers or aircraft left the Japanese abandoned their attack and retreated. The Midway victory was one of the most important battles of the Pacific war, removing Japanese naval air superiority in one day and placing them on the defensive thereafter.

Mihailovič Colnel Draza 1873–1946. Yugoslav soldier; leader of the ◊Chetniks, a nationalist resistance movement against the German occupation. His feud with ◊Tito's communists led to the withdrawal of Allied support and that of his own exiled government from 1943. He turned for help to the Italians and Germans, and was eventually shot for treason.

Milch Field Marshal Erhard 1893–1972. German soldier. Although not a pilot he commanded a fighter group during World War I and 1926 became chairman of Lufthansa, the German national airline. Using this cover, he trained pilots and developed equipment for the future ◊Luftwaffe air force. In 1936 he became General der Flieger of the Luftwaffe and 1941 took over responsibility for aircraft production. Imprisoned as a war criminal, he was released in 1955.

Milne Bay bay on the extreme eastern tip of New Guinea. A Japanese force landed here 26 Aug 1942 intending to move west and take Port Moresby. Japanese intelligence wrongly thought it poorly defended, unaware that it was defended by two Australian infantry brigades, one with experience against the Germans in Africa, and two fighter squadrons of the Royal Australian Air Force (RAAF). The aircraft attacked the transports and escorts, the troops resisted the ground attack strongly, and the Japanese withdrew 6 Sept. It was the first time Allied troops defeated a Japanese attack.

Mitchell Reginald Joseph 1895–1937. British aircraft designer whose design for the ◊Supermarine Spitfire fighter was a major factor in winning the Battle of ◊Britain.

Mitscher Vice Admiral Marc A 1887–1947. US sailor. A pioneer aviator who constantly pressed the cause of naval aviation, in 1941 he commanded the USS *Hornet,* the carrier from which the ◊Doolittle raid on Tokyo was launched. He became Air Commander, ◊Guadalcanal 1943, and in 1944 took command of Task Force 58, a concentration of carriers with its own supply organization which could act independently of the US fleet. This provided air support for the operations in the ◊Marshall Islands, ◊Hollandia, the ◊Marianas, the battles of the ◊Philippine Sea and ◊Leyte Gulf, and the operations at ◊Iwo Jima and ◊Okinawa.

Mitsubishi Japanese aircraft. Mitsubishi built a number of aircraft types, the most famous of which was known to the Allies as the *Zero* or 'Zeke' fighter, introduced 1939. A naval carrier fighter, it could outperform land-based fighters and came as an unpleasant surprise to the Allies. It had a top speed of 565 kph/351 mph, a range of about 2,400 km/1,500 mi, carried two cannon and two machine guns plus 270 kg/600 lb of bombs, and was highly manoeuvrable.

The *G3M (Nell)* was a twin-engine torpedo bomber which sank the British battleships *Prince of Wales* and *Repulse* off Malaya 1941. The *G4M (Betty)* was a twin-engine bomber capable of carrying 1,000 kg/ 2,200 lb of bombs to a range of 4,800 km/3,000 mi; to achieve this level of performance weight was saved by not using armour or self-sealing fuel tanks, making the machine highly vulnerable and so unpopular with its crews.

Model Field Marshal Walter 1891–1945. German soldier. A staff officer during the campaign in France 1940, he became commander of 3 Panzer division and led this in Operation ◊Barbarossa 1941 until given command of a Panzer Corps. He later commanded 2nd Panzer Army and 9th Army at ◊Kursk, after which he was frequently moved to various command positions to restore stability on the Eastern Front, acting as a 'trouble-shooter' for Hitler. He became commander in chief in the West Aug 1944, too late to stop the Allied advances in Normandy after ◊D-Day. Replaced by von ◊Rundstedt, he took over Army Group B and was responsible for defeating the British airborne landing at ◊Arnhem and launching the German offensive in the ◊Bulge. In April 1945 his army was trapped in the Ruhr pocket and, declaring that no German field marshal should permit himself to be captured, he shot himself.

Mogaung small Burmese town W of ◊Myitkyina held by the Japanese which formed a block covering the supply routes. The capture of this town by the ◊Chindit brigade June 1944 took 16 days, broke the Japanese supply lines, and isolated ◊Myitkyina for future attack.

Mohne Dam dam in the valley of the Mohne river, Germany, which, together with the Sorpe Dam, supplied 70% of the water required by the industries in the ◊Ruhr. Attacked by the RAF 16–17 May 1943, both dams were broken, causing severe flooding but with little effect on industrial capacity.

Molotov–Ribbentrop pact nonaggression treaty signed by Germany and the USSR 23 Aug 1939. Under the terms of the treaty both countries agreed to remain neutral and to refrain from acts of aggression against each other if either went to war. Secret clauses allowed for the partition of Poland – Germany was to acquire W Poland, with the east going to the USSR – and for the Russian annexation of the Baltic states. The pact ended when Hitler invaded Russia 22 June 1941 in Operation ◊Barbarossa.

Montgomery Field Marshal Bernard Law, 1st Viscount Montgomery of Alamein 1887–1976. British soldier. He commanded part of the ◊British Expeditionary Force in France 1939–40 and took part in the subsequent evacuation from ◊Dunkirk. In Aug 1942 he took command of the 8th Army, then barring the German advance on Cairo; his victory at El ◊Alamein in Oct turned the tide in N Africa and was followed by the expulsion of Rommel from Egypt and rapid Allied advance into Tunisia. In Feb 1943 Montgomery's forces came under US general Eisenhower's command, and they took part in the conquest of Tunisia and ◊Sicily and the invasion of ◊Italy.

Montgomery was promoted to field marshal 1944 and commanded the Allied armies during the opening phase of the invasion of France June 1944, and from Aug the British and commonwealth troops that liberated the Netherlands, overran N Germany, and entered Denmark. He received the German surrender 3 May 1945 at his 21st Army Group headquarters on Lüneberg Heath. He was in command of the British occupation force in Germany until Feb 1946, when he was appointed Chief of the Imperial General Staff. Created 1st Viscount Montgomery of Alamein 1946.

Morgan General Sir Frederick 1894–1967. British soldier. He was appointed Chief of Staff to plan the future invasion of Europe Jan 1943. His plan was accepted July and with some modifications became the plan for Operation ◊Overlord. He and his staff spent the following year working out the plan in minute detail.

Mortain town in Normandy which became the centre of a German counterattack intended to break through to Avranches on the sea and cut off the US forces to the west Aug 1944. Warned by decrypted ◊Ultra messages, General ◊Bradley was prepared and repelled the attack, manoeuvring the Germans into a position which led to their defeat at the ◊Falaise Gap.

Moscow industrial city, capital of the USSR and of the Moskva region, on the Moskva River 640 km/400 mi SE of St Petersburg. Germans troops came within 30 km/20 mi NW of Moscow Nov 1941, but stubborn Russian defences and severe winter weather forced their withdrawal in Dec. The failure to take Moscow was a severe setback for Operation ◊Barbarossa.

Mountbatten Admiral Louis, 1st Earl Mountbatten of Burma 1900–1979. British soldier and administrator. During the battle for ◊Crete 1941 his ship, HMS *Kelly,* was sunk, and he was picked up from the sea. He became chief of combined operations 1942 and was criticized for the heavy loss of Allied lives in the ◊Dieppe raid. He became commander in chief SE Asia 1943 and concentrated on the reconquest of ◊Burma. The campaign was primarily land-based and was actually conducted by General ◊Slim, beginning with the victories at ◊Imphal and ◊Kohima March 1944 and ending successfully a year later. He accepted the surrender of 750,000 Japanese troops in his area of command at a formal parade in Singapore Sept 1945.

Mulberry harbours prefabricated harbours built in Britain and floated across the English Channel to be moored off the Normandy coast to provide landing facilities for supplies and reinforcements after the ◊D-Day landings 6 June 1944. One was sited off ◊Arromanches, the other, to supply US forces, at St Laurent. During 18–22 June both were damaged by a severe storm, the US harbour so badly that it was never brought back into use. This delayed the Allied build-up of stores for some time.

Munda Japanese airfield on New Georgia Island in the ◊Solomon Islands. Attacked by two US infantry divisions and a Marine corps July 1943, the capture of the island and airfield was a slow and hard-fought process with heavy casualties. The airfield was finally taken 5 Aug and Allied aircraft began operating from it 10 days later.

Munich agreement pact signed 29 Sept 1938 by Neville ◊Chamberlain, Edouard ◊Daladier, Hitler, and ◊Mussolini, under which Czechoslovakia was compelled to surrender its Sudeten-German districts (the *Sudetenland*) to Germany. Chamberlain claimed it would guarantee 'peace in our time', but it did not prevent Hitler from seizing the rest of Czechoslovakia March 1939.

Murmansk ice-free seaport in NW Russia, on the Barents Sea. After the entry of the USSR into the war 1941, it was the winter terminal for supplies from Britain and later from the US; in the summer supplies went to Archangel which was closer to Leningrad.

Mussolini Benito 1883–1945. Italian dictator 1925–43. As founder of the Fascist Movement 1919 and prime minister from 1922, he was known as *Il Duce* ('the leader'). He invaded Abyssinia 1935–36, intervened in the Spanish Civil War 1936–39 in support of ◊Franco, and conquered Albania 1939. He brought Italy into the war June 1940 but defeats in N Africa and Greece, the Allied invasion of Sicily, and discontent at home destroyed his prestige, and he was compelled to resign by his own Fascist Grand Council July 1943. He was released from prison by German parachutists Sept 1943 and set up a 'Republican Fascist' government in N Italy. In April 1945 he and his mistress, Clara Petacci, were captured by partisans at Lake Como while heading for the Swiss border, and shot. Their bodies were taken to Milan and hung upside down in a public square.

For my part I prefer 50,000 rifles to 50,000 votes.
                                                        Benito Mussolini 1921

Mutaguchi Lieutenant General Renya 1888–1966. Japanese soldier. An ambitious and hot-tempered man, he commanded the Japanese force which captured Malaya and Singapore 1941, then went to command the 15th Japanese Army in Burma where he planned and commanded the disastrous offensives against ◊Imphal and ◊Kohima 1944. Following his failure, he was dismissed and was employed in administrative jobs thereafter.

Myitkyina town in N Burma commanding road and rail routes, about 420 km/260 mi N of Mandalay. Held by the Japanese, it was the objective of ◊Stilwell's 1944 operations and the airfield was taken by '◊Merrill's Marauders' and Chinese troops 17 May 1944. British troops came up from the south after the fall of ◊Mogaung and the town was besieged. Never entirely surrounded, the Japanese were able to resupply and reinforce it and in spite of hard fighting the Allies were unable to take it until the Japanese withdrew 3 Aug 1944.

N

Nadzab small town inland from Lae, New Guinea. In order to attack the Japanese garrison at Lae, a US paratroop regiment and Australian artillery were parachuted into Nadzab Sept 1943. They occupied the town, allowing the 7th Australian Division to be flown in and mount an offensive against Lae itself. This was one of the very few airborne operations mounted in the Pacific theatre.

Nagasaki industrial port (coal, iron, shipbuilding) on Kyushu Island, Japan. Three days after the attack on ◊Hiroshima, the second atom bomb was dropped here 9 Aug 1945. Of Nagasaki's population of 212,000, 73,884 were killed and 76,796 injured, not counting the long-term victims of radiation.

Nagumo Vice Admiral Chuichi 1886–1944. Japanese sailor. He was commander of the Fast Carrier Striking Force which attacked ◊Pearl Harbor Dec 1941. A cautious man, after his aircraft had made two raids against Pearl Harbor he refused to mount a third, as urged by his air commanders, which ensured the survival of the vast US Navy oil stores. Had these been destroyed, the US fleet would have been forced to retire to the US Pacific coast. In April 1942 Nagumo entered the Indian Ocean, attacked British naval bases in Ceylon, and sank several British warships. He was decisively defeated at the battle of ◊Midway May 1942, but fared better in the ◊Solomons and at ◊Santa Cruz, although he lost much of his aircraft strength. He was relieved and sent to command the defences of ◊Saipan, committing suicide when this was successfully invaded by US forces July 1944.

Nakajima Japanese aircraft, principally naval. The *B5N (Kate)* was a single-engine carrier bomber which soon became the principal naval bomber; it was used in China and at ◊Pearl Harbor, and sank the US carriers *Yorktown, Lexington, Wasp,* and *Hornet.* It was gradually replaced from 1944 onwards by the **B6N (Jill)** which also acted as a torpedo bomber and early ◊kamikaze machine.

The **J1N (Irving)** was a twin-engine naval escort and night fighter, while the **Ki-27 (Nate)** was perhaps the most numerous wartime fighter, seeing action in China and Manchuria prior to 1940 and from then in every Pacific area. The **Ki-43 (Oscar)** was an army fighter, and the **Ki-44 (Tojo)** was designed to attack high-altitude bombers, though they had little effect on US raids.

Namsos Norwegian seaport about 160 km/100 mi N of Trondheim. A British infantry brigade landed there 16 April 1940 and joined Norwegian troops to advance on Trondheim. German troops landed from destroyers rapidly outflanked them, forcing them into the mountains, where they were then attacked by German aircraft. Obviously doomed to failure, the operation was called off and the troops evacuated by sea 2 Sept.

napalm jellied gasoline used as an incendiary agent in aircraft bombs. The name is derived from the coagulating agents, Naphtha and Palmitic acid.

Narvik town in N Norway. A German force landed here by sea 9 April 1940. A British force was landed nearby 15 April but was not trained or equipped to operate in snow; in spite of French reinforcements they were unable to make any progress against German defences until the commander was replaced. They finally captured the town 28 May, but by that time German successes elsewhere in Norway allowed heavy reinforcement of the Narvik area and on 31 May all Allied troops were forced to evacuate the town.

Nehring General Walter 1892–1969. German soldier. Chief of Staff to ◊Guderian in the 1940 campaigns, he commanded the ◊Afrika Korps 1942 until wounded at ◊Alam Halfa. He later took part in the defence of Tunis, then went to the Eastern Front to command a Panzer Corps and finally a Panzer Army.

nerve gas chemical weapon which attacks the primary nerve centres and is lethal. Three nerve gases, Sarin, Soman, and Tabun, were developed in Germany between 1936 and 1942 as a result of research into organo-phosphoric weedkillers. As similar research had been carried out for agricultural purposes in Britain, the Germans assumed that the British had discovered similar gases, and since no antidote was known at that time there was little likelihood of the gases being used. About 500,000 artillery shells and 100,000 aircraft bombs filled with Tabun were discovered in German dumps after the war.

New Britain main island of the Bismarck Archipelago, NE of New Guinea. Taken by the Japanese 1941, a major base with five airfields was built at ◊Rabaul at the western end of the island. There was also an excellent harbour and the town held a garrison of about 100,000 troops. The Allies originally planned a direct assault on Rabaul, which could have been very costly; instead they landed on the western end of the island 26 Dec 1943 and established forward airfields to dominate the area, isolating Rabaul for the rest of the war.

New Georgia one of the bigger islands of the ◊Solomons, it was occupied by the Japanese 1941. A major airbase was built at Munda, on the south coast, and another at Seqi in the east. US forces made landings on the eastern tip 21 June 1943, close to Munda 2 July, and on the west coast 5 July. These expanded to attack Munda from two directions, an operation hampered by torrential rain and fanatical resistance. Munda was finally taken 5 Aug but the island was not secured until 25 Aug 1943.

New Guinea island in the S Pacific, NW of Australia; one of the largest islands in the world. In 1941 the eastern half was under Australian control and the west under the Dutch, but most of the interior remained unexplored and the terrain was harsh. Japanese forces landed on the north coast at Buna and Gona July 1942 and advanced into the Owen Stanley mountains, aiming for ◊Port Moresby. Held up by Australian and US forces, they fell back to the north coast and established a large beachhead which was contained by the Allies but not completely cleared until May 1945. A landing was also made at ◊Milne Bay in the east of the island but this was defeated by Australian troops and aircraft.

Ngakyedauk Pass pass in the mountains of the ◊Arakan district of Burma, discovered 1943. The British were having difficulty supplying the 7th Indian Division advancing toward Buthidaung at the time. The only available route was a mountain track, until the discovery of the pass allowed engineers to build a road passable by trucks and tanks. A supply base was set up and the line of supply for the second Arakan campaign was secure.

Nimitz Admiral Chester W 1885–1966. US sailor. He was appointed commander in chief US Pacific Fleet on the USA's entry into the war and held this post until the war ended. Under his command US forces advanced through Makin, Tarawa, the Marshalls, and the Marianas; he then joined forces with MacArthur to take the ◊Philippines, followed by ◊Iwo Jima and ◊Okinawa. The Japanese surrender was signed aboard his flagship USS *Missouri* in Tokyo Bay 2 Sept 1945. One of the greatest naval strategists of the century, after the war he became Chief of Naval Operations.

ground forces casualties: NW Europe 1944–45

	killed/missing	*wounded*	*POW*
Canada	10,740	30,910	2,250
France	12,590	49,510	4,730
Poland	1,160	3840	370
UK	30,280	96,670	14,700
US	109,820	356,660	56,630
Germany	128,030	399,860	7,614,790

Normandy *département* in N France forming the southern coastline of the English Channel. It was the objective for the ◊D-Day invasion 6 June 1944. Having landed here, Allied forces broke out through France and the Low Countries to Germany, while forces from Italy attacked from the south and Soviet forces attacked from the east. The landings at Normandy marked the start of the major Allied push to retake German-occupied territory in Europe.

North American US aircraft. The *P-51 Mustang* was designed to an RAF specification 1940, but performed poorly with its original Allison engine. The RAF fitted it with the Rolls Royce Merlin, which transformed its performance and it became an outstanding long-range escort fighter with a top speed of 700 kph/435 mph and armed with six machine guns.

The *B-25 Mitchell* was perhaps the best medium bomber of the war and was used in the ◊Doolittle raid on Tokyo. It had a speed of 440 kph/275 mph, carried up to 2,000 kg/4,400 lb of bombs and was adapted to various roles, including being armed with a 75 mm field gun for attacking submarines.

ground forces casualties: Western Desert 1941–43

	killed/missing	wounded	POW
UK	c. 7,000	?	?
other Allied	c. 8,470	c. 24,000	c. 41,300
Germany	12,810	?	1
Italy	20,720	?	

[1]Axis POWs in Tunisia in 1943 totalled 266,600; totals are not available for earlier actions.

North Africa campaign Allied military campaign 1940–42. Shortly after Italy declared war on France and Britain June 1940, an Italian offensive was launched from Libya toward Egypt and the Suez Canal. In Dec 1940 Britain launched a successful counteroffensive and captured Cyrenaica. After an agreement between Mussolini and Hitler, the German ◊Afrika Korps was established under ◊Rommel. During 1941 and early 1942 the Axis powers advanced, recaptured ◊Tobruk, and crossed the Egyptian border before halting at El Alamein. The British 8th Army under General Montgomery won a decisive Allied victory against Rommel's forces at El ◊Alamein 4 Nov 1942, followed by advances across Libya from Tunisia. British and US troops advanced from French NW Africa and the Allied armies in N Africa converged on Tunis. After a last-ditch defence, the Axis forces surrendered May 1943.

North Cape, Battle of the naval battle between British and German squadrons Dec 1943. The German battle cruiser ◊*Scharnhorst* sailed with five destroyers from Norway to attack a British convoy en route to

◊Murmansk. The convoy was escorted by the battleship *Duke of York*, a cruiser and 18 destroyers, with 3 more cruisers close by. One of these detected the *Scharnhorst* by radar and all three opened fire. The Germans turned away but were again found and bombarded by the three cruisers, although one was damaged by the *Scharnhorst*. The German commander sent his destroyers to search for the British convoy; they failed to find it and returned to their base in Norway, leaving the *Scharnhorst* alone. It was discovered by the British convoy escort and the *Duke of York* and a cruiser opened fire, landing thirteen 14-in shells on the *Scharnhorst* and thoroughly wrecking it. After being torpedoed by destroyers and further bombardment from the battleship, the *Scharnhorst* sank with the loss of all but 36 of her 1,839 crew.

Norway Norway was invaded by Germany 9 April 1940, largely to ensure the supply of Swedish iron ore via Norwegian routes. There was some resistance but much of this was undermined by an active group of Nazi sympathisers under the leadership of ◊Quisling. British and French troops were hastily collected and landed at various points but they were not trained or equipped for warfare in the far north, whereas the Germans were well-established, so they were unable to do much before they had to be evacuated. King Haakon and his government escaped to England and an active resistance movement was established. This and the constant threat of British ◊commando raids on the coastal islands kept a large German garrison in Norway throughout the war. On 7 May 1945 resistance forces seized most of the country's important installations without resistance from the Germans, who surrendered the following day.

Nuremberg Trials the trials of the 24 chief Nazi war criminals Nov 1945–Oct 1946 by an international military tribunal consisting of four judges and four prosecutors: one of each from the USA, Britain, USSR, and France. An appendix accused the German cabinet, general staff, high command, Nazi leadership corps, ◊SS, ◊SA, and ◊Gestapo of criminal behaviour.

The main charges in the indictment were: (1) conspiracy to wage wars of aggression; (2) crimes against peace; (3) ◊war crimes: for example, murder and ill-treatment of civilians and prisoners of war, deportation of civilians for slave labour, and killing of hostages; (4) crimes against humanity: for example, mass murder of the Jews and other peoples, and murder and ill-treatment of political opponents. Of the accused, ◊Krupp was too ill to be tried; Ley (1890–1945) committed suicide during the trial; and ◊Bormann, who had fled, was sentenced to death in his absence. Fritsche (1899–1953), Schacht (1877–1970), and von Papen (1879– 1969) were acquitted. The other 18 were found guilty on one or more counts ◊Hess, Walther Funk (1890–1960), and ◊Raeder were sentenced to life imprisonment; Shirach (1907–1974) and ◊Speer to 20 years; Neurath (1873–1956) to 15 years; and Admiral ◊Dönitz to 10 years. The remaining 11 men, sentenced to death by hanging, were Hans ◊Frank, Wilhelm ◊Frick, ◊Goering (who committed suicide before he could be executed), ◊Jodl, ◊Kaltenbrunner, ◊Keitel, ◊Ribbentrop, Alfred Rosenberg (1893–1946), Fritz Sauckel (1894–1946), Arthur Seyss-Inquart (1892–1946), and Julius Streicher (1885–1946). The SS and Gestapo were declared criminal organizations.

Oakridge town in Tennessee, E USA, on the Clinch River, noted for the Oak Ridge National Laboratory (1943), which manufactures plutonium for nuclear weapons. The community was founded 1942 as part of the ◊Manhattan project to develop an atomic bomb; by the end of the war its population was more than 75,000. Ownership of the community passed to the residents in the late 1950s.

Oboe radar-based blind bombing system adopted by the RAF 1942. It used two transmitters in England; one tracked the bomber, guiding it on a course across the target. The other also tracked the bomber and ordered it to drop its bombs at the computed bomb-release point. Since accuracy was of a very high order, bombing became very accurate, and the system was used by the ◊Pathfinder force to drop marker bombs for the rest of a bombing force.

O'Connor General Sir Richard 1889–1981. British soldier. In 1940 he became commander of the Western Desert Force in Egypt, defeating the Italians at Sidi Barrani Dec 1940. He went on to capture ◊Bardia and destroyed the Italian 10th Army at ◊Beda Fomm. He was captured by the Germans April 1942, but escaped two years later and returned to England. He commanded VIII Corps in the Normandy campaign.

Odessa Soviet seaport on the Black Sea; a prime objective of German and Romanian forces in Operation ◊Barbarossa. Besieged 4 Aug 1941 it resisted for 73 days before being taken and it was incorporated into Romania as a new province, 'Transdniestria'. It was recaptured by Soviet troops 10 April 1944 and returned to the USSR.

OSS Office of Strategic Services. US intelligence organization operating agents and assisting resistance movements in German-occupied Europe. It was the forerunner of the Central Intelligence Agency (CIA).

Okinawa group of islands, forming part of the Japanese ◊Ryukyu Islands in the W Pacific. The principal island, Okinawa, was captured by US troops in the *Battle of Okinawa* 1 April–21 June 1945, with 47,000 US casualties (12,000 dead) and 60,000 Japanese (only a few hundred survived as prisoners). During the invasion over 150,000 Okinawans, mainly civilians, died; many were massacred by Japanese forces. The island was returned to Japan 1972.

Omaha Beach Normandy landing beach used by the US V Corps on ◊D-Day 6 June 1944. In the area of Vierville, it was strongly defended and the ◊landing craft and swimming tanks were launched too far out at sea in choppy conditions, so that many capsized and sank. Naval gunfire support lifted too early so that troops ran into intense fire on landing and were pinned to the beach for some time. However, with brave leadership and hard fighting US troops broke out by the middle of the afternoon and the beach was secured.

Ordzhonikidze town in the Caucasus region of the USSR, about 400 km/250 mi NW of Baku. It became the most easterly point ever reached by German forces Aug 1942, but by Dec the town had been re-taken by the Soviets and the Germans were beginning their march home.

Oslo capital of Norway. It was captured 9 April 1940 by German paratroops landing at the airport and a force of German troops concealed in merchant ships to pass the Oskarsborg fortress guarding the harbour entrance.

OSS abbreviation for ◊Office of Strategic Services.

Overlord, Operation code-name for the ◊D-Day landings in Normandy 6 June 1944 and the subsequent drive to retake German-occupied Europe.

P

Pacific theatres the Pacific Ocean Area comprised the entire space between the USA and China and was under the overall command of US admiral ◊Nimitz. It was subdivided into the Southeast, South, Southwest, and Central Pacific theatres of operation.

ground forces casualties: Pacific Theatre 1941–45

	killed/missing	wounded	POW
USA	55,060	162,230	30,000
Japan	685,230	?	37,280

Pantelleria volcanic island in the Mediterranean, 100 km/62 mi SW of Sicily. Strategically placed, the island was strongly fortified by Mussolini but surrendered to the Allies 11 June 1943 after a month-long air bombardment. Its capture was a vital precursor to the attack on ◊Siciliy.

Panther tank German medium tank devised as an answer to the Soviet ◊T-34. Armed with a long 75 mm gun and notable for its inter-leaved road wheel suspension, it was rushed into production Nov 1942 and so early models were unreliable, but it soon acquired a formidable reputation. It weighed 44 tons, had a top speed of 55 kph/34 mph, and a crew of five.

Panzer (German 'armour') German term for armoured troops, vehicles, formations, or other equipment connected with tanks. A Panzer Army was a mechanized army based on a core of tanks and supported by infantry, artillery, and service troops in vehicles capable of accompanying the tanks.

Panzerbuchse (German 'armour rifle') heavy infantry rifle designed to penetrate tanks, using a 7.92 mm bullet with a special hard core. Such rifles were common pre-1939 but the rapid improvement in tanks during the war rapidly made them obsolete.

Panzerfaust (German 'armour fist') German ◊recoilless launcher designed for anti-tank use. It consisted of a bomb made of a ◊shaped charge of about 130 mm/5 in diameter mounted on a stem with four light steel fins. These fins wrapped around the stem which was then inserted into a light steel tube with a propelling charge. The soldier held it under his arm, took aim, and fired. The charge blew the bomb forward and also exhausted from the rear of the tube, so that there was no recoil force. It was highly effective against any tank, but had a limited range of 30– 100 m (100–330 ft), depending upon the model.

Panzerkampfwagen (German 'armoured fighting vehicle') German term for tanks, abbreviated to PzKw. The *PzKw I* was a 5-ton two-man vehicle carrying a 20 mm cannon. The *PzKw II* was a 9-ton three-man vehicle also with a 20 mm cannon. Both were light tanks and saw little use after 1941, their chassis being adapted to various assault and self-propelled gun designs.

The *PzKw III* was the principal medium tank 1939 and was constantly improved to 1943 when production stopped. In its final form it weighed 20 tons, had a speed of 40 kph/25 mph, 30 mm/1 in armour, a crew of five, and a 50 mm main gun. The *PzKw IV* was a close support tank, carrying a 75 mm howitzer in the turret. Like the PzKw III it was constantly improved, and in its final form weighed 25 tons, had a speed of 42 kph/26 mph, 80 mm/3 in armour, a long 75 mm gun, and a crew of five. The subsequent standard tanks were more usually known by their names – ◊Tiger and ◊Panther.

Panzerschreck (German 'tank terror') German anti-tank rocket launcher copied from the US ◊Bazooka. It fired an 88 mm ◊shaped charge rocket to a maximum range of about 137 km/150 yds and could penetrate 100 mm/4 in of armour plate.

Paris port and capital of France, on the river Seine. It was declared an open city 11 June 1940 and was occupied by the German Army 14 June. In Aug 1944, as Allied forces came close, Hitler ordered the

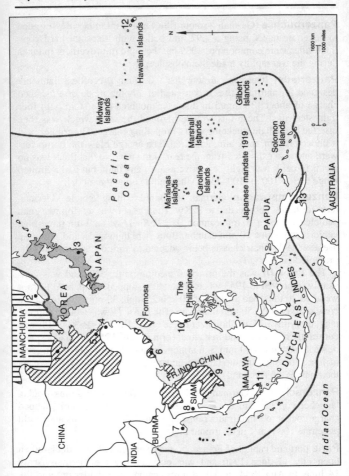

JAPANESE EXPANSION 1928–42

Key

 Japanese Empire before 1928

|||| Occupied by Japan 1928–36

\\\\ Occupied by Japan 1937 – Nov 1941

—— Extent of Japanese conquest 1942

Cities/towns

1	Peking	8	Bangkok
2	Vladivostok	9	Saigon
3	Tokyo	10	Manila
4	Shanghai	11	Singapore
5	Nanking	12	Pearl Harbor
6	Hong Kong	13	Port Moresby
7	Rangoon		

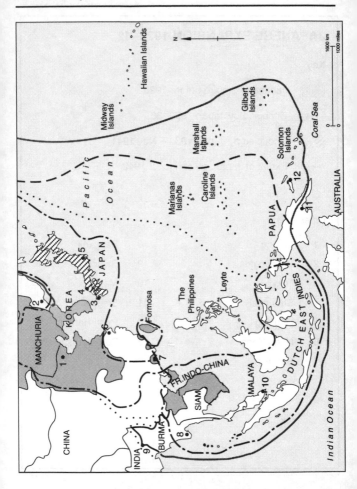

THE DEFEAT OF JAPAN 1942–45

Key

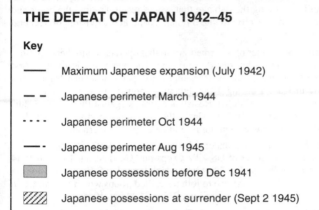

—————— Maximum Japanese expansion (July 1942)

– – Japanese perimeter March 1944

· · · · Japanese perimeter Oct 1944

— - Japanese perimeter Aug 1945

▨ Japanese possessions before Dec 1941

▧ Japanese possessions at surrender (Sept 2 1945)

Cities/towns

1	Peking	7	Hong Kong
2	Vladivostok	8	Rangoon
3	Nagasaki	9	Imphal
4	Hiroshima	10	Singapore
5	Tokyo	11	Port Moresby
6	Shanghai	12	Rabaul

German commandant, General Cholitz, to hold the city at all costs. Cholitz, realizing the damage that would result, ignored the order and surrendered the city to the French Armoured Division of General ◊Leclerc 25 Aug.

partisan member of an armed group that operates behind enemy lines or in occupied territories during wars. The name 'partisans' was first given to armed bands of Russians who operated against Napoleon's army in Russia during 1812, but was applied to Russian, Yugoslav, Italian, Greek, and Polish Resistance groups against the Germans during World War II. In Yugoslavia the communist partisans under their leader, ◊Tito, played a major role in defeating the Germans.

Patch General Alexander McCarrell 1889–1945. US soldier. He became commander of US XIV Corps on ◊Guadalcanal 1942. In 1944 he commanded the US 7th Army which landed in S France and fought northward through Alsace to join the Allied troops which had landed in Normandy. His army crossed the Rhine 26 March 1945.

Pathfinder Force special RAF force of highly experienced and skilled bomber crews carrying the best navigational equipment and used to find and mark targets for the main bombing forces. This economized on navigational equipment and skilled operators, leaving the average bomber crew to go to the selected target area, spot the markers – usually coloured flares – and use these as their aiming mark.

There's one thing you men can say when it's all over and you're home once more. You can thank God that twenty years from now when you're sitting by the fireside with your grandson on your knee, and he asks you what you did in the war, you won't have to shift him to the other knee, cough and say, "I shovelled shit in Louisiana."

General Patton addressing his troops
before D-Day landings June 1944

Patton General George Smith 1885–1945. ('Blood and Guts') US soldier. He served in World War I and formed the first US tank force, leading it in action 1918. He was appointed to command the 2nd Armored Division 1940 and became commanding general of the First Armored Corps 1941. In 1942 he led the Western Task Force that landed at Casablanca, Morocco. After commanding the 7th Army in the invasion of ◊Sicily, he led the 3rd Army across France and into Germany and Czechoslovakia. He played a central role in stopping the German counteroffensive at the Battle of the ◊Bulge Dec 1944–Jan 1945. Patton was an outspoken advocate of mobility and armour but lacked political acumen and was side-lined into command of 15th Army, a paper command, soon after the war ended. He was killed in a traffic accident Dec 1945.

Paulus Field Marshal Friedrich von 1890–1957. German soldier. He was Chief of Staff to the German 6th Army 1939–40 then served as ◊Halder's deputy and took responsibility for much of the detailed planning of Operation ◊Barbarossa. He was promoted to general Jan 1942 and commanded the forces besieging ◊Stalingrad 1942–43. He surrendered Feb 1943, and following the ◊July Bomb Plot 1944 made propaganda broadcasts to Germany urging surrender. He gave evidence for the prosecution at the ◊Nuremberg trials before settling in Dresden, then in East Germany.

Pearl Harbor an inlet of the Pacific Ocean where the US naval base is situated in Hawaii on Oahu Island. It was the scene of a Japanese surprise air attack led by Admiral ◊Nagumo Dec 7 1941 that brought the US into the war. The attack took place while Japanese envoys were holding so-called peace talks in Washington, and caught the Americans unawares. The local US commanders Admiral ◊Kimmel and Lt-Gen Short were relieved of their posts and held responsible for the fact that the base, despite warnings, was totally unprepared at the time of the attack. About 3,300 US military personnel were killed, 4 battleships were lost, and a large part of the US Pacific fleet was destroyed or damaged. The only relief was that the US aircraft carriers had been sent on a training exercise and so were saved to form the nucleus of a new fleet.

The Japanese, angered by US embargoes of oil and other war material and convinced that US entry into the war was inevitable, had opted to strike a major blow in the hope of forcing US concessions. Instead, it galvanized public opinion and raised anti-Japanese sentiment to a fever pitch, with war declared shortly after.

Peenemunde German rocket and aeronautical research station on the Baltic island of Usedom, about 90 km/55 mi NW of Stettin (now Szczecin, Poland). Development of the ◊V2 rocket and the later development of the ◊V1 flying bomb was carried out here, as well as much basic research into the flight of rockets, missiles, and artillery projectiles. It was bombed by the RAF 17–18 August 1943 with 597 aircraft, causing considerable damage, killing 750 workers including some crucial scientists, and setting the programme back several months.

Percival Lieutenant General Arthur 1887–1966. British soldier. Placed in command of British forces in ◊Malaya June 1941, he barely had time to consider his position before the Japanese invaded Dec 1941. He was keenly aware of the deficiencies in his defences but could extract no further support from Britain and was forced to surrender 15 Feb 1942. He was imprisoned in Manchuria but was present aboard the USS *Missouri* to see the Japanese formally surrender 2 Sept 1945.

To make a union with Great Britain would be a fusion with a corpse
Marshal Pétain responding to Churchill's
proposal of Anglo-French union 1940

Pétain Marshal Henri Phillipe 1856–1951. French general and right-wing politician. His defence of Verdun 1916 during World War I made him a national hero. He became head of state 16 June 1940 and signed an armistice with Germany 22 June, convinced that Britain was close to defeat and that France should get the best terms possible. He removed the seat of government to ◊Vichy, a health resort in central France in the unoccupied zone of France, and established an authoritarian regime which collaborated with the Germans, although Dec 1940 he dismissed his deputy Pierre ◊Laval who wanted to side with the Axis powers. The Germans had Laval reinstated April 1942 and in Nov occupied the Vichy area of France, reducing Pétain's 'government' to a puppet regime. When the Allies invaded he was taken to Germany Aug 1944, but returned 1945 and was sentenced to death for treason, although the sentence was later commuted to life imprisonment.

Petlyakov Soviet aircraft. The *Pe-8* was the main Soviet heavy bomber, a four-engine machine with a crew of 11, flying at 440 kph/ 275 mph with up to 4,000 kg/8,800 lb of bombs. The *Pe-2* was an outstanding light bomber and high-altitude fighter. A twin-engine two-man machine, it had a speed of 540 kph/335 mph, carried 500 kg/2,200 lb of bombs, and was armed with five machine guns.

Philippine Islands group of islands in the South China Sea, due south of Taiwan. Originally a US possession, by 1940 they were self-governing. The combined US and Philippine forces were unable to prevent the islands being overrun by the Japanese invasion 8 Dec 1941. They fell back into the ◊Bataan Peninsula and finally to ◊Corregidor, surrendering 6 May 1942. General ◊MacArthur was ordered to escape by submarine to Australia, vowing to return.

He led the US re-occupation of the islands 20 Oct 1944, landing on ◊Leyte Island. The US forces then cleared the islands one by one, liberating ◊Manila 4 March 1945, though isolated pockets of resistance were not cleared until Aug.

Philippine Sea, Battle of decisive US naval victory June 1944. At various times during the war the Japanese naval staff drew up plans to lure the US fleets into a decisive battle. When US forces landed on ◊Saipan June 1944 orders were given to concentrate the Japanese fleet on the Philippine Sea, east of the islands. The orders were intercepted by the Americans, and Admiral ◊Spruance was prepared for the Japanese attack. Spruance had 15 carriers with 896 aircraft; the Japanese 6 carriers and 430 aircraft, and were relying upon the support of ground-based aircraft from ◊Guam.

Locating the US fleet, the Japanese launched 244 aircraft at 08.45 19 June 1944. A US submarine arrived and torpedoed the Japanese carrier *Taiho,* crippling it. The air action which followed became known as the ◊Great Marianas Turkey Shoot; Japan was short of skilled pilots by this time and the US patrolling carrier aircraft shot them down in droves. A second Japanese attempt at launching an air strike was again foiled when a US submarine torpedoed a carrier, which exploded and sank. The *Taiho,* which had been torpedoed in the morning, had filled up with petrol vapour and now exploded, capsized, and sank. The last Japanese aircraft of the day were now launched with orders to attack the US fleet and fly on to Guam. Half were shot down before they found the fleet, the remainder missed the fleet, flew to Guam, and found the airfield there in ruins and surrounded by US fighters which promptly shot them all down.

The two fleets separated overnight, but the next day the Japanese turned back to find the Americans and resume the battle. A US scout found the Japanese late in the afternoon and despite the risk of launching a strike so late in the day, Spruance decided to gamble on a final blow and launched 77 dive-bombers, 54 torpedo-bombers, and 85 fighters. Half an hour later three Japanese carriers were dead in the water, one sinking; one battleship and one cruiser were severely damaged; and the Japanese had only 35 aircraft left. The Japanese fleet refuelling ships had also been found and set on fire and the Japanese commander had no choice but to run for home. The US aircraft returned in the dark, the fleet provided every method of illumination possible, and although 80 aircraft landed in the sea all the crews were rescued. The battle was the last of the great carrier battles, and it broke the back of the Japanese navy.

Ploesti Romanian city about 55 km/35 mi N of Bucharest; it was in the centre of the oilfields and an important source of fuel for the German army. Far from any Allied airfields, it was left untouched until 1 Aug 1943 when it was severely damaged by a force of 177 US Liberator bombers, although 50 were shot down in the long flight over well-defended areas. In April 1944 it became possible to mount bombing attacks on the area from Allied airfields in Italy and Ploesti was finally captured by Soviet troops Aug 1944.

Poland, invasion of following the staged 'raid' on ◊Gleiwicz, Poland was invaded by Hitler 1 Sept 1939, using 1.5 million men in five armies. Army Group North struck from Pomerania into the ◊Polish Corridor and Danzig; 4th Army struck from E Prussia south to Warsaw and west to meet Army Group North and cut off the Polish Pomorze

army; 8th and 10th armies moved northeast from Silesia toward
Warsaw; and the 14th Army struck from Slovakia towards Kraków.
The Poles had placed their armies on the borders, so that once the initial
blow had pierced their lines they were rapidly rolled up and destroyed.

As agreed in a secret clause in the ◊Molotov–Ribbentrop pact, two
Soviet armies marched into Poland from the east 17 Sept and the country was divided between the two invaders, although small outposts
continued to resist until 7 Oct. W Poland was divided; part was
absorbed into Germany and part administered as the *gouvernementgen-
eral*. E Poland became Soviet territory and has remained so ever since.

ground forces casualties: Poland 1939

	killed/missing	wounded	POW
Poland	66,300	133,700	787,000
Germany	13,110	27,280	–
USSR	900	?	?

Polikarpov Soviet aircraft. The *I-15* was a biplane fighter with four
machine guns and a speed of 400 kph/250 mph, but by 1941 it was
becoming obsolete and was employed mainly as a light bomber. It was
replaced by the *I-16*, a monoplane capable of 525 kph/325 mph and
armed with two 20 mm cannon and two machine guns. This could also
carry bombs and rockets and was a useful ground-attack machine.

Polish Corridor strip of land about 110 km/70 mi wide separating E
Prussia from Germany, with the free city of ◊Danzig at its coastal end,
giving Poland access to the Baltic. Germany resented this partitioning
of E Prussia and one of the primary causes of the invasion of Poland
was the German demand to be permitted to build a road and rail connection across the Corridor, in a zone to be granted extra-territorial
rights, a demand which the Poles implacably refused.

Polish Home Army clandestine resistance force which began forming as soon as the invasion of Poland ended Sept 1939. Properly
organized into districts and commands, at its maximum it numbered
about 600,000 men and women armed with weapons hidden at the time
of the Polish collapse 1939, dropped by British aircraft, or stolen from

the Germans. They assisted the Soviets as they began to advance into Poland 1943, but soon found that once the Poles had served their purpose they were either abandoned, arrested, or shot out of hand. The ◊Warsaw Rising 1944 revealed the Soviets' true intentions, which was to permit the Home Army and the Germans to wipe each other out and then move in with Soviet puppets once the hard work had been done.

Port Moresby seaport on the S coast of ◊New Guinea. It was a prime Japanese objective, since occupation would have given them control of N Australia, and was the target of a Japanese campaign May 1942, when it was subject to heavy bombing attacks. However, the Battle of the ◊Coral Sea destroyed their direct invasion force and their later attempts to attack from the north by the ◊Kokoda Trail and from the east at ◊Milne Bay both failed.

Portal Air Chief Marshal Sir Charles 1893–1971. British airman. Chief of Air Staff 1940–45, he was an advocate of strategic bombing and at the ◊Casablanca Conference Jan 1943 reached agreement with the US on a Combined Bomber Offensive to destroy German military industrial capability. Unfortunately Portal was unable to control ◊Harris, commanding RAF Bomber Command, who considered such a policy a 'panacea' and instead preferred simple area bombing. Had Portal been able to control Harris and make him direct his attacks at the German oil industry, the war could probably have been shortened.

Potsdam Conference conference held in Potsdam, Germany, 17 July–2 Aug 1945 between representatives of the USA, Britain, and the USSR. They established the political and economic principles governing the treatment of Germany in the initial period of Allied control at the end of the war, and sent an ultimatum to Japan demanding unconditional surrender on pain of utter destruction.

Pound Admiral Alfred Dudley Pickman Rogers 1877–1943. British sailor. As First Sea Lord and chief of the British naval staff 1939–43, he was responsible for the effective measures taken against German U-boats and to protect convoys. Unfortunately he suffered from a brain tumour which clouded his judgement, as when he ordered convoy PQ17 to disperse while under attack, resulting in massive losses: of 34 merchantmen only 11 survived and the lost cargo included 210 aircraft, 430 tanks, and 3,550 vehicles. He resigned due to ill health Oct 1943 and died 3 weeks later.

prisoners of war (POWs) troops captured in war, who have fallen into the hands of, or surrendered to, an opponent. Such captives may be held in prisoner-of-war camps. The 1929 Geneva Convention guaranteed several basic rights for POWs including humane treatment, limits to the nature and extent of interrogation, and restrictions on the duties which they could be forced to perform. All major combatants were signatories to the Convention with the exception of the USSR and Japan, and in general the signatories abided by its terms.

However, no such protection was afforded to ◊partisans or members of ◊resistance movements, and any who fell into German hands were handed over to the ◊Gestapo and were often tortured and executed. The Germans also felt no obligation toward Soviet captives many of whom were massacred by the ◊Einsatzgruppen or sent to slave labour camps, where a high proportion died of overwork, starvation, or simply brutal treatment. For their part, the Soviets were equally scornful of the rights of POWs, as the massacres at ◊Katyn Wood attest, and few German troops survived capture by the Soviets.

The Japanese regarded capture as a matter of dishonour and so few Japanese troops were taken prisoner, most preferring suicide to surrender. By the same token, they regarded any prisoners they took as having forfeited any right to respect. The ill-treatment of POWs by the Japanese became notorious; thousands died from sheer sadistic brutality as in the ◊Bataan Death March, others from neglect (e.g., insufficient rations or medical provision), or forced labour. Many of the Allied troops who survived Japanese POW camps remained permanently broken men, both mentally and physically.

proximity fuse artillery or aerial bomb fuse which operates by sensing how near the target is. Designed in Britain and developed in the USA, the fuse used a tiny radio to transmit a signal which was reflected from the target indicating the distance; once the target was within lethal distance the fuse fired the explosive in the bomb or shell. It was first used as an anti-aircraft fuse in the Pacific by the US Navy, and was then found effective in bringing down ◊V-1 flying bombs over Britain 1944. It was first used against ground troops in the Battle of the ◊Bulge Dec 1944.

Q

Québec Conference actually two conferences of the Allied leaders Roosevelt, Churchill, Mackenzie King, and Tse-ven Soong in the city of Québec. The *first conference* 1943 approved British admiral ◊Mountbatten as supreme Allied commander in SE Asia and made plans for the invasion of France, for which US general ◊Eisenhower was to be supreme commander. The *second conference* Sept 1944 adopted plans for intensified air attacks on Germany, created a unified strategy against Japan, and established a postwar policy for a defeated Germany.

Quisling Vikdun 1887–1945. Norwegian politician. Leader of the Norwegian Fascist Party from 1933, he aided the Nazi invasion of Norway 1940 by delaying mobilization and urging non-resistance. He was made premier by Hitler 1942, and was arrested and shot as a traitor by the Norwegians 1945. His name became a generic term for any traitor who aids an occupying force.

R

Rabaul town at the NE end of the island of ◊New Britain; a major Japanese air and naval base. Before the US invasion of the ◊Philippines could take place this base had to be isolated and so the island was invaded from the west by US Marines 26 Dec 1943. They gradually expanded east, compressing the Japanese into the eastern end. At the same time the nearby ◊Admiralty Islands were captured by US forces, so isolating Rabaul by sea. With US airfields established on the Admiralty islands and a ground force keeping the Japanese contained on New Britain, Rabaul ceased to be any threat to US operations.

radar (*ra*dio *d*irection *a*nd *r*anging) method of detecting aircraft by transmitting a pulse of radio energy and measuring the time that a reflection takes to return. Since the speed of radio waves is known, the distance can be calculated very accurately. By suitable antenna design the radio pulses can be sent in a narrow beam, giving an indication of the aircraft's direction as well as its distance. Developed independently in Britain, France, Germany, and the USA in the 1930s, it was first put to practical use for aircraft detection by the British, who had a complete coastal chain of radar sets installed by Sept 1938. It proved invaluable in the Battle of ◊Britain 1940, when the ability to spot incoming German aircraft did away with the need to fly standing patrols.

Raeder Admiral Erich 1876–1960. German sailor. Chief of Staff in World War I, he became commander in chief of the German Navy 1935 and evaded the restrictions of the Versailles treaty while expanding the navy. He was behind the successful U-boat campaign against Britain and launched attacks against the Arctic convoys supplying the USSR. Following the humiliation of the Battle of ◊Barents Sea Dec 1942 Hitler threatened to remove big guns from battleships and install them as coastal defence weapons. This was too much for Raeder and he resigned 1943. He was sentenced to life imprisonment at the ◊Nuremberg trials 1946 but was released 1955 on grounds of ill health.

Ramsay Admiral Sir Bertram 1883–1945. British sailor. In 1940 he was responsible for organizing Operation Dynamo, the evacuation of about 350,000 British and Allied troops from ◊Dunkirk in the face of the German army. He then served with the Allied force which invaded N Africa 1942 and planned the Allied landings in ◊Sicily 1943. In 1943 he became naval commander in chief for the ◊D-Day landings and supervised the amphibious aspects of the operation. He commanded the naval side of the clearing of the ◊Scheldt Estuary late 1944. He was killed in an aircraft accident Jan 1945.

Rangers US Army equivalent to the British ◊commandos. The 1st Ranger Battalion was trained at the British commando training centre in Scotland 1942, and four more battalions were then raised. They served in the landings in ◊N Africa, ◊Sicily, ◊Italy, and ◊Normandy with distinction. However, some US commanders failed to appreciate their special role and employed them as ordinary infantry. They were disbanded soon after the war.

Rangoon capital of ◊Burma, on the Gulf of Mataban. Occupied by the Japanese 8 March 1942, it became the principal supply port for their armies in the country, and as such it was the Allies' prime objective in their operations to retake Burma 1944. By March 1945, with most of Burma in Allied hands and the Japanese in general retreat, General ◊Slim ordered an offensive against Rangoon before the rains came and made progress impossible. The city was finally taken by 26 Indian Division who approached by sea, landed south of the city 2 May 1945, and occupied it on the following day.

Rapido River river running SW through ◊Cassino to meet the Garigliano river. It became a major German defensive obstacle in the ◊Gustav Line. The first US attempt to cross 20 Jan 1944 was a failure, with over 1,000 killed and 600 wounded; this engagement was known as the ***Battle of Bloody River***. The second attempt took place 24 Jan north of Cassino where the river was shallower; it took two days to establish a bridgehead, after which reinforcements were put across and the Gustav Line was broken.

rationing restricted allowance of provisions or other supplies in time of war or shortage. Food rationing, organized by the government, began in Britain 1940. Each person was issued with a ration book of coupons. Bacon, butter, and sugar were restricted, followed by other goods, including sweets, petrol, clothing, soap, and furniture. Some people tried to buy extra on the black market. In 1946 the world wheat shortage led to bread rationing. All food rationing finally ended in Britain 1954.

Ravensbruck German ◊concentration camp in Mecklenburg, NW of Berlin, established 1936 and used for women prisoners. Medical experiments were carried on here using Polish victims, and it was also the place of execution for Allied female agents.

recoilless guns first used by German airborne troops in ◊Crete 1941, recoilless guns direct some of the explosion of the propellant cartridge backwards, balancing the recoil due to the ejection of the projectile forwards. When correctly designed the result is a gun which does not recoil; this saves weight in the construction of the mounting. Their principal defect is short range and prominent backblast, both due to the propellant gases being ejected to the rear. The principle was adopted by the British and US armies, but only the latter managed to get guns into service before the war ended, using 57 mm and 75 mm weapons on ◊Okinawa.

They were a good deal more popular with their designers than they ever were with the troops.
                                    German officer on *recoilless guns*.

Reichenau Field Marshal Walther von 1884–1942. German soldier. He commanded 10th Army in the invasion of ◊Poland and 6th Army in the invasion of Belgium and France. He remained in command of 6th Army and led it in Operation ◊Barbarossa 1941, playing a major role in the victory at ◊Kiev. He was rewarded with the command of Army Group South but suffered a heart attack shortly after and died.

Reichswald, Battle of the the Reichswald was a German state forest situated around Cleve, close to the Dutch border, about 25 km/15 mi

W of Nijmegen between the Waal and Maas rivers. In the winter of 1945 the Germans released the sluices on these rivers so that the areas north and south of the forest were flooded and impassable. As part of the advance into Germany, the 2nd Canadian Corps and the British XXX Corps were required to advance through this area Feb 1945. Unable to manoeuvre due to the floods, the attack was preceded by an immense artillery barrage, over 6,000 tons of shells being fired on the first day of the attack. In spite of the difficult terrain the attack went well and took the initial objectives, after which German resistance stiffened and it was not until 21 Feb that the entire area was cleared.

There was no room for manoeuvre and no scope for cleverness; I had to blast my way through three defensive systems, the centre of which was the Siegfried Line.

General Sir Brian Horrocks on his tactics in the *Reichswald*.

Remagen small town on the Rhine, 20 km/12 mi SE of Bonn. On 7 March 1945 a patrol of the US 9th Armored Division discovered that the Ludendorff Bridge across the river had somehow escaped destruction. Calling up troops of 87th Division they seized the bridge, giving them a valuable crossing point. The bridge had been bombed earlier in the war by the Allies; it was also bombed now by the Germans and this, coupled with the heavy traffic of tanks across it, caused it to collapse some days later, but by that time other crossings had been secured.

Renault French light tanks. The *FT-17* had been used in World War I and though long obsolete, several were used by the French 1940, and they were also used against the Allied landings in N Africa 1942. A five-ton two-man vehicle armed with a single machine gun, it was quite useless by that time.

The *R-35* was a modern machine developed 1935 using cast armour. Weighing 10 tons, it was armed with a 37 mm turret gun and one machine gun. Some 2,000 were built and it saw extensive use in 1940, though it was no match for the German tanks.

Rendova island in the ◊New Georgia group in the Pacific. As part of the US attack on the group 30 June 1943 it was first to be assaulted by a specially trained 'Barracuda' commando-style force. Unfortunately the US Navy landed them in the wrong place, and by the time they had got back to their objective the island had been invaded and secured by the main force.

reporting names names given to ◊Japanese aircraft by US forces 1941 and retained even after their real names were discovered.

Republic US aircraft. The *P-47 Thunderbolt* was a single-seat fighter with an enormous 2,800 hp radial engine and eight machine guns. It had a speed of 689 kph/428 mph and could carry 1,100 kg/2,500 lb of bombs or rockets. It was a highly successful escort and ground-attack fighter which was used in Europe and the Pacific.

resistance movement opposition movement in a country occupied by an enemy power. Resistance in E Europe took the form of guerrilla warfare, for example in Yugoslavia, Greece, Poland, and by ◊*partisan* bands behind the German lines in the USSR. In more industrialized countries, such as France (where the underground movement was called the *maquis*), Belgium, and Czechoslovakia, sabotage in factories and on the railways, propaganda, and the assassination of Germans and collaborators were the main priorities. Most resistance movements in the war were based on an alliance of all anti-fascist parties, but there was internal conflict between those elements intent only on defeat of the enemy, and those who aimed at establishing communist governments, as in Yugoslavia and Greece.

Reynaud Paul 1878–1966. French politician. He succeeded Edouard ◊Daladier as prime minister March 1940 but resigned in June after the German breakthrough. He was imprisoned by the Germans until 1945, and again held government office after the war.

Rhine, crossing of the the river Rhine was the principal obstacle to the Allied advance into Germany 1945. The first crossing was a bridge at Nijmegen in Holland, acquired as a by-product of the ◊Arnhem operation and held by the Canadian Army. The US 3rd Army under ◊Patton then crossed near Mainz 21 March 1945. The principal crossings were planned to give access to the ◊Ruhr, so as to threaten the German industrial base. The British crossed at Wesel and the Americans near Rheinberg, both 23 March. Both these crossings were preceded by heavy artillery and air bombardment of the German side, parachute landings to secure bridgeheads, and preliminary attacks by ◊commando and ◊Ranger forces.

Ribbentrop Joachim von 1893–1946. German Nazi politician. Awarded the Iron Cross in World War I, he joined the Nazi party 1932 and acted as Hitler's adviser on foreign affairs; he was German ambassador to Britain 1936–38 and foreign minister 1938–45 during which time he negotiated the Non-Aggression Pact between Germany and the USSR (see ◊Molotov–Ribbentrop pact). He was tried at Nuremberg as a war criminal 1946 and hanged.

River Plate, Battle of the naval battle in the South Atlantic between a British cruiser squadron of three ships and the German pocket battleship *Admiral ◊Graf Spee* Dec 1939. Although the British cruisers were no match for the battleship, Admiral Harwood launched an attack. German fire seriously damaged HMS *Exeter,* put half of HMS *Ajax's* guns out of action, and then damaged HMS *Achilles,* but the cruisers did sufficient damage to the German ship to make her captain break off and run for shelter in Montevideo, Uruguay. The British followed, and waited in international waters outside the neutral port. The Uruguay government ordered the Germans to leave after 72 hours. Hitler, reluctant to risk the *Graf Spee* being sunk by heavier British warships which were sailing for the River Plate, ordered the captain to scuttle her. He did so 17 Dec 1939 and three days later shot himself.

Rjukan Norwegian electric power station about 160 km/100 mi N of Oslo. It produced 'heavy water' which at that time was valuable as a material for conducting experiments in the development of atomic bombs. In order to prevent the Germans using the material, a party of saboteurs from the SOE (◊Special Operations Executive) destroyed the plant 28 Feb 1943. It was back in production after five months and 16 Nov 1943 was attacked by the US Air Force who destroyed the power station but not the heavy water plant. In Jan 1944 a shipment of heavy water was despatched to Germany but SOE saboteurs sank the ferry carrying the cargo across Lake Tinnsjoe, effectively ending any German research into nuclear physics.

Rokossovsky Marshal Konstantin 1896–1968. Soviet soldier. He came to prominence as commander of the 16th Army defending Moscow 1941. In 1942 he took command of the Don Front which pinned the German 6th Army in ◊Stalingrad Nov 1942. He then commanded the Central Front at ◊Kursk, holding the German attack and then counterattacking in an offensive which carried him to the line of the river Dniepr. In the 1944 offensive he commanded the 1st Byelorussian Front and advanced to ◊Warsaw where he paused while the ◊Polish Home Army rose against the Germans in anticipation of being assisted by the Soviets. Instead the Soviets waited until the Home Army had been virtually destroyed before taking Warsaw Jan 1945. He then advanced across Poland, took Danzig, and isolated the German armies in ◊Kurland, finally making contact with the British army at Wismar 5 May 1945. Following the war, he was appointed commander in chief of the Soviet forces in Poland, not the most tactful appointment Stalin ever made.

Rolls Royce British industrial company manufacturing cars and aeroplane engines. Famous for its luxury cars, during the war it produced the Merlin engine, used in Spitfires and Hurricanes, and latterly produced jet engines, which became an important product of the company.

Rommel Field Marshal Erwin 1891–1944. German soldier. He served in World War I, and in World War II played an important part in the invasions of central Europe and France. He was commander of the N African offensive from 1941 (when he was nicknamed 'Desert Fox') but was defeated in the Battles of El ◊Alamein 1942. He retreated to Tunisia and defeated US forces at ◊Kasserine Pass Feb 1943 before being finally defeated himself at ◊Medenine the following month. He was assigned to the defence of N Italy 1944 and then moved to France as commander of Army Group B, strengthening coastal defences prior to the ◊D-Day landings June 1944. He was forced to commit suicide after being implicated in the ◊July Bomb Plot.

The ordinary soldier has a surprisingly good nose for what is true and what is false.

Field Marshal Erwin Rommel

Roosevelt Franklin Delano 1882–1945. 32nd president of the USA 1933–45, a Democrat. He endeavoured to use his influence to restrain Axis aggression, and to establish 'good neighbour' relations with other countries in the Americas. Soon after the outbreak of war, he launched a vast rearmament programme, introduced conscription, and provided for the supply of armaments to the Allies on a 'cash-and-carry' basis. Re-elected 1940, he announced that the USA would become the 'arsenal of democracy'. The slaughter at ◊Pearl Harbor 7 Dec 1941 inflamed public opinion, and the USA entered the war on the side of the Allies. From this point on, Roosevelt concerned himself solely with the conduct of the war. He introduced ◊lend-lease for the supply of war materials and services to the Allies and drew up the ◊Atlantic Charter of solidarity with Churchill. He participated in the Washington 1942 and ◊Casablanca 1943 conferences to plan the Mediterranean assault, and the conferences in ◊Québec, Cairo, and ◊Tehran 1943, and ◊Yalta 1945, at which the final preparations were made for the Allied victory. He was re-elected for a fourth term 1944, but died 1945.

We must be the great arsenal of democracy.
                                                    Franklin D Roosevelt speech 1940

Rossler Rudolf 1897–1958. German spy working for the Allies. He moved to Switzerland 1933 and set up in business as a publisher. An ex-soldier, he had many friends in high places who were as opposed to the Nazi party as he was, and he received valuable information from them. He had advance notice of many German operations, and with the aid of Swiss military intelligence this information was passed to the Allies. He was recruited by the Soviet director of intelligence in Switzerland under the code-name 'Lucy', after which his information was relayed directly to Moscow, including details of the German plans at ◊Stalingrad and ◊Kursk. Eventually the operations of the 'Lucy Ring' became too blatant for the Swiss to tolerate and they moved against it 1944, ending Rossler's activities. He never revealed the names of his contacts in the German High Command.

Rostov city on the river Don in S USSR close to the Sea of Azov. In late 1941 it was defended by the 9th Soviet Army against an attack by the 1st German Panzer Army under von ◊Rundstedt. After a hard battle the city was captured 21 Nov 1941. The River Don was frozen hard, and the Soviets were able to cross the ice and establish two bridgeheads to begin a counterattack, while other Soviet units moved to the flanks and began threatening the German supply lines. Von Rundstedt abandoned the city 29 Nov and fell back to a better defensive position. Hitler ordered him to cancel his orders to retire and stand firm, whereupon von Rundstedt resigned. It was the first military setback in Operation ◊Barbarossa, and the loss of von Rundstedt was a serious blow to the army.

Rotmistrov Marshal Pavel 1901–1990. Soviet soldier and tank specialist. He commanded VII Tank Corps at ◊Stalingrad 1942 and played a vital role in preventing the relief of the 6th German Army. After this he commanded the 5th Guard Tank Army at ◊Kursk and led the advance across the USSR, liberating ◊Kharkov. By this time 5th Guards was regarded by Stalin as his elite force and he ordered it north to clear the Baltic states 1944. After the war Rotmistrov became Marshal of Armoured Troops and Deputy Commander of Armoured Forces.

Rotterdam capital city of the Netherlands and seaport. It was heavily bombed by the Luftwaffe 14 May 1940 to reinforce a German demand for surrender. The ferocity of this attack against an undefended city persuaded the Dutch to surrender rather than see the same treatment meted out to the rest of their country.

Ruhr Germany's main industrial centre, encompassing Dusseldorf, Dortmund, and Essen. The area was named after the River Ruhr and the seven dams across the river were constantly bombed by the Allies throughout the war in an attempt to flood the area (e.g., with the ◊'bouncing bombs'), although without success.

The Ruhr had abundant supplies of coal and iron and was a hub of Germany's transport network, making it ideal for heavy industry. Consequently, much of Germany's steel and munitions industry was based in the area and it was a major Allied target. Montgomery advocated making the Ruhr the primary objective for the entire thrust of the

Allied invasion following the ◊Normandy landings, but Eisenhower overruled the plan in favour of an advance on a broad front. The area was encircled by US 1st and 9th Armies April 1945, finally falling 18 April.

Rundstedt Field Marshal Karl Rudolf Gerd von 1875–1953. German soldier. He was largely responsible for the German breakthrough in France 1940, although it was also his arguments that persuaded Hitler to ignore the Allied pocket at ◊Dunkirk, allowing the mass evacuation to take place. He was promoted to field marshal and commanded Army Group South during Operation ◊Barbarossa. He was defeated on the Ukrainian front 1941 and resigned Nov due to Hitler's order that there should be no withdrawals. He was rehabilitated as commander in chief in France from 1942, and was responsible for the construction of the ◊Atlantic Wall and the defence of 'Fortress Europe'. He resisted the Allied invasion 1944 but had his hands tied by having to have every decision approved by Hitler. He recognized the position as hopeless and told ◊Keitel there was no alternative but to make peace. He was dismissed but again recalled Sept 1944 and in Dec launched the temporarily successful Ardennes offensive, although at Hitler's instigation. He was captured 1945 and charged with war crimes at ◊Nuermberg but these charges were dropped 1949 owing to his ill-health.

Ruweisat Ridge range of hills which were the principal tactical feature of the British defensive line at El ◊Alamein. British forces on this ridge were able to drive off ◊Rommel's armoured forces in the First Battle of El Alamein, July 1942, ending the German threat to Egypt.

Ryukyu islands southernmost island group of Japan, stretching toward Taiwan and including ◊Okinawa, Miyako, and Ishigaki. US operations against this area began Oct 1944 with naval bombardments and attacks by carrier-borne aircraft, and landings on the various islands commenced April 1945.

S

SA (German *Sturm Abteilung* 'Storm Battalion') also known as Storm Troopers or Brownshirts, the SA were the disciplinary force of the Nazi party. Originally uniformed stewards to organize demonstrations, they became street brawlers who dealt with any political opposition to party marches and demonstrations. When the Nazi party gained power 1933 their strength was about 400,000 and they considered themselves the rival to the German Army. At the instigation of the Army and ◊SS leaders, Hitler had all the SA's leaders murdered 29–30 June 1934, the 'Night of the Long Knives', and the organization disbanded.

Saint Nazaire French seaport on the Bay of Biscay, used as a base by the German navy. It was raided by British ◊commandos March 1942; the ex-US destroyer *Campbeltown,* loaded with explosives, was sailed against the gates of the sea-lock giving access to the docks and detonated, wrecking the gates and putting the docks out of action for most of the war.

Saipan island of the ◊Marianas group about 1,900 km/1,200 mi N of New Guinea. It was invaded by US forces 17 June 1944, before the Japanese had completed their planned fortifications. An airfield was captured on the first day, allowing US fighters to provide instant air support, but the clearing of the island was a slow and hard fight which lasted until 17 July. Even then numbers of Japanese troops hid in the more remote areas until the war ended. The operation was notable for the mass suicide of the Japanese civil population, several hundred of whom threw themselves over a cliff rather than be captured.

Sakurai Lieutenant General Seizo. Japanese commander in Burma. His troops captured Rangoon 1942 and he was then placed in command of the ◊Arakan area and the delta of the ◊Irrawaddy river. He was defeated

1944 and forced to retreat to the Sittang river, losing about two-thirds of his 18,000 strong force in the process.

Salamaua seaport on the N coast of New Guinea. The Japanese launched their attack on ◊Port Moresby over the ◊Kokoda Trail from here and when this failed, the port became a major Japanese supply base. It was eventually attacked by Australian troops flown into Wau, about 40 km/25 mi away. Japanese reinforcements failed to arrive and the town was taken 11 Sept 1943.

Salerno Italian port about 65 km/40 mi SE of Naples. The US 5th Army and British X Corps landed there 8 Sept 1943 as a base to attack Naples. Expecting little opposition because of the Italian surrender, they ran into two German Panzer divisions who resisted so strongly that there were thoughts of abandoning the venture. However, the British 8th Army then arrived from the south, forcing the Germans to pull back to the ◊Gustav Line, and X Corps entered Naples 1 Oct 1943.

Sangro River Italian river, rising in the Apennines and flowing NE to the Adriatic near Ortona. German troops set up a defensive line on the river Nov 1943 which was then attacked by the British 8th Army. Severe rains led to flooding which made the river almost impassable and the British had to wait three.weeks before being able to establish a bridgehead. By the end of Nov tanks were across the river and the British advanced on Ortona, which they took 27 Dec 1943.

Santa Cruz, Battle of naval engagement between US and Japanese fleets N of the ◊Solomon Islands Oct 1942. A Japanese force waiting for the recapture of ◊Henderson Field and a US force intent on preventing Japan reinforcing ◊Guadalcanal found each other and flew off air strikes against each other almost simultaneously. The aircraft met and fought, and the survivors continued on to attack the enemy fleets. The USS *Hornet* was struck by two torpedoes, six bombs, and two suicide aircraft, and was abandoned on fire and later sunk by the Japanese. The USS *Enterprise* was also hit, while two Japanese carriers were severely damaged. The battle meant the US Navy no longer had an operational aircraft carrier in the Pacific area.

Savo Island, Battle of naval battle between a Japanese cruiser force and a US-Australian force protecting US transports reinforcing

◊Guadalcanal 8–9 Aug 1942. The Japanese achieved complete surprise, and in two engagements sank three US and one Australian cruiser and damaged two others. The Japanese commander, fearful of air strikes as dawn broke, then withdrew without attacking the transports which were at his mercy. He was reprimanded for his temerity.

Scharnhorst German battle cruiser. It had a displacement of 31,850 tons, a speed of 32 knots, and a crew of 1,840. It was heavily armed with nine 28 cm guns, twelve 15 cm guns, fourteen 10.5 cm guns, sixteen 37 mm and thirty-eight 20 mm anti-aircraft guns, and six 53 cm torpedo tubes, and was protected by a 300 mm/12 in armour belt. Launched 1936, it took part in the ◊Norway campaign 1940, and cruised the North Atlantic sinking 22 merchant ships. It was based at Brest in France until Feb 1942 when it broke out in the ◊Channel Dash and returned to Germany. It was damaged by gunfire and finally sunk by torpedoes in the Battle of the ◊North Cape Dec 1943.

Scheldt Estuary the mouth of the river Scheldt runs from Antwerp to the North Sea between the Dutch mainland and the islands of ◊Walcheren and Beveland. In order for the Allies to use ◊Antwerp as a supply port they had to clear the Germans from the estuary. The Germans realized the strategic importance of the estuary and were determined to defend it for as long as possible. The clearance of the area was carried out by the 1st Canadian Army and involved hard fighting against determined troops in well-built fortified positions. The operations included a land attack across Beveland and waterborne assaults against Beveland and Walcheren. The clearance was finally completed 8 Nov with the taking of Walcheren.

Schellenberg General der SS Walter 1911–1952. German SS officer. He joined the ◊SD 1934 and formed the first ◊Einsatzgruppen 1938. In 1939 he organized the kidnapping of three British Secret Service agents in Holland. After the fall of Admiral ◊Canaris 1944 he became head of the Combined Intelligence Service and was involved with ◊Himmer's abortive attempt to arrange peace talks with the Allies. He escaped to Sweden but later surrendered to the Allies, and was sentenced to six years' imprisonment 1949.

schnorkel device to permit submarines to draw air from and emit fumes to the surface while running diesel engines underwater. It consisted of a tube fitted with a valve which closed automatically if water entered. Invented 1938 by a Dutch naval engineer and fitted to some Dutch submarines, the idea was adopted by the Germans 1942–43 to allow their submarines to run on diesels and charge batteries while remaining submerged, so as to avoid detection by radar.

Schweinfurt Bavarian town 95 km/60 mi E of Frankfurt. During the war it was the centre of the German ball-bearing industry and so a valuable strategic target. It was attacked in a daylight raid 17 Aug 1943 by the US Air Force, who lost 15.5% of their force to fighters and anti–aircraft fire. A second raid 14 Oct was accompanied by fighters as far as Aachen, after which they had to turn back and the bombers went on alone. This raid lost 60 out of 291 aircraft, with 138 damaged. Such heavy losses were unacceptable and the USAF discontinued long-range attacks until they had fighters capable of escorting bombers all the way to their targets.

Scoones General Sir Geoffrey Alan Percival 1893–1975. British soldier. He was commander of the British IV Corps on the India–Burma border 1944 and was responsible for the defence of ◊Kohima and ◊Imphal and the defeat of the Japanese Ha-Go offensive against India. After this he led IV Corps in an offensive which drove the Japanese across the ◊Chindwin river and into central Burma. In Dec 1944 he was given command of central India and knighted.

SD (German *Sicherheitsdienst* 'security force') the security arm of the ◊SS established 1931 to hunt down political enemies and dissenters within the Nazi party. This function was gradually taken over by the ◊Gestapo and the SD became the party's intelligence service, controlling foreign spies and overseeing the politics and loyalties of the German population.

seabees nickname for US Navy Construction Battalions (CBs). Their primary role was the construction of airfields and similar facilities on captured islands. So that they could begin work as soon as possible after the initial assaults, they were trained to fight as infantry to deal with any counterstrokes aimed at disrupting their work.

Second Front battle line opened against Germany with the ◊D-Day landings 6 June 1944. Following Germany's invasion of the USSR June

1941 (the 'first front'), Stalin constantly pressured Britain to invade the European mainland, to relieve pressure on Soviet forces.

Senio River Italian river flowing NE from the Apennines to the Adriatic a few miles W of Ravenna. It was adopted as a defensive line by the Germans in the winter of 1944, but contrary to orders the German commander decided to hold the river lightly and concentrate his forces some miles back out of the range of Allied artillery. When the Allies attacked with a massive artillery bombardment 9 April 1945, the light German defence on the river was crushed and the Allies had crossed the river and punched a hole in the German line inside three days.

Sevastopol Black Sea port, resort, and fortress in the Crimea, Ukraine. The German advance into the ◊Crimea Nov 1941 isolated it and the Germans left it to concentrate on ◊Moscow and ◊Leningrad. In May 1942 they began a siege, bringing up super-heavy artillery including the 800 mm ◊Gustav gun, and 540 mm and 600 mm self-propelled howitzers. Air strikes and a naval blockade added to the pressure and on 7 June infantry and tanks made the initial assault. After bitter house-to-house fighting, the Soviets ordered their troops to fall back into the inner city 23 June. By now the defenders were short of food and ammunition, and on 30 June the Germans broke into the city, at which the Soviets authorized evacuation and were able to get most of their troops away by small boats before the Germans completed the occupation 3 July. It remained in German hands until recaptured by the Soviet Army April 1944.

shaped charge munitions cylindrical charge of explosive which has one end hollowed out into a cone or hemisphere and lined with metal or glass. When the explosive is detonated from the other end, the advancing detonation wave collapses the liner into a jet of molten metal and explosive gas moving at very high velocity. The momentum of this jet will penetrate armour plate or other hard targets. Although the phenomenon was known in the 1880s it was not until the late 1930s that it was put to any practical use, and from 1940 all combatants developed shaped charge artillery shells, grenades, bombs, and rocket warheads to defeat tanks and reinforced concrete defences.

Sherman tank US Medium Tank M4. After putting the Medium Tank M3 ◊Grant into production the US Army took the basic hull and chassis design and added a new turret with a 75 mm gun. This became the M4 Sherman, standardized 5 Sept 1941. Mass production began March 1942 and 49,234 were built between then and June 1945. It was used by all Allied armies, and although no match for the German ◊Tiger or ◊Panther until given a heavier gun, it proved reliable, easy to operate and maintain, and a suitable basis for several variations such as rocket-launchers, mine-clearers, swimming tanks, and self-propelled guns. In its basic form it weighed 32 tons, had a speed of 40 kph/25 mph, and a crew of five men.

Sicily Sicily was invaded by General ◊Patton's US 5th Army and ◊Montgomery's British 8th Army 10 July 1943. US forces landed on the southern coast and advanced NW to take Palermo 22 July, then turned east to clear to island. The British force landed on the southeast tip and advanced north toward Messina. The initial assault was to be supported by airborne operations, but due to poor navigation most of the glider forces crashed into the sea and paratroops were dropped in the wrong places. The island was strongly held by German troops who mounted a determined resistance and were able to evacuate the bulk of their troops to Italy before Messina fell 17 Aug 1943.

Sidi Barrani Egyptian village close to the Libyan border. In Sept 1940 Italian forces crossed the border and set up a fortified camp with five infantry divisions, artillery, and tanks. On 8 Dec the British 4th Indian and 7th Armoured divisions, under General ◊O'Connor, launched an attack. The Indian division made a frontal assault while the armour swung round and set up a road block. Between them they captured 38,000 prisoners, 237 guns, and 73 tanks.

Sidi Rezegh village in Cyrenaica SE of ◊Tobruk, with a small airfield. Taken by the British 19 Nov 1941 during Operation ◊Crusader, it was fiercely attacked by 15 and 21 Panzer Divisions 22 Nov and almost recaptured, but the Germans were forced to withdraw as they were running short of ammunition and fuel. A second battle took place on 27 Nov when 15 Panzer Division were halted by dug-in tanks and artillery and then driven off by 4th Armoured Division.

Siegfried Line German defensive line along the borders of France and

Holland. Originally intended as a series of strongpoints opposing the
◊Maginot Line to slow down any French offensive rather than offer solid
resistance, in 1938 Hitler ordered it to be strengthened with permanent
works. Very little was actually done other than planting a thick belt of
concrete anti-tank obstacles backed by pillboxes and artillery emplace-
ments, and work stopped 1940. When the Allies invaded ◊Normandy
1944 some hurried additions were made but the line was never a formidable obstacle, though it was taken seriously by the Allies as they lacked
detailed knowledge of the defences.

Sikorski General Wladislav 1881–1943. Polish soldier and politician;
prime minister 1922–23, and 1939–43 head of the Polish government in
exile in London. He was in Paris when the Germans took Poland and
became commander in chief of the 100,000 strong Free Polish Forces,
who he took to Britain 1940. Following the German invasion of the
USSR 1941, he concluded an agreement with the Soviets to re-establish
Poland's pre-war boundaries, but the treatment of Polish prisoners in
Soviet hands soured relations. The revelation of the ◊Katyn Wood massacre 1943 nearly caused a serious rift, only averted by strong
intervention from Churchill. He was killed in an aeroplane crash near
Gibraltar in suspicious circumstances 4 July 1943 and the government-
in-exile's influence declined from then on.

Singapore island and British naval base at the tip of the Malayan
peninsula. The base had been slowly constructed during the 1930s and
was never fully completed. It was well protected against sea attack by
coastal artillery, but had no landward defences (although the coast guns
could, and did, fire inland). When ◊Malaya fell, the collapse of
Singapore was inevitable and it surrendered 15 Feb 1942.

Skorzeny Lieutenant-Colonel Otto 1908–1975. German soldier. An
early advocate of irregular warfare, he commanded the German group
which rescued ◊Mussolini from imprisonment Sept 1943. In Oct 1944
he kidnapped the son of Admiral ◊Horthy, forcing Horthy to abdicate
and thus foiling his plan to sue for a separate peace. In Dec 1944 he
caused chaos in the Battle of the ◊Bulge with the deployment of squads
of English-speaking soldiers, dressed in US uniforms and driving US
vehicles, inserted behind the US lines to mystify and confuse. He was
tried for war crimes at ◊Nuremberg and acquitted.

Slim Field Marshal Sir William Joseph, 1st Viscount 1891–1970. British soldier. He was wounded in the Sudan 1941 and then led the 10th Indian Division in operations in the Middle East. He commanded the 1st Burma Corps 1942–45, stemming the Japanese invasion of India, and defeated the offensive against ◊Imphal and ◊Kohima, forcing the Japanese out of ◊Burma 1945. He was governor general of Australia 1953–60.

In a battle nothing is ever as good or as bad as the first reports of excited men would have it.
Field Marshal Sir William Joseph Slim Unofficial History

Smith General Holland M 1882–1967. US Marine. His ruthless drive and personality earned him the nickname of 'Howling Mad' but he perfected the art of amphibious warfare while commanding V Amphibious Corps in the Pacific, leading them in the ◊Aleutian Islands, Tarawa, Kwajalien, ◊Saipan, and Tinian. He was given command of the Fleet Marine Force Aug 1944 and directed the landings on ◊Guam and ◊Iwo Jima.

Smolensk Soviet city and rail junction 400 km/250 mi W of Moscow, an objective of German Army Group Centre during Operation ◊Barbarossa 1941. Aided by an encircling movement of Army Group North, the Germans captured 310,000 men, 3,200, tanks and 3,000 guns. However, this delayed the forward thrust of Army Group Centre, allowing the Soviets to organize the defence of Moscow. Smolensk remained in German hands until re-taken by Soviet troops 25 Sept 1943.

Sobibor German extermination camp NW of Lublin, established March 1942. An estimated 250,000 Jews were sent there and murdered before the camp was closed 1943. Its closure was unique since it was forced by a rebellion of prisoners led by a Soviet prisoner-of-war.

SOE see ◊Special Operations Executive.

Sokolovsky Marshal Vasiliy 1897–1968. Soviet soldier. Chief of Staff to the West Front Army from 1941, he took command of it 1943, led it in the counteroffensive after ◊Kursk and liberated ◊Smolensk. His progress then slowed and he was removed from command and became Chief of

Staff to the 1st Ukrainian Front. In 1945 he became Deputy Commander of 1st Byelorussian Front for the attack on ◊Berlin, captured the Führerbunker, and verified Hitler's corpse from dental records. After the war he became commander in chief of Soviet Forces in Germany.

Solomon Islands group of Pacific islands E of New Guinea, including ◊Bougainville, ◊Guadalcanal, ◊New Georgia, Choiseul, and Santa Isabela. Occupied by the Japanese during their advance of 1941–42, the Allied forces began clearing the islands with the landing on Guadalcanal 7 Aug 1942. This provided them with a close support airfield and in June ◊New Georgia was taken, followed by Choiseul in Oct and Bougainville in Nov.

sonar (acronym for *so*und *na*vigation and *r*anging) method of locating underwater objects by the reflection of ultrasonic waves. The time taken for an acoustic pulse to travel to the object and back to the source enables the distance to be found since the velocity of sound in water is known. The Allies developed and perfected an apparatus for detecting the presence of enemy U-boats beneath the sea surface by the use of ultrasonic echoes. It was originally named ASDIC, from the initials of the Allied Submarine Detection Investigation Committee responsible for its development, but the name was changed to sonar 1963.

Spaatz General Carl 1891–1974. US airman. Sent to Britain as an observer 1940, he studied RAF organization before returning to the USA. As commander of the US 8th Air Force 1942 he launched a daylight bombing offensive against Germany and then moved to N Africa 1943 to control air support over Tunisia and Sicily. He was placed in charge of Strategic Air Forces Europe Jan 1944 and controlled the air offensive prior to the ◊D-Day landings. He then turned to strategic bombing of German fuel supplies and railways before going to the Far East to command the Strategic Air Forces Pacific. After the war he became Chief of Staff to the US Air Force.

Special Air Service (SAS) British unit formed in Egypt 1941 to conduct raids on German and Italian airfields in N Africa. Assisted by the ◊Long Range Desert Group, it destroyed some 400 Axis aircraft together with dumps of fuel, bombs, and other vital stores. From the initial small unit it expanded to a number of squadrons and carried out commando-style raids in Sicily and Italy, then operated with the ◊Maquis in occupied France. After the invasion of Normandy 1944, units operated behind German lines, disrupting communications, and after the Allies crossed the German border 1945 they were used to capture German war criminals.

Special Boat Squadron (SBS) originally a sub-unit of the ◊Special Air Service, the SBS became a separate unit 1943 and operated chiefly in the Adriatic and Aegean Seas, raiding and gathering intelligence. They were also used to conduct beach reconnaissance prior to amphibious landings. Disbanded 1945, the unit was later revived.

Special Operations Executive (SOE) British intelligence organization established June 1940 to gather intelligence and carry out sabotage missions inside German-occupied Europe. Some 11,000 agents were eventually employed, but screening was careless and a number of German agents infiltrated the organization, fatally damaging many operations before they were detected and removed.

Speer Albert 1905–1981. German architect and government minister. He was appointed Hitler's architect and in 1942 became Armaments Minister. He raised the index of arms production from 100 Jan 1942 to 322 by July 1944. In the latter months of the war he concentrated on frustrating Hitler's orders for the destruction of German industry in the face of the advancing Allies. At the ◊Nuremberg Trials he was sentenced to 20 years' imprisonment for his employment of slave labour.

Spitfire see ◊Supermarine.

Spitzbergen group of islands 610 km/380 mi N of Norway, containing extensive coal mines operated by a Soviet company. Britain, Norway, and the USSR agreed to deny this valuable resource to the Germans; since a garrison could not be maintained there, the Soviet and Norwegian citizens were removed, the mines wrecked, and the coal stocks set on fire in a raid by Canadian troops 25 Aug 1941. The islands remained uninhabited for the rest of the war.

Spruance Vice Admiral Raymond A 1886–1969. US sailor. He took over 5 Cruiser Division at ◊Pearl Harbor 1941 and in 1942 was promoted to command Task Force 16, assigned to protect Midway Island.

During the Battle of ◊Midway, Spruance took over command when Admiral ◊Fletcher's flagship was crippled and sank all four Japanese carriers. He then became Chief of Staff to Admiral ◊Nimitz and was given command of the 5th Central Pacific Fleet Aug 1943, leading it at Tarawa, Kwajaliewn, Truk, the Battle of the ◊Philippine Sea, ◊Okinawa, and ◊Iwo Jima. He was involved in the planning for the invasion of Japan, and after the war succeeded ◊Nimitz as commander in chief of the Pacific Fleet.

SS Nazi elite corps (German *Schutz-Staffel* 'protective squadron') established 1925. Under ◊Himmler its 500,000 membership included the full-time armed ◊*Waffen-SS* (armed SS). The SS performed state police duties and was brutal in its treatment of the Jews and others in the concentration camps and occupied territories. It was condemned as an illegal organization at the ◊Nuremberg Trials of war criminals.

Stalin Josef (adopted name (Russian 'steel') of Joseph Vissarionovich Djugashvili) 1879–1953. Soviet dictator. A member of the October Revolution Committee 1917, Stalin became general secretary of the Communist Party 1922. After Lenin's death 1924, Stalin clashed with Trotsky over the future of the Soviet revolution but won the ideological struggle by 1927. He eliminated any remaining opposition in the Great Purge 1936–38 which decimated the Soviet Red Army with the slaughter of thousands of officers.

   Stalin was well aware of German plans to turn against the USSR, but agreed to the ◊Molotov–Ribbentrop pact to gain time and territory. During the war, he took charge of the military direction of the campaigns against Germany but unlike Hitler was prepared to take advice from the professional soldiers. He had uneasy relations with the Western Allies, threatening to come to a separate peace unless they opened a ◊second front. He met Churchill and Roosevelt at ◊Tehran 1943 and at ◊Yalta 1945 where postwar spheres of influence were agreed, and took part in the ◊Potsdam conference. After the war, Stalin quickly turned E Europe into a series of Soviet satellites and maintained an autocratic rule domestically. He not only brought the USSR out of the war but as a superpower, but only at an immense cost in human suffering to his own people. He was denounced after his death 1953 by Khrushchev and other members of the Soviet regime.

Stalingrad Soviet city on the river Volga (now Volgograd), a major industrial centre and the objective of German Army Group B during the 1942 campaign to occupy the Caucasus region. The city was reinforced by the Soviets, and General von ◊Paulus, the commander of German 6th Army, began attacking with units as and when they arrived instead of waiting until all his army had reached the area. As a result the Soviets were able to concentrate and destroy them one by one, whereas they might not have resisted a massed attack. Von Paulus halted his piecemeal attacks, waited for reinforcement by 4th Panzer Army, and launched the first major assault 19 Aug 1942. The initial advance through the suburbs was relatively smooth, but once into the built-up areas it became a house-to-house battle which went on for two months without either side gaining any advantage. While staving off the Germans the Soviets were preparing a massive counterattack with 1 million men, 13,500 guns, and 894 tanks commanded by Marshal ◊Zhukov. This was launched 19 Nov and swept around the flanks of the 6th Army and encircled it. Fending off German attempts to relieve von Paulus, the Soviets then set about destroying the 6th Army until it surrendered 31 Jan 1943 with the loss of 1.5 million men, 3,500 tanks, 12,000 guns and mortars, 75,000 vehicles, and 3,000 aircraft.

Stauffenberg Colonel Claus von 1907–1944. German soldier and one of the main conspirators in the ◊July Bomb Plot 1944. He planted the bomb in Hitler's headquarters conference room in the Wolf's Lair 20 July 1944, but Hitler was merely injured and the conspiracy collapsed. Stauffenberg and 200 others were later executed.

Sten gun British submachine gun. Designed 1940 by two officers named Shepherd and Turpin, the name derives from their initials and the EN of Enfield, the Royal Small Arms Factory. A cheap and easily made weapon, it was turned out in millions and armed all three British services as well as being dropped wholesale to resistance groups all over Europe. Firing a 9 mm pistol cartridge, common throughout Europe, it used a 32-shot magazine firing at about 500 shots a minute. A silenced version was also made for use by ◊commando raiders and clandestine agents.

Stilwell General Joseph Warren 1883– 1946. US soldier, nicknamed

'Vinegar Joe.' Stilwell became US military representative in China 1942, when he commanded the Chinese forces cooperating with the British (with whom he quarrelled) in ◊Burma; he later commanded all US forces in the Chinese, Burmese, and Indian theatres until recalled to the US 1944 after differences over nationalist policy with ◊Chiang Kai-shek. Stilwell sought the engagement of 30 divisions of Chinese nationalist troops in battle against the Japanese. Chiang Kai-shek refused, preferring to reserve his forces for use against the Chinese Communists in the anticipated Chinese civil war. At Chiang's insistence, President F D ◊Roosevelt recalled Stilwell, giving him command of the US 10th Army on the Japanese island of ◊Okinawa.

Stopford General Sir Montagu 1892–1971. British soldier. He commanded an infantry brigade in France and Belgium 1940 and was given command of 33 Corps in India 1943. With this corps he relieved ◊Kohima and ◊Imphal 1944 and then advanced into central Burma to capture Mandalay 25 March 1945 and continued to ◊Rangoon. He was appointed Commander of 12th Army just before the war ended.

strategic bombing bombing of enemy territory with the aim of disrupting its economy and destroying morale. During World War II strategic bombing of cities was extensively used by both the Axis and the Allied powers. ◊Rotterdam in the Netherlands, ◊Warsaw in Poland, and Hamburg in Germany all experienced heavy bombardment.

Student Colonel General Kurt 1890–1958. German airman. He served as a pilot in World War I and remained in the German Army, transferring to the ◊Luftwaffe when it was formed. He was selected to organize and train a parachute force and examine the possibilities of gliders for landing troops. He developed this force into the 7th Air Division which operated in Norway, Holland, and Belgium, while his glider troops executed a brilliant coup in their capture of Fort ◊Eben Emael, breaking the Belgian defensive line 1940. Student was wounded in Holland, but in 1941 he was again in the front line, leading his paratroops in the invasion of ◊Crete. This led to such heavy casualties that Hitler forbade future parachute operations, and his plans for an airborne invasion of ◊Malta were cancelled. He commanded the 1st Parachute Army in Holland and Germany 1945, though by that time they were operating as ordinary infantry.

Sturmgeschutz (German 'assault gun') German armoured self-propelled gun, usually based on a tank chassis with a fixed superstructure rather than a turret and so able to carry a heavier gun than it could as a tank. Developed as a means of bringing heavy firepower forward to assist infantry in overcoming strongpoints, they also came to be used as tank destroyers.

Sturmgewehr (German 'assault rifle') German automatic rifle developed 1942–43 around a 7.92 mm short cartridge. Battle experience showed that soldiers rarely fired at targets more than about 400 m/1,300 ft away, so there was no reason to have a rifle and cartridge capable of firing 2,000 m/6,500 ft. A lighter cartridge led to a lighter rifle and meant troops could carry more ammunition. The result was a light rifle capable of firing single shots or automatic, originally known as the *Maschinen Pistole* 43 for political reasons but later known as the *Sturmgewehr* 44. Popular and efficient, it became the forerunner of a new generation of rifles which equipped the world's armies in the post-war years.

Supermarine British aircraft company famous for one product, the Supermarine *Spitfire*; this single engine, eight-gun monoplane was designed by R J ◊Mitchell 1936 and went into service with the RAF Aug 1938. It was the only British combat aircraft to remain in production throughout the war years, over 20,000 being built, and 19 squadrons were equipped with it in the Battle of ◊Britain 1940. It was progressively improved, adopting cannon instead of machine guns, and was modified into an attack bomber, photo-reconnaissance aircraft, and, as the *Seafire*, a naval carrier fighter. The Mark IX of 1944 flew at 655 kph/408 mph, carried cannon and .5 in machine guns, and had a range of 700 km/435 mi.

Syria although nominally independent, the French took control of Syria under a Mandate from the League of Nations 1922. In 1940 the French High Commissioner supported the ◊Vichy government and provided facilities for German aircraft. Fearful of a German occupation, British and Free French forces invaded 8 June 1941 and occupied the country after a five-week campaign. The Free French took control of the country and remained there until 1946.

T

T-34 tank Soviet medium tank. Developed 1939–40 and produced from June 1940, it became the premier Soviet wartime tank and probably the best tank of the war. Powered by a 3.8 litre v-12 diesel engine producing 500 hp, it weighed 26 tons, had a speed of 50 kph/31 mph, 45 mm/2 in thick armour, and a powerful 76 mm gun in the turret. The suspension was on large wheels, based on the US ◊Christie design, giving it a very good cross-country performance at speed, and the wide tracks gave it excellent flotation in mud and snow conditions. Its performance astonished the Germans whose first reaction was simply to copy a captured specimen, but this was found to be impossible and instead hasty upgrading programmes and the development of the ◊Panther tank were put under way. The T-34 was upgraded 1944 by substituting an 85 mm gun for the original weapon. Production continued well after the war, and the T-34 was used in Korea and supplied to communist-backed regimes in various parts of the world.

tank destroyer self-propelled anti-tank gun, generally resembling a tank but usually with a fixed superstructure so that it can mount a much heavier gun than a tank of similar size. The US policy was to use an open-topped turret, allowing a more powerful gun to be fitted. Effective in ambushes, and to allow guns to be moved rapidly or to stalk tanks, they fell out of use in postwar years when tanks were designed to mount more powerful guns.

Taranto seaport and naval base in S Italy. It was raided by British torpedo bombers launched from an aircraft carrier 11 Dec 1940. Three Italian battleships were torpedoed and damaged, one beyond repair, and several other ships damaged. The Italian fleet withdrew to bases on the west coast, further from the scene of action but less liable to be attacked.

Tarawa atoll in the Gilbert islands, consisting of a number of small islands bound by a coral reef. Attacked by US 2nd Marine division and US Army 27th Division 20 Nov 1943, the landing used amphibious tractors to ferry the men ashore. Due to tidal changes the second wave beached on the reef and the troops had to wade ashore, leading to excessive casualties. The pre-landing air and naval gunfire support was badly coordinated and the Japanese defence formidable and it took three days of hard fighting to capture the island. The US forces suffered over 1,000 killed and 2,100 wounded.

Tedder Air Marshal Arthur William, 1st Baron Tedder 1890–1967. British airman. He was air officer commanding RAF Far East 1936–38 and Middle East 1941–43, where his method of pattern bombing became known as 'Tedder's carpet'. As deputy supreme commander under US general Eisenhower 1943–45, he was largely responsible for the initial success of the 1944 ◊Normandy landings.

Tehran conference conference held 1943 in Tehran, Iran, the first meeting of the Allied leaders Churchill, Roosevelt, and Stalin. The chief subject discussed was coordination of Allied strategy in W and E Europe.

Terauchi Field Marshal Count Hisaichi 1879–1945. Japanese soldier. He commanded the Southern Army from Sept 1941 to the end of the war, with headquarters in Saigon. He was not a strategist and frequently persisted in reinforcing operations which had no chance of success, wasting manpower. Totally indifferent to human life, he sacrificed his troops and wasted no sympathy on prisoners. He was responsible for building the Burma railway, in which 17,000 prisoners of war died. He died from a stroke Sept 1945.

Thoma General Wilhelm Ritter von. German soldier. He commanded a Panzer Regiment in Poland 1939, then joined the Mobile Troops Office in General Headquarters. He led the 6th and then 20th Panzer Divisions in the invasion of the USSR 1941 and Sept 1942 was given command of the Afrika Korps. He was captured by the British 4 Nov 1942 during the Second Battle of El ◊Alamein.

thousand-bomber raid RAF raid against the German city of Cologne, 31 May 1942. It was organized by Air Marshal ◊Harris shortly after he took over Bomber Command as a means of reviving the morale of the Command and demonstrating the ability of the RAF as a strategic bombing force. It required the use of training and spare aircraft and the drafting-in of crews from different commands to make up the required numbers. The target was selected as it was well known and lightly defended. Some 898 bombers actually arrived over Cologne and dropped 1,455 tons of bombs, starting 1200 fires; 18,440 buildings were destroyed and over 56,000 people made homeless. The raid was followed by two similar attacks, one on Essen and one on Bremen, which were less successful.

Tiger tank German heavy tank. Designed to meet an army demand for a 'breakthrough' tank, the Tiger went into production 1942. Heavily armoured, it mounted an 88 mm gun and used torsion-bar suspension with wide tracks. Weighing 55 tons, it had a speed of 37 kph/23 mph and a five-man crew. Its 100 mm/4 in armour made it impervious to Allied tank guns except at suicidally short ranges. Production ended Aug 1944 after 1,350 had been built, since the Tiger B began production Feb 1944. This was even heavier and better protected, weighing 69 tons and was armed with a longer and more powerful 88 mm gun. It was known to the Allies as the 'Royal' or 'King' Tiger. A total of 484 were built before the war ended.

Timoshenko Marshal Semyon K 1895–1970. Soviet soldier. An old companion of Stalin and one of the few people he was prepared to trust. After commanding a sector in the war against ◊Finland 1939–40 he became Commissar of Defence. When the German invasion took place 1941 he took command of the West Front but was too late to do more than delay the German advance. Transferred to the Southwest Front he mounted a powerful but mistimed offensive to recapture ◊Kharkov which was soundly defeated by the Germans who then swept him aside and advanced to ◊Stalingrad and the ◊Caucasus. Timoshenko was then moved to a less active area for a short time before being assigned to Moscow to work on strategic planning for the rest of the war.

Tinian island in the ◊Marianas group. It was a difficult target, unusual among Pacific islands in having a cliff-bound coastline with only a few small beaches. It was attacked 24 July 1944 by US Marines who made a mock attack against the main beach and settlement while actually landing on small beaches no more than 45 m/50 yds wide several miles away. Over 15,000 men got ashore against light resistance and by nightfall had secured a beachhead at a cost of only 15 killed and 225 wounded. The Japanese launched a counterattack during the night but suffered severe loses and the island was completely secured by 1 Aug.

Tirpitz German battleship, launched 1939 as a sister ship to the ◊*Bismarck*. It sailed to Norway Jan 1942 and remained there, a permanent threat to Allied convoys bound for the USSR. It frequently sailed out to scatter convoys but was never brought to action. In Sept 1943, accompanied by the ◊*Scharnhorst* and 10 destroyers, the *Tirpitz* sailed to ◊Spitzbergen and bombarded the various mining and shore installations there, to no particular purpose since the Allies had already wrecked them; this was the only time it saw any form of action. On returning to anchorage in Kaafjord, Norway, it was attacked by British midget submarines 23 Sept 1943, and was further damaged by an air strike launched from a British carrier April 1944. The RAF attacked with ◊Lancaster bombers Sept 1944 and in Nov it was towed to a new and more secure hide near Tromso. On 12 Nov the RAF attacked with 5,500 kg/12,000 lb armour-piercing bombs, and the *Tirpitz* capsized and sank.

Tito (adopted name of Josip Broz) 1892–1980. Yugoslav communist politician, in effective control of Yugoslavia from 1943. Tito served in the Austrian army during World War I, was captured by the Russians, and fought in the Red Army during the civil wars. Returning to Yugoslavia 1923, he became a prominent communist and in World War II organized the National Liberation Army to carry on guerrilla warfare against the German invasion 1941, and was created marshal 1943. In 1943 he established a provisional government and gained Allied recognition (previously given to the ◊Chetniks) 1944, and with Soviet help proclaimed a federal republic 1945. As prime minister 1945–53 and president from 1953, he followed a foreign policy of 'positive neutralism'.

Tobruk Libyan port 96 km/60 mi W of Bardia. Occupied by Italy 1911, it was taken by Britain in Operation ◊Battleaxe 1941, and

unsuccessfully besieged by Axis forces April–Dec 1941. It was captured by Germany June 1942 after the retreat of the main British force
to Egypt, and this precipitated ◊Auchinleck's replacement by
◊Montgomery as British commander. Montogomery recovered it after
the second battle of ◊Alamein and it remained in British hands for the
rest of the war.

Todt Fritz 1891–1942. German engineer. He was responsible for
building the first *autobahns* (motorways) and, in World War II, the
◊Siegfried Line and the ◊Atlantic Wall. He joined the Nazi party 1922
and was appointed Inspector General of Road Construction 1933. His
success in this post led to Hitler putting him in charge of completing the
Siegfried Line 1938. His ***Organisation Todt,*** formed for this task, continued constructing defences on the Atlantic Coast using forced labour
until 1944. He was made minister for arms and munitions 1940. In
1942, alarmed at the attrition of equipment on the Eastern Front, he
advised Hitler to end the war with the USSR. Returning by air from this
meeting his aircraft crashed in mysterious circumstances and he was
killed.

Tōjō Hideki 1884–1948. Japanese general and premier 1941–44.
Promoted to Chief of Staff of Japan's Kwantung army in ◊Manchuria
1937, he served as minister for war 1940–41. In this post he was pivotal
in negotiating the tripartite Axis alliance with Germany and Italy 1940.
His main concern was winning the war in China, but he and the Army
felt this was being hampered by the Western powers denying Japan
vital resources. As a result he brought Japan into the war to take Allied
colonial possessions in the Pacific and SE Asia, which he and the Army
believed could be swiftly taken, in order to put Japan in a position of
strength in subsequent negotiations.

As part of this strategy, he ordered the occupation of Indo-China
1941 and maintained peace negotiations with the USA right up until the
attack on ◊Pearl Harbor 1941. As the war progressed, he was held
responsible for defeats in the Pacific, particularly the fall of the
◊Marianas, and was forced to resign 18 July 1944. After Japan's defeat,
he attempted suicide but was captured by US forces and was tried and
hanged as a war criminal 1948.

Tokyo capital of Japan, on Honshu Island. It was raided by a small force of US bombers led by Col ◊Doolittle 18 April 1942. The city was then left until Nov 1944 when 111 B-29 bombers attacked an aircraft engine factory. Due to the long flight from the US airfields in the Marianas, the bomb load was small, to allow for the weight of fuel, and it was decided that incendiary bombs would do more damage. The first fire raid took place 9 March 1945 when 279 B-29 bombers dropped 1,650 tons of incendiary bombs, devastating the centre of Tokyo and killing over 100,000 people – more than were killed by the atomic attacks on Hiroshima or Nagasaki. Raids continued against Tokyo until 14 Aug 1945, with over 1,000 bombers being used on some attacks.

Tolbukhin Marshal Fedor Ivanovitch 1894–1949. Soviet soldier. Chief of Staff to the Transcaucasian District 1941 he began the war by organizing the Soviet thrust into ◊Iran late 1941. He then planned the landing of two armies into the ◊Crimean peninsula to relieve ◊Sevastopol, but this venture failed and he was dismissed. He proved that the disaster was not his fault and was given command of the 57th Army at ◊Stalingrad 1942 and led it in the subsequent Soviet counteroffensive. In March 1943 he was given command of the South Front and liberated the ◊Crimea, taking 67,000 prisoners. He then moved to command the 3rd Ukrainian Front and held this post to the end of the war, liberating Belgrade and handing it over to ◊Tito's troops, then moving on to liberate Budapest, defeat the German forces in Hungary and occupy Vienna.

Totenkopfverbande the 'death's head' units of the Nazi ◊SS organization. Originally used to guard concentration camps from 1935, during the war they became an elite combat division attached to the Waffen-SS.

Toulon French naval base on the Mediterranean coast, SE of Marseilles. After the Allied landings in N Africa 1942, Vichy France was occupied by the German Army. On 19 Nov Hitler gave orders to seize the French fleet of 60 warships lying in Toulon harbour. Admiral ◊Darlan ordered the fleet to escape to ◊Dakar but his order was countermanded by the fleet commander, Admiral Laborde, a supporter of ◊Pétain. On 27 Nov II Panzer Corps began to attack the dockyard.

Laborde immediately ordered all captains to scuttle their ships and except for five submarines which escaped, the remainder of the fleet sank or was set on fire.

Treblinka German extermination camp 80 km/50 mi NW of Warsaw. Originally built 1940 as a forced labour camp for political prisoners, from June 1941 it was rebuilt and had gas chambers and crematoria installed, and by the summer of 1942 was receiving shipments of Jews from the ◊Warsaw ghetto. About 800,000 were killed here before a mass escape took place April 1943 in which many of the SS guards were killed by the inmates. After severe reprisals the camp was closed down and dismantled in Nov 1943.

Truk group of about 55 volcanic islands surrounded by a coral reef in the E Caroline islands of the W Pacific. Originally a German possession it was mandated to Japan 1920 and turned into a heavily fortified air and naval base. Its use as a naval base was discontinued Feb 1944 after a series of heavy raids mounted by a US carrier task force under Admiral ◊Mitscher in which several warships and 150,000 tons of merchant shipping were sunk but it continued in use as an air base. As the focus of US operations moved further away it became a backwater and was left in isolation.

Truman Harry S 1884–1972. US politician and 33rd president of the USA 1945–53. Became vice-president in the 1944 elections and president following the death of President ◊Roosevelt 12 April 1945. In July 1945 he attended the ◊Potsdam Conference with Churchill and Stalin and while returning from this meeting announced his intention to drop the atomic bomb on ◊Hiroshima in order to convince the Japanese of Allied strength and persuade them to end the war. After the end of the war, he implemented the Marshall Plan to revitalize Europe.

Truscott General Lucian K Jr 1895–1965. US soldier. He commanded the forward headquarters in the N African campaign 1942 and was then given command of the 3rd Infantry Division for the attack on ◊Sicily and Italy 1943. He replaced General Lucas as commander of US VI Corps Feb 1944 and later led the advance on Rome. In Aug 1944 VI Corps formed part of 7th Army and landed in S France, advancing rapidly up the Rhone valley. Truscott returned to Italy April 1945 to command the US 5th Army in the final phases of the campaign.

Tulagi island in the Florida group in the ◊Solomon Islands, a few miles N of ◊Guadalcanal. Captured by the Japanese May 1942, it became a major seaplane base, intended to provide support for their projected operations against ◊Port Moresby. At a late stage in the planning of the assault on Guadalcanal it was decided to take Tulagi, and at short notice the 1st Marine Raiders were given the task. They landed on 8 August 1942 and were met by fanatical resistance and some bitter fighting before the island was taken.

Tunisia French colony in N Africa. Tunisia was invaded by British and US forces in Operation Torch 8 Nov 1942. Slow progress by the Allies allowed German reinforcements to be flown in from Sicily and a strong defensive line was set up. The intention was to make a rapid thrust to join up with the British 8th Army, then driving ◊Rommel westwards towards Tunisia, but the strength of German forces foiled this idea and the campaign became a long and difficult affair before Tunis was finally captured 7 May 1943.

Turner Admiral Richmond Kelly 1885–1961. US sailor. A specialist in amphibious warfare, Turner was Commander South Pacific Amphibious Force July 1942 and conducted the US landings at ◊Guadalcanal Aug 1942. He then directed the landings in ◊New Georgia and the Gilbert Islands. Transferred to the Central Pacific Theatre 1944, he was responsible for operations in the Marshall Islands and the ◊Marianas, and in 1945 for the landings on ◊Iwo Jima and ◊Okinawa.

Twining General Nathan F 1897–1971. US airman. He commanded the US 13th Air Force in the Pacific theatre 1943, and was then sent to Italy to command the 15th US Air Force and conduct a strategic bombing campaign against targets in S Germany and Central Europe. In 1945 he returned to the Pacific to command the 20th Air Force, using B-29 bombers to raid Japan.

U-boats (German *Unterseeboots*) general name for German submarines. There were a number of different types, ranging from small coastal to large seagoing boats. The most prolific type was the Type *VIIC,* of which over 600 were built. This displaced about 850 tons, was 67 m/220 ft long, had a top speed of 17 knots, and carried up to 24 torpedoes. The final design was the Type *XXI* displacing 1,800 tons, 77 m/251 ft long, travelling at 15 knots, with a range of 19,300 km/12,000 mi, and carrying 23 torpedoes. This latter version was also fitted with the ◊schnorkel, allowing it to proceed submerged on its diesel engines to avoid detection while charging batteries.

Ultra abbreviation of *Ultra Secret*, term used by the British from spring 1940 to denote intelligence gained by deciphering German signals enciphered by the ◊Enigma machine.

Urquhart Major General Robert Elliot 1901–. British soldier. Served with the 51st Highland Division in N Africa 1942 and then in Sicily and Italy. He returned to Britain and in 1944 was given command of 1st Airborne Division which he led at ◊Arnhem.

USO (United Services Organization). A US welfare organization which sent concert parties and entertainers to all parts of the world where US troops were serving.

Utah Beach Normandy landing beach on the extreme right flank of the Allied landings, close to the village of La Madelaine. It was the target of US VII Corps under General ◊Collins. Opposition was light and the assault troops soon left the beaches to link up with airborne troops who had landed ahead of them near Vierville.

V-bombs (German *Vergeltungswaffe* 'revenge weapons') German flying bombs of World War II, launched against Britain 1944 and 1945. The *V1,* also called the doodlebug and buzz bomb, was an uncrewed monoplane with an explosive warhead, powered by a simple kind of jet engine called a pulse jet. The *V2,* a rocket bomb with a preset guidance system, was the first long-range ballistic missile, also called the ◊A4.

strategic rockets and missiles 1944–45

V-1 (Fieseler FZG 76)		
	power	V-1 (Fieseler FZG 76)2
	max speed	560 kph/350 mph
	range	260 km/160 mi
	warhead	850 kg/1,870 lb
	no. launched	8,900 against UK
		12,000 against W Europe
V-2 (Peenemünde A-4)	power	liquid-fuelled rocket motor
	max speed	610 kph/380 mph
	range	305 km/190 mi
	warhead	1,000 kg/2,200lb
	no. launched	2,650 total

Valentine tank British medium tank, so named because it was approved for production on St Valentine's Day 1938. It had been designed by Vickers Armstrong as a private venture and over 8,000 were eventually built in Britain and Canada, 1,300 of which were sent to the USSR. It was first used in Operation ◊Crusader in N Africa 1941 and soon acquired a reputation for reliability. Weighing 17 tons, it was initially fitted with a 2-pounder (40 mm) gun but this was later replaced by a 6-pounder (57 mm) weapon. It was not used in Europe, though a conversion into a ◊tank destroyer, mounting a 17 pounder gun, was of considerable value. After N Africa it saw service in Madagascar and on the ◊Arakan front in Burma.

Vandegrift Lieutenant-General Alexander A 1887–1972. US Marine. He commanded the 1st US Marine Division which landed on ◊Guadalcanal and successfully resisted Japanese counterattacks, securing ◊Henderson Field and keeping it open. He was then made commander of 1st Marine Amphibious Corps, leading them in the landings at ◊Bougainville. In 1944 he returned to the USA to become Commandant of the Marine Corps.

Vasilevsky Marshal Alexandr M 1895–1977. Soviet soldier. Appointed Chief of Staff 1942 he was responsible for planning most of the major Soviet operations of the war, including the ◊Stalingrad counteroffensive and the defence of the ◊Kursk salient. In March 1945 he took command of the 3rd Byelorussian Front when its commander was killed and completed the conquest of E Prussia and the Baltic states. In May 1945 he was appointed commander in chief Far East, and planned and executed the invasion of ◊Manchuria, Korea, and the ◊Kurile and Sakhalin islands of Japan.

Vatutin General Nikolai A 1901–1944. Soviet soldier. Appointed commander of the Southwest Front 1942 he took part in the action at ◊Stalingrad and the destruction of the German 6th Army. He attempted an offensive but was soundly defeated by von ◊Manstein. After this he conducted a successful defence of the southern sector of the ◊Kursk salient and then counterattacked to ◊Kharkov and liberated much of the Ukraine. A further advance liberated ◊Kiev, but he was ambushed by anti-Soviet partisans near Rovno Feb 1945 and fatally wounded.

Venlo town in Holland on the German border, 48 km/30 mi NW of Dusseldorf. In Nov 1939 two British intelligence officers were induced to cross the German border to meet a party of anti-Nazi sympathizers. These turned out to be SS men who kidnapped the two and, under torture, forced them to give information which damaged Allied intelligence sources in Europe.

Veritable, Operation combined British–Canadian offensive between the Maas and Waal rivers and through the ◊Reichswald Forest and ◊Siegfried Line Feb 1945.

Vian Admiral Sir Philip 1894–1968. British sailor. He commanded a destroyer flotilla off the Norwegian coast Nov 1940. Under direct orders from Churchill, he sailed into the Josenfjord in Norwegian waters to rescue 299 British merchant seamen captured from ships sunk in the Atlantic by the *Admiral Graf Spee* who were being held on board the German supply ship ◊*Altmark*. Vian successfully rescued them in a daring surprise attack. He later evacuated British troops from Norway, attacked the *Bismarck* with torpedoes, escorted commandos to ◊Spitzbergen, and then moved to the Mediterranean to escort convoys to ◊Malta. In 1943 he commanded a naval force covering the invasion of ◊Sicily and then a carrier support force during the invasion of Italy. In 1944 he commanded the Eastern Task Force in the ◊D-Day landings invasion and then went to the Far East to command the Pacific carrier squadron, taking part in the landings at ◊Okinawa.

Vichy government right-wing government of unoccupied France after the country's defeat by the Germans June 1940; it was named after the spa town of Vichy, France, where the national assembly was based under Prime Minister ◊Pétain until the liberation 1944. *Vichy France* was that part of France not occupied by German troops until Nov 1942. Authoritarian and collaborationist, the Vichy regime cooperated with the Germans even after they had moved to the unoccupied zone Nov 1942. It imprisoned some 135,000 people, interned another 70,000, deported some 76,000 Jews, and sent 650,000 French workers to Germany.

Vickers British armament company and aircraft manufacturer. Their most notable wartime aircraft was the *Wellington* bomber, a twin-engine machine using a method of construction devised by Barnes ◊Wallis which gave it immense strength. It could carry 3,000 kg/6,600 lb of bombs, had a top speed of 410 kph/255 mph, was armed with six machine guns, and had a crew of six. It entered service 1938 and was the principal British bomber until replaced by heavier four-engine machines 1942. It was then converted for other duties including mine-laying, magnetic mine detection, anti-submarine patrols, and torpedo-bombing.

Vieitinghoff Colonel General Heinrich von. German soldier. He commanded the German 10th Army in Italy from 1943, conducting a brilliant fighting defence. He fell back to the ◊Gustav Line as soon as it was apparent that the Allied landings were secure, and after the fall of ◊Cassino withdrew north of Rome and set up a formidable defence on the ◊Gothic Line. In Feb 1945 he was sent to command Army Group Kurland, but once this had become encircled he was directed back to Italy to replace ◊Kesselring as Army Group Commander. Once his defensive front was broken he had no option but to surrender 2 May 1945.

Vlasov Lieutenant-General Andrey 1900–1946. Soviet soldier. After serving as a military adviser in China, he commanded a mechanized corps against the Germans 1941 and escaped from the encirclement at ◊Kiev. Given command of 20th Army during the defence of Moscow, he then went to the Crimea and was captured near ◊Sevastopol May 1942. He felt he had been badly treated by Stalin and began making anti-Soviet broadcasts for the Germans. In Nov 1944 he began forming a 'Russian Liberation Army' from disaffected prisoners-of-war. He was captured by the Soviets May 1945 and executed for treason.

Volkssturm German civilian home defence organization, similar to the British ◊Home Guard, established Sept 1944. All civilian males between 16 and 60 capable of bearing arms were liable for service. Although organized and trained on military lines, the shortage of weapons and instructors made it largely ineffective. In Jan 1945 Hitler ordered it should be amalgamated with regular army units, which accounted for the number of schoolboys and old men taken prisoner by the Allies in the final days of the war.

Voroshilov Marshal Klimenti 1881–1969. Soviet soldier and politician. An old comrade of Stalin, he became minister of defence 1934 and was responsible for the equipment and organization of the Soviet Army. In 1940 he was replaced by ◊Timoshenko and became deputy chairman of the defence committee. When Germany invaded he was given active command of the Northwest Front. With little military ability he failed to prevent the Germans reaching Leningrad and was replaced by ◊Zhukov. His friendship with Stalin prevented him being publicly condemned, but he was moved into various staff and liaison roles for the remainder of the war.

Vought US aircraft. The *F4U* Corsair was a naval carrier fighter and the first US combat aircraft to exceed 400 mph. A single-engine gull-wing monoplane, it was initially rejected by the US Navy but adopted by the Marines, who put it to good use in the ◊Solomon Islands campaign. Its success against Japanese fighters convinced the Navy, who adopted it as a night fighter and later a day fighter and dive bomber. With a 2450 hp engine it could reach 725 kph/450 mph, carried 910 kg/ 2,000 lb of bombs or rockets and was armed with four 20 mm cannon or six .5 in machine guns.

Vultee US aircraft. The *A-35 Vengeance* was a two-man naval dive bomber designed to meet a British specification 1940, but by the time they appeared in service the dive-bombing concept was no longer held in much esteem in Europe. They were therefore sent to the Far East where local air superiority allowed them to be used as bombers by the RAF and Australians in ◊New Guinea and ◊Burma. With a speed of 440 kph/275 mph it could carry 910 kg/2,000 lb of bombs and was armed with six machine guns.

Vyazma–Bryansk Line Vyazma is a Russian town on the Moscow–Smolensk railway about 240 km/150 mi W of Moscow; Bryansk is about 210 km/130 mi due south. In 1941 a defensive line, the Vyanzma–Bryansk Line, ran between the two and was held by the Soviet Army to block the route to Moscow. It was broken by IV Panzer Group during the second phase of the advance to Moscow Sept 1941, after which the Germans swung round, encircled the two towns, and captured 633,000 prisoners, 1,240 tanks, and 5,200 guns.

W

Waffen SS military arm of the ◊SS. The first such unit was Hitler's personal bodyguard, the 'Liebstandarte Adolf Hitler', a 120-man company formed 1933. By the end of 1944 the Waffen SS numbered 600,000 men in 34 divisions. Originally very stringent physical conditions ensured a high quality of recruit, but as the war progressed the requirements were relaxed. As German recruits dwindled, ◊Himmler began recruiting from Scandinavian and Dutch volunteers and then abandoned the pure Aryan requirements to recruit from any occupied country, resulting in 'Waffen SS Legions' from Latvia, Ukraine, Albania, Hungary, and other places. In general the Waffen SS fought as motorized infantry, but by the end of 1944 the 6th Panzer Army was a Waffen SS formation.

Wainwright Lieutenant-General Jonathan 1883–1953. US soldier. He served in the Philippines 1940 as commander of the North Luzon Force of four infantry divisions, a cavalry regiment, and supporting artillery. Under the command of ◊MacArthur he fell back into the ◊Bataan peninsula when the Japanese invaded 1941 and held out until April 1942. He then fell back on the island of ◊Corregidor, but was unable to withstand the Japanese invasion, and surrendered 5 May 1942. He took part in the ◊Bataan Death March, survived to be imprisoned in Manchuria for the remainder of the war, and was present to see the Japanese surrender signed on board USS *Missouri* 2 Sept 1945.

Wake Island small island 3,200 km/2,000 mi W of Hawaii. In 1941 it had a radio station, a small airstrip with 12 fighters, and a garrison of 525 US Marines. A Japanese air raid 8 Dec destroyed eight of the aircraft and on 11 Dec a Japanese force of two cruisers, four destroyers, and four troop transports arrived. The Marines opened fire with 5 in coastal defence guns and severely damaged a cruiser, blew up a destroyer, set one transport on fire and damaged all the others. The Japanese withdrew, pursued by the four remaining US fighters, one of which landed a bomb on the stern of a destroyer, detonating its load of depth charges and blowing off its stern. This spirited defence gave US morale a much-needed boost after the fiasco of ◊Pearl Harbor. The Japanese reappeared in much greater strength 25 Dec; the defences were swamped with troops and the US force was obliged to surrender. The casualties did not reflect a Japanese victory: while there were 120 US dead, the Japanese lost two warships, 21 aircraft, and 820 dead.

Walcheren island on the north side of the ◊Scheldt estuary, Holland, mostly below sea level and occupied by strong German coast defences. When the Allies began the clearance of the Scheldt, this strongpoint was the most difficult target. In order to isolate the defences the RAF bombed the dykes, breached them, and allowed the sea to flood into the centre of the island. They also dropped 9,000 tons of bombs on the German gun batteries and flew 250 fighter-bomber sorties. A landing was then made by ◊commandos to establish a small beachhead, through which infantry and pack artillery was landed. A further landing was made on the western shore, supported by naval gunfire, in which amphibious carriers, tanks, and rocket launchers were landed. After a six-day battle the island was finally secured 8 Nov 1944.

Wallis Barnes Neville 1887–1979. British aeronautical engineer. He designed the airship R-100, and the geodetic construction system used in Wellington and Lincoln bombers. He perfected the ◊'bouncing bombs' used by the RAF to destroy the German ◊Mohne and Eder dams 1943. He was knighted 1968.

war crime offence (such as murder of a civilian or a prisoner of war) that contravenes the internationally accepted laws governing the conduct of wars, particularly The Hague Convention 1907 and the Geneva Convention 1929. A key principle of the law relating to such crimes is that obedience to the orders of a superior is no defence.

War crimes became a major issue in the aftermath of World War II. The United Nations War Crimes Commission was set up 1943 to investigate German atrocities against Allied nationals. Leading Nazis were tried in ◊Nuremberg 1945–46, while high-ranking Japanese defendants were tried in Tokyo before the International Military Tribunal, and others by the legal section of the Allied supreme command. In the light of these investigations the Geneva Convention was revised 1949.

Warsaw Capital city of Poland. Occupied by the Germans 1939, it was the scene of two notable risings. The Germans had established a Jewish area (the *Warsaw ghetto*) in the centre of Warsaw into which some 433,000 people were crowded. In July 1942 shipments of Jews to the extermination camp at ◊Treblinka began. On 19 April 1943 a detachment of SS were sent into the ghetto to round up the remaining inhabitants and destroy the buildings. Rather than submit, the Jews fought back with small arms and grenades they had managed to acquire. Resistance ended 16 May when the main synagogue was blown up. Many Jews escaped via the sewers and joined the ◊Polish Home Army.

In Aug 1944 the German army began withdrawing from Warsaw in anticipation of the arrival of the Soviet Army. The Home Army rose in rebellion with the intention of keeping the German troops occupied and thus making it easier for the Soviets to enter the city. Street fighting began 1 Aug, but on the following day the Soviet attack was halted and the Germans were free to turn their full power against the rebellion, and fighting continued until Oct. In spite of appeals for help the Soviets made no move to assist the Poles and would not permit Allied aircraft flying in arms and supplies to the Poles to land in Soviet territory. Home Army detachments from outside Warsaw which attempted to go to the city's aid were surrounded and disarmed by the Soviets. Eventually the Poles realised the Soviets were waiting for the Poles and Germans to wear each other out so they could impose their own regime with no resistance and they surrendered 2 Oct 1944.

Wau village about 50 km/30 mi inland from Salamaua. In Aug 1943 the Japanese in Salamaua decided to occupy Wau in order to control a route into the interior of the island. Australian troops were flown from ◊Milne Bay to Wau Jan 1943 in time to set up defences. Bad weather prevented Allied air activity and by 29 Jan the Japanese had got to within 45 m/50 yds of the Australian positions around the airfield. The weather then improved and 57 Australian aircraft were able to land and deliver sufficient reinforcements to repel the Japanese and force them to retreat.

Wavell Field Marshal Sir Archibald, 1st Earl Wavell 1883–1950. British soldier. In 1939 he was put in command of the Middle East, an area stretching from Syria to Italian Somaliland. When the Italians invaded Egypt 1940 Wavell defeated them at ◊Sidi Barrani, captured ◊Bardia and ◊Tobruk and destroyed what was left of the Italian Army at ◊Beda Fomm. He then removed the Italians from E Africa, restored the Emperor of Abyssinia, ◊Haile Selassie, and was then ordered to send most of his army to Greece.

The failure in Greece was followed by the loss of ◊Crete 1941 and the arrival of Rommel and the German army in Africa, recapturing Cyrenaica and putting Tobruk under siege. Wavell, with limited resources, launched two attacks to relieve Tobruk, but both failed, after which he was replaced by ◊Auchinleck. Sent to India as commander in chief, he became Allied Supreme Commander after Japan entered the war but, again with limited resources, was unable to prevent the Japanese conquest of ◊Malaya and ◊Burma. In late 1942 he began an offensive in the ◊Arakan and was promoted to field marshal, but the Japanese counterattacked March 1943 and regained all they had lost. At this point Churchill lost what faith he had in Wavell as a military commander and 'promoted' him to Viceroy of India.

Werewolf projected Nazi movement founded 1945 ◊Goebbels as a resistance force against the Allied invasion of Germany. It only succeeded in attracting a few diehard Nazi fanatics and, with no broad support, collapsed when the Allies rounded up the remaining Nazi leaders.

Weygand General Maxime 1867–1965. French soldier. Chief of Staff to Marshal Foch during World War I, he rose to commander in chief of the French Army and retired 1935. Recalled 1939, he was given command of French forces in Syria and the Lebanon. In May 1940 he was called back to France to replace ◊Gamelin as Supreme Commander. A staff officer all his life, he had never commanded troops in the field and was quite unable deal with the German invasion. He managed to assemble troops on the river Somme to form a defensive line but this was easily broken by the Germans, whereupon he urged ◊Pétain to seek the best terms he could. After the surrender Weygand became minister of national defence in the Pétain government and commander in chief of French Forces in N Africa, but the Germans demanded his removal from this post Nov 1941 as his sympathies were suspect. He was arrested by the Vichy government 1942 and imprisoned in Germany for the rest of the war. On his return to France he was tried for treason and acquitted.

Wilson Field Marshal Sir Henry Maitland 1881–1964. British soldier. In 1940 Wilson was commander of British troops in Egypt. After the defeat of the Italian forces in North Africa he commanded the force sent to Greece 1941. Faced with overwhelming German strength he skilfully manoeuvred and extracted the British and Commonwealth troops, after which he conducted the campaigns in ◊Syria and ◊Iraq. In 1943 he replaced Alexander as commander in chief Middle East, but after the death of Sir John ◊Dill was sent to the USA in charge of the British Military Mission.

Wingate Major-General Orde 1903–1944. British soldier. An unconventional soldier, Wingate began studying guerrilla warfare 1936 when he organized special detachments in Palestine to counter Arab insurgents. In 1940–41 he commanded 'Gideon Force', a guerrilla group which organized local tribesmen to rise against the Italians in Abyssinia. In 1942 he was summoned to India by ◊Wavell and instructed to organize a deep penetration operation behind Japanese lines which became known as the ◊Chindits. His first operation Feb 1943 was in brigade strength and was soon the target of ferocious counterattacks by the Japanese, leading to excessive losses in men and equipment for very little strategic gain. Nevertheless, the experience gained enabled him to prepare a much larger force of six brigades which began the second Chindit operation Feb 1944. This proved more successful, but Wingate was killed in an air accident 24 March 1944 and the operation was then conducted by General ◊Lentaigne.

Witzleben Field Marshal Erwin von 1881–1944. German soldier. He commanded the 1st German Army in France 1940 and was promoted to field marshal. In May 1941 he became commander in chief in the West but retired for health reasons 1942. He had long been involved with a circle of officers opposed to Hitler and was drawn into the ◊July Bomb Plot, being nominated as the future commander in chief after Hitler had been killed. When the plot failed he was arrested and hanged Aug 1944.

women's services the organized military use of women on a large scale. In many countries in the war, women replaced men in factories, on farms, and in other noncombat tasks; they are now found in combat units in many countries, including the USA, Cuba, Britain, and Israel.

In Britain there are separate corps for all three services: the *Women's Royal Army Corps* (WRAC) created 1949 to take over the functions of the ◊Auxiliary Territorial Service, established 1938 – its World War I equivalent was the Women's Army Auxiliary Corps (WAAC); *Women's Royal Naval Service* (WRNS) 1917–19 and 1939 onwards, allowed in combat roles on surface ships from 1990; and the *Women's Royal Air Force* (WRAF) established 1918 but known 1939–48 as the Women's Auxiliary Air Force (WAAF). There are also nursing services: Queen Alexandra's Royal Army Nursing Corps (QARANC) and Naval Nursing Service, and for the RAF Princess Mary's Nursing Service.

The USA had a separate Women's Army Corps (WAC), established 1948, which developed from the wartime Women's Army Auxiliary Corps (WAAC); but women are now integrated into the general structure of all three services. There are separate nurse corps for the three services.

Wurzburg German early warning ◊radar set, one of the first designs developed 1936. It went into service 1940 and became the standard German air defence warning equipment.

X-4 German wire-guided air-to-air missile. Development began 1943 and production late 1944, though this was never completed due to Allied air raids destroying the factory manufacturing the rocket motors. About 2 m/6 ft long, it was propelled by a liquid-fuel rocket and had a 22 kg/48 lb explosive warhead. With a range of about 2,750 m/3,000 yds it could have been a formidable air defence weapon.

X-7 German wire-guided anti-tank missile. This was developed as a spin-off from the ◊X-4 programme. Gyro-stabilized and wire-guided like the X-4, it carried a ◊shaped charge warhead capable of penetrating over 200 mm/8 in of armour plate. Weighing 10 kg/22 lb it had a range of 1 km/1,100 yds. Development was not completed before the war ended, but it can be considered as the ancestor of all the present-day anti-tank missiles.

X-craft British midget submarines. Introduced 1943 they were intended to enter restricted harbours and lay time-fused explosive charges beneath enemy ships. Displacing about 30 tons, they had a four or five man crew and were propelled by electric motors giving a speed of 6 knots. They were used to immobilize the ◊Tirpitz Sept 1943 and also against Japanese ships in Singapore harbour July 1945.

X-Gerat German radio bombing system used against Britain 1940. It depended upon a transmitter sending out a narrow beam over the target, along which the bombers flew. Three other beams were directed across the guide beam; one at 50 km/31 mi from the target to warn pilots, the second at 20 km/12 mi and the third at 5 km/3 mi. The signals from the second and third beams were fed into a calculator and gave an accurate measurement of the bomber's speed, from which the calculator worked out the optimum bomb release point and told the bomb-aimer when to drop. It was eventually countered by electronic jamming.

Y

Yakovlev Soviet aircraft. The *Yak-1* was a single-seat monoplane fighter which entered service 1941. Production was delayed by the need to shift the factory deeper into the USSR to avoid capture by the Germans. Adopted as the standard fighter, it had a speed of 600 kph/375 mph and was armed with a 20 mm cannon, two machine guns and six rockets. The *Yak-3* was an improved model, lighter but stronger, which appeared 1943 and became the scourge of the Luftwaffe on the Eastern Front. With a speed of 725 kph/450 mph it carried the same cannon and machine gun armament. The *Yak-9* was another modification of the Yak-1 which became a ground-attack fighter, light bomber, and long-range escort fighter and in time became the most numerous of all the Yak designs. It had a speed of 700 kph/435 mph, a 20 mm cannon, two machine guns, and could carry 200 kg/440 lb of bombs.

Yalta conference meeting at which the Allied leaders Churchill, Roosevelt, and Stalin completed plans for the defeat of Germany 1945 and the foundation of the United Nations. It took place in Yalta, a Soviet holiday resort in the Crimea.

Yamamoto Admiral Isoroku 1884–1943. Japanese sailor. He became chief of naval aviation 1938 and chief of the combined fleet 1939. Long convinced that Japan would eventually fight the USA he began planning the attack on ◊Pearl Harbor early 1940. After the raid he was quick to appreciate the significance of the US carrier force escaping the damage, and prepared plans to entrap and destroy them, but this backfired and instead he lost most of his own carriers in the Battle of ◊Midway. In 1943 he planned a series of naval offensives and set out on a tour of bases in the Solomon Islands to explain his strategy and raise morale.

The Americans intercepted signals giving his itinerary and sent out fighters which shot his aircraft down 18 April 1943.

Yamashita Lieutenant General Tomoyuki 1885–1946. Japanese soldier. He commanded the 25th Army in the invasion of ◊Malaya and ◊Singapore 1941, conducting a quick and effective campaign which earned him the title 'Tiger of Malaya' in Japan. This angered the premier ◊Tōjō who thought Yamashita was seeking his place, and he was sent to Manchuria to command an army group. After Tōjō fell from grace 1944, Yamashita was brought out of obscurity and sent to defend the Philippines. He conducted a skilful defensive campaign but was eventually forced to surrender after the Japanese capitulation Sept 1945. He was arrested for war crimes and executed 1946.

Yamato Japanese battleship class, consisting of the *Yamato* and the *Musashi*. Designed to be bigger and more powerful than any other warship in the world, they displaced 64,170 tons, had a speed of 27 knots, armour 400 mm thick, carried nine 460 mm, twelve 155 mm, and twelve 127 mm guns, and had a crew of 2,500.

The *Yamato* appeared at the battles of ◊Midway, the ◊Philippine Sea, and ◊Leyte Gulf, and was sunk by US carrier aircraft off the Japanese coast when en route to Okinawa 7 April 1945. The *Musashi* also saw action in the ◊Philippine Sea and was sunk by torpedoes dropped by US aircraft during the battle of ◊Leyte Gulf, 24 Oct 1944.

Yeremenko Marshal Andrey 1892–1970. Soviet soldier. An armour specialist, he commanded a mechanized cavalry corps in ◊Finland 1939–40 and was then sent to command the Red Banner Army in E Siberia. Recalled after the German invasion 1941 he was given command of the Bryansk Front but was severely wounded. In Aug 1942 he became commander of the ◊Stalingrad Front, leading it in the entrapment of the German 6th Army and the subsequent counteroffensive. In 1943 he commanded the Baltic Front for a time, then moved south to command the Independent Coastal Army which removed the Germans from the ◊Crimea 1944. He then returned to the Baltic Front, conquering Latvia, then took command of the 4th Ukrainian Front to conquer Czechoslovakia and destroy the remains of the German Army Group Centre 1945.

Yokosuka Japanese aircraft. The *D4Y (Judy)* was a fleet dive bomber but was designed with an in-line engine, unusual for Japan; this gave a good deal of trouble and it was replaced by a radial engine and some of this design were then used as night fighters. It had a speed of 580 kph/360 mph and was armed with two 20 mm cannon or three machine guns, and could carry 320 kg/700 lbs of bombs.

The *E14Y1 (Glenn)* was an unusual floatplane, designed to fold up and be carried in a submarine for spotting purposes. Its top speed was only 170 kph/105 mph but this was adequate for its role. The *P1Y (Frances)* was a twin-engine bomber, torpedo bomber, or reconnaissance machine with good speed and long range, but it appeared late in the war and the shortage of skilled pilots and fuel by that time limited its usefulness.

The *MXY-7 (Baka)* was the most unusual of all wartime aircraft, being designed purely as a suicide (◊kamikaze) machine. Made of wood, cheap, simple, and propelled by a rocket motor of limited duration, it was packed with 1,205 kg/2,645 lbs of high explosive and carried beneath a converted 'Betty' bomber to within 80 km/50 mi of its target and then released in a gliding path. When in sight of the target the pilot prayed, lit the rocket motor, put the machine into a steep dive, and steered it to impact at about 915 kph/570 mph.

Z

Z batteries British anti-aircraft rocket batteries. The British began work on air defence rockets 1936 and perfected a 3-in solid-fuel rocket carrying a 12 kg/28 lb high-explosive warhead. A simple two-rocket launcher was produced and these were organised into 56-launcher batteries around ports and other important targets. Siting was important, since after a 128-rocket salvo was launched into the sky, 128 spent motors would shortly return to earth, and it was necessary to locate the battery so that these fell into the sea or onto open country. First employed 1942, they were usually operated by ◊Home Guard units.

Zeitzler General Kurt 1895–1963. German soldier. A staff officer in the Polish and French campaigns 1939–40, his logistic and organizational skills led to his appointment as Chief of Staff to 1 Panzer Army for Operation ◊Barbarossa. A favourite of Hitler, in 1942 he was appointed Chief of the General Staff and in this position he supported von ◊Paulus' request to withdraw from ◊Stalingrad. Hitler refused, von Paulus was destroyed, and thereafter Hitler paid more attention to his Chief of Staff. Zeitzler then planned Operation Zitadelle, the elimination of the ◊Kursk salient, which ended in defeat. After a few more defeats at Soviet hands, Hitler lost patience and July 1944 replaced him with ◊Guderian.

Zhukov Marshal Georgi Konstantinovich 1896–1974. Soviet soldier and minister of defence 1955–57. Zhukov joined the Bolsheviks and the Red Army 1918 and led a cavalry regiment in the Civil War 1918–20. His army defeated the Japanese forces in Mongolia 1939. As chief of staff from 1941, he defended Moscow 1941, counterattacked at ◊Stalingrad 1942, organized the relief of ◊Leningrad 1943, and led the offensive from the Ukraine March 1944 which ended in the fall of Berlin. He headed the Allied delegation that received the German surrender 1945, and subsequently commanded the Soviet occupation forces in Germany.

History shows that risks should be taken but not blindly.
Marshal Zhukov 1965

Zyklon-B poison gas used in German extermination camps. A cyanide compound originally developed for fumigation purposes in the 1920s, Zyklon-B was actually a crystalline compound which gave off hydrogen cyanide gas when exposed to the air. It was first used against humans in a German euthanasia programme 1939, aimed at ridding Germany of lunatics, incurable invalids, and other 'undesirables'. The victims were induced to enter a 'shower bath', Zyklon-B was released, and the gas killed them in a few minutes. When the extermination camps were set up, this method was adopted as standard and was responsible for several million deaths. The inventor, Dr. Bruno Tesch, was convicted of war crimes and executed for his manufacture and supply of the substance to the camps.

Appendices

The Asian War 1940–45

1940	Aug	British withdraw from Shanghai and northern Chinese garrisons
	Sept	Japanese forces begin to arrive in French Indo-China
		Japan joins in triple pact with Germany and Italy
	Oct	US places embargo on export of iron and steel scrap to Japan
1941	Apr	Japan and USSR join in neutrality agreement
	Dec 7	Japanese attack Pearl Harbor, Hong Kong, and Malaya followed by US and British declaration of war on Japan
	Dec 11	Germany and Italy declare war on US
1942	Jan–June	Japanese occupation of Malaya, Indonesia, Solomon Islands, Philippines, Timor, part of Aleutian islands, part of New Guinea
	Feb 15	Fall of Singapore
	May 7 and June 4–7	Battles of Coral Sea and Midway
	Aug 7	US landings in Solomon islands
1943	July	Opening of US South Pacific offensive
1944	Feb	US forces take Marshall islands
	June	Systematic bombing of Japan begins
	Oct	US landings in Philippines
1945	Feb–Mar	US capture of Iwo Jima
	Apr	Completion of British destruction of Japanese forces in Burma
	Apr–June	US capture of Okinawa
	Mar–Aug	Major phase of air offensive against Japan
	Aug 6	Atomic bomb dropped on Hiroshima
	Aug 8	USSR declares war on Japan and invades Manchuria
	Aug 9	Atomic bomb dropped on Nagasaki
	Aug 10	Japanese cabinet decides to surrender
	Sept 12	Final signature of surrender

The European War 1939–45

1939	Sept 1	German invasion of Poland
	Sept 17	Soviet invasion of Poland
	Sept 27	Polish resistance comes to an end
	Nov 30	Soviet attack on Finland
1940	Mar 12	Finland makes peace with USSR
	Apr	British and French mine Norwegian waters to hinder German shipping
	Apr 9	Germans invade Norway and Denmark
	May 3	Allied forces withdraw from Norway
	May 10	German invasion of Netherlands, Belgium, Luxembourg
	May 14	Dutch army lays down arms
	May 26	Belgian forces ordered to capitulate
	May 28– June 4	Evacuation of British forces and 140,000 French from Dunkirk
	June 10	Italy declares war on France and Britain
	June 22	French armistice with Germany (and June 24 with Italy)
	July 9	End of French Third Republic; formal initiation of new regime at Vichy
	Aug 8–Oct 10	Battle of Britain
	Oct 8	German troops enter Romania
	Oct 28	Italian attack on Greece from Albania
	Nov	Hungary and Romania join German-Italian-Japanese pact
1941	March	Bulgaria joins Axis
	Apr 6	German invasion of Yugoslavia and Greece
	Apr 17	Yugoslav capitulation
	Apr 23	Greek armistice with Germans; German forces withdrawn
	May 20	Successful German airborne attack on Crete begins
	June 22	German invasion of USSR. By end of October German forces have occupied Odessa and Kharkov, entered the Crimea, and are on the outskirts of Moscow
1942	July 2	Opening of German summer offensive – capture of Sevastopol and entry of Northern Caucasus
	Nov 8	Anglo-American landings in North Africa provoke occupation of Vichy by Germans and scuttling of French fleet at Toulon
	Nov 19	At height of German success, Russian counter-offensive begins
1943	Jan	Soviets raise siege of Leningrad
	Feb 2	German surrender at Stalingrad

	March	German spring offensive begins
	July	Soviet summer offensive opens
	July 10	Allied landings in Sicily
	Sept 3	Allied invasion of Italy and armistice with new Italian government
	Nov 6	Russian recapture of Kiev
	Dec 31	Russian recapture of Zhitomir
1944	**Feb**	Soviet forces enter former Estonia
	Mar	Crimea retaken by Soviet forces
	June 4	Anglo-American forces enter Rome
	June 6	Anglo-American landings in Normany open the invasion of northern Europe
	August	Soviet forces enter Poland, Romania, and East Prussia
	Aug 15	Allied landings in south of France
	Aug 24	Surrender of Romanian government
	Sept 2	Liberation of Brussels
	Sept 12	American forces enter German territory near Eupen
	Sept 25	USSR declares war on Bulgaria: surrender three days later
	Oct 20	Russians enter Belgrade
	Dec 16–25	German counteroffensive in France defeated
1945	**Jan–Apr**	Battle of Germany
	Jan 17	Soviet forces take Warsaw
	Feb 7	Yalta conference
	Feb 13	Russians near Berlin
	Mar 7	Allied forces cross the Rhine
	Apr 20	Russians enter Berlin
	Apr 25	US/USSR forces meet on the Elbe
	Apr 28	German forces in Italy surrender
	May 1	Death of Hitler announced
	May 7	German surrender
	May 8	VE day – the end of the war in Europe
	June 5	Allied Control Commission takes control of German territory as of 31 December 1937

declarations of war 1939–45

declared by	against	date
Germany	Poland	None; invaded 1 Sept 1939
UK, France, Australia, New Zealand	Germany	3 Sept 1939
Canada	Germany	10 Sept 1939
USSR	Poland	None; invaded 17 Sept 1939
USSR	Finland	13 Nov 1939
Germany	Denmark, Norway	None; invaded 9 Apr 1940
Germany	Holland, Belgium	None; invaded 10 May 1949
Italy	UK, France	10 June 1940
Italy	Greece	None; invaded 28 Oct 1940
Germany	Greece, Yugoslavia	None; invaded 6 Apr 1941
Italy	Yugoslavia	None; invaded 6 Apr 1941
Germany	USSR	None; invaded 22 Jun 1941
Italy, Romania	USSR	22 Jun 1941
Hungary, Slovakia	USSR	23 Jun 1941
Finland	USSR	26 Jun 1941
UK	Finland, Hungary, Romania	5 Dec 1941
Japan	UK, USA	7 Dec 1941
USA	Germany, Italy	11 Dec 1941
Brazil	Germany, Italy	22 Aug 1942
Bolivia	Germany, Italy, Japan	7 Apr 1943
Iran	Germany	9 Sept 1943
Italy	Germany	13 Oct 1943
Liberia	Germany, Japan	25 Jan 1944
Romania	Germany	25 Aug 1944
Bulgaria	Germany	8 Sept 1944
Ecuador	Germany, Japan	2 Feb 1945
Peru	Germany, Japan	13 Feb 1945
Chile	Japan	14 Feb 1945
Venezuela	Germany, Japan	16 Feb 1945
Turkey	Germany, Japan	23 Feb 1945
Uruguay	Germany, Japan	23 Feb 1945
Egypt	Germany, Japan	24 Feb 1945
Syria	Germany, Japan	26 Feb 1945
Lebanon	Germany, Japan	27 Feb 1945
Saudi Arabia	Germany, Japan	1 March 1945
Iran	Japan	1 March 1945
Finland	Germany	4 March 1945, but a state of war was held to have existed from 15 Sept 1944
Argentina	Germany, Japan	27 March 1945
Brazil	Japan	6 June 1945
USSR	Japan	8 Aug 1945

Codenames of World War II

Few wars in history can have produced as many codewords as World War II and they are frequently used by historians as a convenient shorthand, particularly when referring to operations. Some of the more common are listed here.

Aberdeen	British attack on the Cauldron 1942
Accolade	British attack on the Dodecanese Islands 1943
Adlertag	(Eagle Day) German attack on British air defences 13 Aug 1940
Alpenveilchen	(Alpine Violet) Axis invasion of Albania Jan 1940
Anklet	Commando raid on the Lofoten Islands Dec 1941
Anton	German occupation of S France 1942
Anvil	Allied plan for invasion of S France 1944; the plan was carried out under the operational name 'Dragoon'
Apostle	Anglo-French operation in Norway May 1940
Atlantic	British-Canadian holding operation Normandy 1944
Avalanche	Allied landings at Salerno Sicily Sept 1943
Barbarossa	German invasion of the USSR 22 June 1941
Battleaxe	British offensive in Libya June 1941
Baytown	British crossing of the straits of Messina to invade Italy 1943
Bigot	Security classification covering the Allied plans for D-Day
Blackcock	British offensive against the Ruhr Jan 1945
Blissful	US landing on Choiseul, Solomon Islands Oct 1943
Bluecoat	British offensive at Caumont, Normandy, Aug 1944
Bodyguard	Allied deception plans for Operation Overlord
Bolero	Allied plan for build-up of US and Canadian troops in Britain 1942
Brassard	Allied landing on Elba June 1444
Braunschweig	German offensive against Stalingrad and the Caucasus 1942
Brevity	British offensive in Libya May 1941
Cartwheel	Allied plan to isolate the Japanese naval base at Rabaul 1944
Catchpole	US landings on Eniwetok, Marshall Islands 1944
Champion	Allied plan for offensive in Burma 1943
Chariot	British Commando raid on St Nazaire March 1942
Cherryblossom	US landing on Bougainville, Solomon islands Nov 1943
Clarion	Allied air offensive against German communications Feb 1945
Claymore	British commando raid on Lofoten islands March 1941
Cobra	US break-out from the Normandy beachhead 1944
Compass	British offensive in Libya Dec 1940
Corkscrew	Allied occupation of Pantellaria June 1943

Cromwell	Codeword to alert British home forces in the event of German invasion 1940
Diver	British air defence plan against V-1 flying bombs
Doomsday	Allied liberation of Normandy 1945
Downfall	US plan for the invasion of Japan 1945
Dracula	British amphibious assault on Rangoon 1945
Dragoon	Allied invasion of S France 1944
Dynamo	Evacuation of Allied troops from Dunkirk 1940
Edelweiss	German offensive against the Baku oilfields 1941
Eiche	German plan to rescue Mussolini 1943
Elkton	US strategic plan for the elimination of the Japanese naval base at Rabaul 1943
Epsom	British offensive from Caen June 1944
Fall Blau (Plan Blue)	German plan for offensive in S USSR 1942
Fall Gelb (Plan Yellow)	German plan for the invasion of France and the Low Countries 1940
Fall Rot (Plan Red)	German plan for the second phase of the invasion of France 1940
Fall Schwarz (Plan Black)	German plan for the establishment of a strong defensive position in Italy Aug 1943
Fall Weiss (Plan White)	German plan for the invasion of Poland 1939
Fat Boy	Plutonium bomb dropped on Nagasaki 9 Aug 1945
Felix	German plan to capture Gibraltar 1940
Flintlock	US invasion of the Marshall islands 1944
Forager	US invasion of the Marianas islands 1944
Fortitude	Deception plan for Operation Overlord
Galvanic	US assault on the Gilbert islands 1943
Gauntlet	British Commando raid on Spitzbergen Aug 1941
Gomorrah	Series of RAF raids on Hamburg July 1943
Goodtime	New Zealand brigade attack on the Treasury Islands 1943
Goodwood	British offensive east of Caen July 1944
Grenade	US offensive against the Rhine 1945
Gymnast	Allied plan for invasion of French N Africa 1942
Ha-Go	Japanese counteroffensive in the Arakan, Burma 1944
Herakles	German-Italian plan for the invasion of Malta
Iceberg	US invasion of Okinawa 1945
I-go	Japanese air offensive against Guadalcanal March 1943
Infatuate	Allied capture of Walcheren and clearance of the Scheldt estuary Oct 1944

Jubilee	British-Canadian raid on Dieppe Aug 1942
Judgement	British naval air attack on Taranto, Italy Nov 1940
King II	US liberation of Luzon, Philippine Islands Oct 1944
Lightfoot	Second battle of El Alamein Oct 1942
Little Boy	The first atomic bomb dropped on Hiroshima 6 Aug 1945
LumberJack	US drive to the Rhine following Operation Grenade 1945
Mailed Fist	Planned recapture of Singapore 1945
Manhattan	Cover name for the development of the atomic bomb
Manna	(1) British landing in Greece Oct 1944; (2) Air drops of food to starving Dutch April 1945
Margarethe	German occupation of Hungary 1944
Market Garden	British-US offensive to cross the Meuse, Waal, and Neder-Rjin rivers Sept 1944. Commonly applied to the airborne landings at Arnhem which was an essential part of this plan and as far as the operation got.
Matador	British plan for the defence of N Malaya 1941
Merkur	German invasion of Crete May 1941
Millenium	RAF thousand-bomber raid on Cologne May 1942
Mincemeat	Allied deception plan for the invasion of Sicily 1943
Mo	Japanese plan for attack on Port Moresby 1942
Morgenluft	Afrika Korps offensive against Gafsa, Tunisia Feb 1943
Neptune	Naval part of the plan for Operation Overlord June 1944
Noball	RAF operations against German V-weapons 1944
Nordlicht	German plan to capture Leningrad 1942
Ochsenkopf	German counteroffensive in Tunisia Feb 1943
Olive	British offensive against the Gothic Line Italy 1944
Olympic	US plan for the invasion of Kyushu Japan 1945
Overlord	Allied invasion of Normandy 8 June 1944
Plunder	British crossing of the Rhine by 21 Army Group 1945
Pugilist	British 8th Army attack on the Mareth Line, Tunisia 1943
Punishment	Gennan invasion of Yugoslavia April 1941
Ratweek	Allied air offensive against German communications in the Balkans Sept 1944
Reckless	Allied assault on Hollandia April 1944
Retribution	Allied naval operations off the coast of Tunisia to stop the escape of German and Italian troops by sea 1943
Romulus	British offensive in the Arakan, Burma Dec 1944
Rosselsprung	German attack on Tito's headquarters in Yugoslavia May 1444
Roundup	Initial Allied plan for the invasion of Europe 1942
Rupertforce	Allied expedition to Narvik, Norway April 1940

Sealion	German plan for the invasion of Britain 1940
Shingle	Allied landing at Anzio, Italy Jan 1944
Sho-Go	Japanese naval plan for the defence of the Philippines 1944
Siegfried	German advance on Stalingrad 1942
Sinyavino	Soviet plan to relieve Leningrad Sept 1942
Slapstick	British landing at Taranto, Italy Sept 1943
Sledgehammer	Allied plan to invade N France 1942
Sonnenblume	German plan to send assistance to the Italians in N Africa 1941
Stamina	Air supply of British troops in Imphal and Kohima, Burma 1944
Starvation	US Navy mining of Japanese waters March 1945
Strangle	Allied bombing offensive against German communications in Italy March–April 1944
Supercharge	British breakthrough after Second Battle of El Alamein 1942
Talon	British assault on Akyab island, Burma 1945
Thunderclap	Allied bombing offensive aimed at breaking German civilian morale 1945
Thursday	Second Chindit operation in Burma 1944
Tidal Wave	Allied air attacks on Ploesti oilfields, Romania Aug 1943
Toenails	US landings on New Georgia 1943
Torch	Allied invasion of French N Africa Nov 1942
Totalize	Phase 1 of the Canadian offensive toward the Falaise Gap Aug 1944
Tractable	Phase 2 of the Canadian offensive toward the Falaise Gap Aug 1944
Tradewind	US assault on Morotai, Philippine Islands 1944
Trinity	Test of the first atomic bomb New Mexico 1945
Tube Alloys	British code name for the early work on the atomic bomb
U-Go	Japanese offensive against Imphal and Kohima, Burma 1944
Uranus	Soviet counteroffensive at Stalingrad 1942
Varsity	Allied airborne operations east of the Rhine crossing March 1945
Veritable	British-Canadian offensive between the Maas and Rhine rivers Feb 1945
Wacht am Rhein	German offensive in the Ardennes (Battle of the Bulge) 1944
Watchtower	US landings on Guadalcanal, Tulagi, and the Santa Cruz Islands Aug 1942
Wilde Sau	German night fighter system of air defence 1943-44
Wintergewitter	German attempt to relieve their units trapped in Stalingrad 1942
Wolfschanze	Hitler's command headquarters in East Prussia
Zeppelin	German plan to assassinate Stalin July 1944
Zipper	British plan for the reconquest of Malaya 1945
Zitadelle	German plan for the elimination of the Kursk salient 1943

leading fighter aces 1939–45

nationality	name	victories
British	Group Captain J E Johnson	38
French	Squadron Leader P H Clostermann (RAF)	33
German	Major Erich Hartmann	352
German	Hauptmann Hans-Joachim Marseille	158 (W Europe only)
Japan	Hiroyishi Nishizawa	87
USA (USAAF)	Major Richard I Bong	40 (Asia only)
USA (USAAF)	Colonel Frances S Gabreski	31 (W Europe only)
USSR	Ivan Kozhedub	62

military aircraft production 1939–45

year	UK	USA	USSR	Allied total	Germany	Italy	Japan	Axis total
1939	7,940	(5,856)	(10,382)	7,940	8,295	(1,692)	(4,467)	8,295
1940	15,049	(12,804)	(10,565)	15,049	10,826	2,142	(4,768)	12,968
1941	20,094	26,227	15,735	62,106	11,776	3,503	5,088	20,367
1942	23,672	47,836	25,436	96,944	15,556	2,818	8,861	27,235
1943	26,263	85,898	34,845	147,006	25,527	967	16,693	43,454
1944	26,461	96,318	40,246	163,025	39,807	–	28,180	68,760
1945	12,070	49,761	20,052	81,883	7,544	–	8,263	15,807

tank and self-propelled gun production 1939–45

year	UK	USA	USSR	Allied total	Germany	Italy	Japan	Axis total
1939	969	–	(2,950)	969	247	(40)	–	247
1940	1,399	(331)	(2,794)	1,399	1,643	250	(315)	1,893
1941	4,841	4,052	6,590	15,483	3,790	595	595	4,980
1942	8,611	24,997	24,446	58,054	6,180	1,252	557	7,989
1943	7,476	29,497	24,089	61,062	12,063	336	558	12,957
1944	4,600	17,565	28,963	51,128	19,002	–	353	19,355
1945	?	11,968	15,419	27,387	3,932	–	137	4,069

merchant shipping losses 1939–45

year	Allied – Atlantic	Allied – elsewhere	Axis – Mediterranean	Japanese
1939	755,531 (220)	706 (1)	–	–
1940	3,654,511 (1,007)	525,162 (52)	186,631 (46)	–
1941	3,295,819 (875)	1,035,729 (424)	714,410 (178)	57,758 (12)
1942	6,150,340 (1170)	1,638,528 (492)	522,082 (148)	1,065,398 (229)
1943	2,170,410 (363)	1,219,724 (244)	767,734 (225)	1,820,919 (434)
1944	505,759 (117)	539,870 (88)	–	3,891,019 (969)
1945	366,777 (91)	70,238 (12)	–	1,782,140 (701)

Figures indicate total tonnage lost; figures in brackets indicate number of ships.

naval losses 1939–45

	aircraft carriers	battleships	cruisers	destroyers	escorts	submarines
UK	8	5	33	120	71	77
USA	11	2	10	71	10	53
USSR	–	1	3	33	–	c100
Germany	–	9 (3)	7 (3)	44 (6)	–	785 (17 + 221 in 1945)
Italy	–	1	11	84	–	84
Japan	19	8	37	134	–	130

Figures in brackets indicate vessels scuttled.